W9-BCC-157

The Author

M. REJAI is Assistant Professor of Government at Miami University, Oxford, Ohio. He holds a Ph.D. from the University of California, Los Angeles, where he was associated with the Institute of Government and Public Affairs. Professor Rejai has written for professional and scholarly journals and is a contributor to *The New Communisms,* co-author of the forthcoming *Twentieth-Century Political Ideologies,* and editor of the forthcoming *Mao Tse-tung on Revolution and War.*

DEMOCRACY

The Contemporary Theories

DEMC

M. Rejai

CRACY

The Contemporary Theories

ATHERTON PRESS
NEW YORK · 1967

Address all inquiries to:
Atherton Press
70 Fifth Avenue
New York 10011

Library of Congress Catalog Card Number 67-18278

Second Printing 1968

Manufactured in the United States of America
Designed by JoAnn Randel

Preface

It is a striking fact that while conceptions of democracy have rapidly multiplied—particularly since World War II—no single source containing a variety of material on this subject is within easy access of student and layman alike. It is a matter of serious concern that while dozens of post-war books bring together, interpret, and document the various developments in Marxism, communism, nationalism, no single volume seeks to perform a similar service for democracy.

This volume marks an attempt to bring together a representative selection of readings from the vast literature of recent democratic theory. The objective is to integrate a wide range of material on this subject within the framework of some explicit themes that are explored throughout. The reading selections illustrate and document the basic themes, as laid out in the introductory chapters of the book.

The volume does not seek to develop a "new" theory of democracy; its major task is to present, describe, and analyze some existing theories. Similarly, since the objective is an *understanding* of the various meanings of democracy, no systematic attention will be paid to *justification* of democratic government. It is of course true—as we shall soon see—that in some formulations of democracy, explanation and justification are inseparably fused (perhaps even confused). Our task, however, is analytical; we shall seek, as much as possible, to avoid defense and justification. The assumption will be made that democracy is a desirable form of government.

The opening chapter examines briefly the historical evolution of democratic ideas since ancient times. Part One considers some major definitions of democracy, while Part Two analyzes the various preconditions necessary for the emergence and survival of democratic government. The concluding chapter highlights some implications of recent changes in the theories of democracy. The book is offered in the hope of stimulating a fuller appreciation of the richness and variety of democratic political theories, particularly as they have evolved in the postwar period.

The literature on democratic theory is rich and varied and, since we were not interested in compiling an exhaustive encyclopedia of the subject, there was no alternative but to impose *some* kind of limitation on the available material. An initial and fairly simple decision called for structuring the book exclusively around the Western theories of democracy to the exclusion of all non-Western and Communist conceptions.[1] As this did not prove greatly helpful, it was decided to delimit the scope of the volume to twentieth-century theories, with special reference to the postwar period. It soon became apparent, however, that a rounded appreciation of the contemporary theories of democracy—as well as some balance in the book—would not be attained unless the twentieth-century conceptions were placed in context and compared and contrasted with such older or "classical" theories as those developed by John Locke, Jean-

1 A second volume focusing on non-Western conceptions of democracy is planned. The more useful sources currently available include: Marguerite J. Fisher, "New Concepts of Democracy in Southern Asia," *Western Political Quarterly*, XV (December 1962), pp. 625–640; Paul E. Sigmund, Jr., ed., *The Ideologies of the Developing Nations* (New York: Frederick A. Praeger, 1963); Fred R. von der Mehden, *Politics of the Developing Nations* (Englewood Cliffs, N.J.: Prentice-Hall, 1964).

Jacques Rousseau, Thomas Jefferson, Abraham Lincoln, and John Stuart Mill. A separate chapter has been devoted to these writers; its function is merely to set the stage and provide a point of departure.

Delimiting in this fashion the area of our concern proved helpful with the problem of manageability, but did not solve it completely. Since the twentieth-century writings on democracy fill literally dozens of volumes by themselves, further limitations had to be imposed.

The problem was to develop suitable criteria for inclusion (or exclusion) of the material at hand. Two criteria were eventually used: (1) the uniqueness of the statement in question, and (2) the effectiveness and economy of the language with which it was made. We need not apologize for being primarily interested in those statements on democratic theory that are somewhat distinctive. We prefer succinct and direct statements to ambiguous and rambling ones. In a few instances, however, the two criteria were not mutually attainable and in every such instance distinctiveness was placed before brevity.

Undoubtedly we have not succeeded in satisfying all readers, by excluding some of their "favorites" or including some they dislike. The bibliography of books, monographs. and articles not specifically used in the volume is arranged in parallel structure with the topical outline of the book and, it is hoped, will aid those readers who want to explore the subject further.

The reader will note that some of the quotations used in the introductory chapters are immediately documented, while others are not. Those quotations not immediately documented reappear in the reading selections, whereas the others do not. For the latter, the original source is specified. This practice helped avoid unnecessary cluttering of the introductory texts.

I have received a great deal of advice and assistance in

the preparation of this volume, and I am happy to have the opportunity to thank those who have helped me. Much of the thinking underscoring the entire enterprise was done in the course of two seminars with James S. Coleman and Thomas P. Jenkin while I was a student at U.C.L.A. I am pleased to acknowledge the enduring intellectual stimulation that those seminars provided. In addition, Thomas Jenkin was kind enough to read and criticize an earlier version of the material that makes up the introductory chapters of this book.

I am also grateful to David Spitz of Ohio State University whose comments and suggestions materially improved the study. A number of colleagues at Miami University read and commented upon the manuscript. Special thanks are due to Reo M. Christenson and Howard White who gave me the benefit of their careful criticisms, and to James R. Woodworth who did much to provide the time and facilities necessary for completion of the study. For financial assistance in the preparation of the manuscript, I should like to thank the Committee on Faculty Research, Miami University. Finally and as usual, I am heavily indebted to my wife, Cynthia, who has read, edited, and criticized the many drafts through which the manuscript has gone.

Responsibility for any shortcomings of the volume rests with me alone.

M. R.

Oxford, Ohio

Contents

DEMOCRACY

The Contemporary Theories

Evolution of Democratic Ideas in the West

For twenty-five hundred years, political theory has been concerned with "democracy" as a form of political organization. The concept did not become the subject of sustained theoretical discourse, however, until the nineteenth century. Since then, it has attracted widespread attention in every part of the globe. The present century has witnessed a singular concern with democratic theory. Fresh theoretical attempts have been made, particularly in the postwar period, to throw new light on a topic of immense complexity.

Analytically, democratic theory has had two fairly distinct features. In one sense, it has dealt with certain definitional components or core concepts; in another, it has been concerned with certain preconditions or prerequisites deemed essential for the emergence and flourishing of democratic political orders. The two aspects are closely interrelated, the preconditions often being treated as integral parts of the definition.

This volume undertakes an analysis of some of the major conceptions associated with political "democracy" in the West; in so doing, it develops a typology of the various formulations of democracy, as well as a classification of the major prerequisites deemed necessary for the emergence and survival of democratic political systems. This endeavor will enable us, first, to identify some of the common denominators implicit or explicit in the various conceptions of democracy and, second, to treat with a degree of precision some of the major issues of democratic political theory—particularly as they have evolved in recent times. The point must be reiterated, however, that "definition" and "precondition" overlap at many points, making it impossible to draw a rigid line of demarcation between the two. Thus, the distinction between Part One and Part Two of the present volume is intended to be suggestive and indicative, not dogmatic and absolute.

Before undertaking the major task before us, let us consider briefly the evolution of democratic ideas since their initial appearance in the ancient world. The historical sketch that follows is necessarily selective; it treats only the most important ideas. These include self-government and popular sovereignty, constitutionalism and the rule of law, equality and liberty, individualism and natural (or inalienable) rights, the consent basis of government and citizen participation in community affairs.

DEMOCRATIC IDEAS IN ANTIQUITY

The word "democracy" was coined by the Greek historian Herodotus in the fifth century B.C. and appeared for the first time in his *History*. It combined two Greek words: *demos,* meaning "the people," and *kratein,* meaning "to rule." Thus the original meaning of democracy was, in the literal sense, "rule of the people"; among its specific features Herodotus included equality before the law, popular deliberation, and popular control of public officials.[1] With the possible exception of Pericles, however, subsequent Greek thinkers did not look with favor upon democracy.[2]

1 *History*, III, 80.

2 Pericles' main ideas are set forth in his Funeral Oration, delivered

Plato's attitude, for example, was decidedly hostile, while Aristotle accepted it with severe qualifications.

The central focus of Greek political thought was the concept of the *polis* (the city-state or the city-community), and it is here that some of the nondemocratic features of Greek thought become apparent. To begin with, the *polis* was viewed as a political, moral, and ethical entity, with none of the modern distinctions between nation, state, society, community, church. In lumping together all these units, the *polis* did not permit independent centers of authority.

The doctrine of inequality is a major component of Greek political thought. Both Plato and Aristotle divided the populace into two groups, citizens and noncitizens, the latter consisting, for the most part, of the slaves. The citizenry was further subdivided into several classes (rulers, soldiers, artisans), each of which was deemed fit for a specific task, assigned to a specific function, and required to remain within its own sphere. In fact, as far as Plato and Aristotle were concerned, the main problem of political life was to identify each man's proper station in the *polis*.

Citizenship, to the extent to which it existed, meant political participation and involvement. In fact, Aristotle defined a citizen as one who participates, for any period of time, in a public office. It is important to note, however, that citizenship in ancient Greece did not entail the possession of rights. The concept of rights had not developed and the individual was not seen as having any claims against the political community. Civic obligation, social responsibility, devotion to the *polis*—these were the basic requirements of citizenship.

In addition to emphasizing the importance of political participation and the value of common life, Greek thinkers contributed to democratic ideas by denouncing tyranny and

---

in Athens in 431 B.C., eulogizing those who had fallen in the first year of the Peloponnesian War. The Oration, originally appearing in Thucydides, *History,* II, 35–46, is conveniently appended in William H. Riker, *Democracy in the United States,* second edition (New York: The Macmillan Co., 1965), pp. 345–350.

stressing respect for law. In Greek thought, there is a definite recognition of the necessity of legal restraints upon political power. This is true even of the later writings of Plato, particularly *The Laws*. In Aristotle, respect for law took the form of an explicit emphasis upon constitutionalism, although his conception of constitutionalism was broader than today's and incorporated the entire way of life of the *polis*.

Finally, both Plato and Aristotle viewed the *polis* as an educational enterprise. While differing in details, they both regarded education as indispensable for self-development and effective citizenship. Since the *polis* was a moral community, one of its important functions was the development of rational and moral capacities of its citizens.

Following the Greeks, serious discussions of democracy became something of a rarity in political thought. Although a number of democratic ideas may be identified, the term "democracy" itself did not make a sustained appearance until the nineteenth century.

Rome's major contribution to democratic government consisted in the further development of the concept of constitutionalism and in the emphasis on law as a system of norms binding on the ruler as well as the ruled. The Roman mind's fascination with legal matters was perhaps a consequence of the attempt to identify a concrete basis for unifying and regulating the far-flung empire.

The Roman lawyers, particularly Cicero, succeeded in developing a full-fledged legal system based on three types of law: *jus naturale, jus gentium,* and *jus civile*. The first was the universal law of nature common to all men. The second was the law of nations or international law, regarded as a product of custom and convention. The third was municipal or constitutional law characteristic of individual states and valid for the citizens of a particular community. The second and third types of law, it was specified, were binding only to the extent to which they did not interfere with natural law.

The concept of natural law is one of Cicero's most important contributions, and is a recurring theme in democratic theory.

The earliest expression of natural law is found in the Greek Sophists, who were contemporaries of Socrates. Among the more important of the Sophists were Antiphon, Georgias, Glaucon, Protagoras, and Thrasymachus, some of whom make frequent appearances in Platonic dialogues. It was the Sophists who spelled out for the first time the distinction between the law of nature and the law of man, between natural law and convention. The law of nature was associated with universal reason and held above the laws of men.

With Cicero the concept of natural law became a permanent fixture in political thought. Ciceronian ideas may be summarized in terms of a number of concrete propositions: (1) The cosmos is rational and governed by an underlying principle of order. (2) The cosmic process is moral and a part of the divine plan. Natural law is an expression of divine reason; it precedes the state and is superior to all legislation. (3) Being moral and rational, men can discover and comprehend natural law and govern their lives accordingly. (4) Before the law of nature all men are equal and enjoy equal rights. Natural law applies equally to all individuals because they are equally possessed of reason and equally capable of virtue. (5) Natural law endows men with certain rights that are "natural." These rights precede the state because natural law precedes the state.

In Cicero, in short, not only do we have the systematization of the concept of natural law, but also the first explicit formulation of a theory of natural rights. Since these rights are imparted by natural law, a denial of natural rights amounts to a denial of natural law.

THE MIDDLE AGES

The fall of Rome in the fifth century signaled the collapse of the civilization of antiquity and the increasing predominance of religion over all aspects of life. The overriding characteristic of the Middle Ages is found in one theme and an infinite number of variations: the relationship or the struggle between the "two realms" (secular and spiritual), the "two swords" (temporal and ecclesiastical), the "two laws" (imperial and papal). As neither of the two realms was sufficiently strong to score a decisive victory over the other, the stalemate dragged on for nearly a millennium.

Some parallels between Christian and Roman ideas were potentially conducive to democratic government. These included the conception of a moral law of nature, the quest for a universal society, and the belief in the dignity and equality of men. It must be remembered, however, that Christian ideas had distinctly spiritual implications. Christian equality, for example, referred to the moral equality of all men before God.

Another important insight of Christianity—again, one that was an offshoot of its transtemporal orientation—lay in the belief that obedience to political authority is conditional, not absolute. This accounts, for example, for the advocacy of tyrannicide by John of Salisbury (1110–1180): the notion that if the ruler exceeds his earthly authority and violates the law of God, he may be lawfully slain.

The great synthesizer of medieval times was of course St. Thomas Aquinas. His particular importance for us is that he succeeded in giving natural law a distinctively religious flavor. The law of nature was viewed as the reason of God, the law of creation, the plan of divine wisdom by which the entire world is governed. It is eternal because God's rule is eternal. It represents, at the same time, the participation of all rational creatures in comprehending God's rule. Man, by virtue of his rationality, can participate in divine providence; he must grasp the law of God and order his life accordingly. Natural law was viewed as the final arbiter of conduct; it applied to the ruler and the subjects alike.

The most significant sociopolitical development of the Middle Ages was feudalism. Feudal institutions dominated the medieval period as thoroughly as the *polis* had dominated the ancient world.

Feudalism was essentially a series of relationships between the king, the lord, and the vassal. Too weak to control his land in its entirety, the feudal king distributed its largest portion among the lords in return for loyalty and fidelity. Each feudal unit consisted of a landed estate or a territorial entity in which the lord exercised complete authority. Each lord in turn divided his land among a number of vassals, thereby creating a network of highly personal relationships. The central institution from which the word "feudalism" derives was the *feudum* or the fief: a grant of land by the lord to the vassal in return for services. The vassal pledged loyalty to the lord, in return for which he was given the fief and granted protection. This exchange of services for protection is the very essence of feudalism. Emerging from it are ideas of contract and mutual obligation. These contractual relationships were at first informal and revocable by the lord; later, they became formalized, institutionalized, and irrevocable.

One of the central institutions of feudalism—one that helped formalize the network of feudal relationships—was the court system, through which everyone, including the king (theoretically), was subject to law. There were two types of courts, the lords' courts and the king's courts, each emphasizing trial by equals. The lords' courts were composed of a number of vassals before whom other vassals accused of breaches of contract were tried. The king's courts were composed of a number of lords before whom other lords, even the king himself, could be tried. The king, under the principle of *primus inter pares,*[3] was considered morally obliged to honor his commitments to his personal vassals and to the lords. In case of violation, however, there was no effective means for redress. The important point for our purposes is that the feudal court system has generally been regarded as the forerunner of kings' councils, representative assemblies, and British parliamentarianism.

EARLY MODERN PERIOD

The feudal period began, generally speaking, with the decline of towns and commercial centers following the collapse of Rome; it ended with the revival of towns in the twelfth, thirteenth, and fourteenth centuries. The growth of trade and commerce coincided with the emergence of a "middle class" composed of merchants, shopkeepers, and bankers. Because the towns were defended by the king, the middle class had no need for the protection offered by the lords. Increasingly powerless vis-à-vis the lords, the king attempted to compensate for his inferiority by forming alliances with the rising classes in towns, in return for which he granted protection and the opportunity to participate in community affairs. It soon became clear that the interests of the middle class could only be advanced by a fairly strong central government capable of ordering the domestic economy and regulating commerce and trade.

The revival of towns and commercial centers coincided with the increasing ascendancy of the secular order and the gradual undermining of the spiritual. By the fourteenth century the authority of the Church was being seriously challenged. Marsilio of Padua (1275–1343), for example, explicitly asserted the supremacy of the temporal realm over the ecclesiastical. He had little sympathy with religion, as

3 As the feudal lords gained in power, the position of the king was increasingly undermined until it became one of *primus inter pares* —"first among equals."

he believed that the existence of the Church had prevented the establishment of a unified Italy. Distinguishing between divine law and the law of state, Marsilio argued that the state need not rely on the former at all. The state is the source of its own law and its law must be obeyed.

Other important contributions of Marsilio had to do with the conceptions of consent and representation. His basic arguments were that political authority must rest on agreement, that governmental power must be exercised with restraint, that the various interests in society must find representation in the ruling circles, and that those who are not represented in the making of decisions may choose not to obey them.

The increasing secularization of life was further reinforced by the intellectual revival that swept Europe in the twelfth and thirteenth centuries, and led to the establishment of great universities in Italy, France, England, and elsewhere. By the middle of the fourteenth century, the Copernican revolution had shattered the foundations of religious belief. It resulted, among other things, in a decisive shift of focus from the affairs of the next world to this, from theology to politics.

The Protestant Reformation was the religious counterpart of a host of social, political, and economic changes that all pointed toward individualism. The Reformation stressed the primacy of personal conscience and the possibility of direct relationship between man and God. It meant, particularly for Luther, elimination of the Church as the intermediary between the individual and his Creator. It provided each man with the opportunity to interpret the scriptures for himself.

The Protestant Reformation did not give a single answer to the problem of man's life and destiny. For Luther, human sinfulness was beyond remedy and salvation could be attained through faith alone. Calvin, by contrast, while subscribing to the notion of human depravity, regarded the individual as capable of doing a great deal to achieve salvation. Whereas for Luther salvation was a matter of divine forgiveness, for Calvin it was a question of individual effort and hard work. Success in this world, particularly in the economic field, was seen as a concrete indication of the possibility of redemption. In this lies the basis for the coalescence between Protestantism and the growing capitalist economic system. As Max Weber and R. H. Tawney have argued, Protestantism not only sanctified individual initiative and exertion, it rationalized man's acquisitive impulse into a moral duty and a "calling." According to Weber, Calvin's emphasis on personal achievement as fulfilling the command of God proved especially congenial to the "spirit of capitalism."[4] Tawney makes the point that one of the most distinctive features of Calvinism as a religion was that "It assumed an economic organization which was relatively advanced, and expounded its social ethics on the basis of it."[5]

Calvinism found its most vigorous supporters in the industrial, commercial, manufacturing, and business classes, whose interests could best be advanced in an orderly and fairly permissive political environment and whose existence was eventually deemed necessary for the emergence of democratic government. We shall return in Chapter 6 to the relationship between Protestantism and capitalism. For the moment, the basic notion is that Protestantism was congenial to the development of capitalism, which was in turn conducive to the emergence of democratic government.

The Renaissance witnessed the intensification of optimism about the future of man; it led to further expressions of individualism, particularly in the intellectual and artis-

4 *The Protestant Ethic and the Spirit of Capitalism,* translated by Talcott Parsons with a Foreword by R. H. Tawney (New York: Charles Scribner's Sons, 1958), p. 108 *et passim.*

5 *Religion and the Rise of Capitalism* (New York: The New American Library, 1947), p. 91.

tic fields. The Renaissance saw the dramatic emancipation of man from religious and medieval ties. As Jacob Burckhardt, perhaps the most noted historian of the Renaissance, has pointed out, the core of the Renaissance was the discovery of man and the emphasis on individual self-expression, self-realization, glory, and fame.[6] Only the Renaissance could have produced the "universal man" who took it upon himself fully to develop his potentialities and give expression to all aspects of his personality.

One of the central contributions of the Renaissance was the concept of the secular state. Its chief theoretician was Machiavelli, whose main objective was the unification of Italy, a goal that he believed, with Marsilio, had been undermined by the Church. The major theme of Machiavelli's thought is the stability and instablity of political orders; *The Prince* is a handbook for creating a stable, secular state.

Following Machiavelli, the concept of the state was further developed by a host of writers, including Jean Bodin, Hugo Grotius, and Thomas Hobbes. When combined with the notion of "sovereignty," the state became a definite impediment to the development of democratic government. "Sovereignty" referred to the quality of supreme, final, absolute, and ultimate power in the hands of the ruler or the state. The conception of ruler-as-sovereign, or state-as-sovereign, fitted neatly into the scheme of monarchical absolutism. It provided the monarch with rationalization and justification for establishing absolute control over society. This concentration of power was manifestly detrimental to the development of democratic ideas.

THE THEORY OF THE SOCIAL CONTRACT

The seventeenth and eighteenth centuries witnessed a resurgence of democratic ideas. The scene was England and France, and the chief spokesmen were Locke and Rousseau.

6 *The Civilization of the Renaissance in Italy* (London: G. G. Harrap & Co., 1929).

The formula—"social contract"—proved to be of crucial importance for modern government.

The theory of the social contract did not originate with Locke and Rousseau, although they did much to popularize it. The notion was explicit or implicit in both the Greek Sophists and the Roman lawyers. The Sophists distinguished between natural law and convention and argued that the latter originates in agreement among individuals. Such agreements, they maintained, were not binding upon those who had not participated in their original formation.

In making a distinction between state and society, and in viewing man as naturally gregarious, the Roman lawyers (particularly Cicero) regarded society as natural to man. State, on the other hand, was looked upon as a product of consent (perhaps tacit) among individuals. Proceeding from the people, they held, political authority must be employed in such a way as to further their collective interests. Power was grounded in law and before law all citizens were considered to possess equal rights. Cicero, in fact, described the state as a "community of law."

The immense popularity of the social contract in the seventeenth and eighteenth centuries has been attributed to a number of causes. Most important perhaps, the social contract was an expression of revolt against sovereignty, absolute government, and monarchical rule. It signified the assertion of the freedom of the individual, the consent basis of government, and the justification of rule over men. Government, in other words, was viewed as an agent of the governed; it does what it is specifically authorized to do. It is not an end in itself.

Both Locke and Rousseau stressed the intrinsic value of the individual, although in the latter the individual has often been interpreted as submerged in the collectivity. Both emphasized that the key to political order lies in agreement among men. Rousseau in fact goes a step further by insisting that mere agreement is too passive and that what is required is active and voluntary participation of each individual in the creation of political society.

The Lockean theory of the social contract is based explicitly on natural law as a moral, universal, and eternal phenomenon, comprehensible to all men of reason. The law of nature is seen to impart certain rights that are natural, inalienable, and absolute—including "life, liberty, and estate." For Locke, men are "by nature all free, equal, and independent"; they are born "with a title to perfect freedom." As such, no man may legitimately subject another to his will, nor may he be subjected to the will of another. The formation of political society is a consequence of man's desire to eliminate certain "inconveniences" or "wants" of the "state of nature"—particularly the want of a "common judge" as the arbiter of disputes. The purpose of the state is to provide the kind of protection that is not available in the state of nature. The "great and chief end" of men in forming governments, according to Locke, is the preservation of their property—"property" defined so broadly as to include "lives, liberties and estates." The political society is a "trust" and government is an agent of the governed: it merely does what it is told to do. It follows that if the ruler exceeds his political authority and violates the trust, he may be rightfully overthrown through revolution and violence.[7]

For Rousseau the central problem of political life is spelled out in the opening sentence of Chapter I, Book I, of *The Social Contract:* "Man is born free; and everywhere he is in chains." Rousseau's declared objective is to identify the conditions under which the "chains" may be legitimized. He attempts to do this by constructing a political utopia in which the nature of man and the functions of government are harmonized, a society in which there is no compulsion

7 All this, needless to say, represents the conventional interpretation of Locke. For a treatment of Locke's thought as Hobbesian philosophy in disguise, see Richard H. Cox, *Locke on War and Peace* (Oxford: The Clarendon Press, 1960).

and force. Rousseau's argument is that the transition from the state of nature to civil society takes place through a social compact that is the product of man's act of willing: through the contract, the moral man voluntarily chooses to live in society. Unable to live alone, man wills to be a part of a larger system of social and emotional commitments. In and out of society, in other words, man obeys himself.

The formation of the political society coincides with the creation of the "general will." In constructing a political society, Rousseau argues, each and every man surrenders himself completely. Each man contributes all of his rights toward the creation of the "general will"; "each man, in giving himself to all, gives himself to nobody." The surrender of rights is total; the recipient is the general will.

Though the vaguest concept in Rousseau, the general will appears to refer to the collective moral entity that emerges from the contract. It is infallible, flawless, always for the common good, and never wrong. Above all, it is the supreme embodiment of man's act of willing. Its very existence justifies the change from nature to society, and makes the "chains" legitimate.

The concept of sovereignty, nowhere used in Locke, reappears in Rousseau but it is now lodged in the people themselves and is regarded as an attribute of the general will. Sovereignty, says Rousseau, is "nothing less than the exercise of general will." It is absolute, limitless, indestructible, indivisible, and inalienable. In specifying the people as the source of sovereignty, Rousseau seeks to reverse the traditional relationship between the ruler and the ruled.

Rousseau's over-all emphasis is on an ethical, moral, and perfectly unified community. He envisions the complete psychic and emotional identification of the individual with the collectivity. Man obeys the state because the state is the embodiment of the general will. Thus, in obeying the state, man obeys himself. It is in this sense that he may be "forced to be free." And it is for this reason that Rousseau is sometimes interpreted as the forerunner of "totalitarian democracy."[8]

Locke and Rousseau, it should be apparent, are in disagreement over many issues. They do agree, however, in denouncing authoritarian rule, asserting the rights of the individual, attempting to reconcile the conflicting claims of liberty and order, and delineating the basis of political legitimacy and the grounds for man's obedience to the state.

DEMOCRATIC THEORY IN THE NINETEENTH CENTURY

Democratic theory came of age in the nineteenth century. The French Revolution shattered the foundations of absolutism and swept aside remnants of the feudal order. With it, liberty, equality, and fraternity became the catchwords of democracy; they were formalized in the Declaration of the Rights of Man and Citizen (August 26, 1789), a document that followed closely the pattern set in the Declaration of Independence.

Prior to the nineteenth century, as we have seen, a number of ideas could be identified as democratic or predemocratic, but seldom was there a systematic attempt to develop a theory of democracy. In fact, the word "democracy" rarely appeared in the literature. The systematization and elaboration of democratic theory in the nineteenth century is primarily the work of four men: Thomas Jefferson, Abraham Lincoln, John Stuart Mill, and Alexis de Tocqueville. The first three, together with Locke and Rousseau, are generally identified as the "classical" theorists of democracy. We shall clarify this term in Chapter 1 and employ it as a basis for comparing the nineteenth-century theories of democracy with their twentieth-century counterparts. For the moment,

8 The most sustained argument to this effect is in J. L. Talmon, *The Origins of Totalitarian Democracy* (New York: Frederick A. Praeger, 1960), pp. 38–49 *et passim*.

let us complete our review of the evolution of democratic theory by briefly summarizing the major ideas associated with Jefferson, Lincoln, de Tocqueville, and Mill.

Much of Jeffersonian political thought is a paraphrasing of the Lockean position. For Jefferson, as for Locke, the world is governed by a moral and universal law of nature. This law imparts equally to all rational men certain inalienable rights, among which "life, liberty, and the pursuit of happiness" are included. For Jefferson, Locke's "life, liberty, and estate" was apparently too narrow; "pursuit of happiness" is a more comprehensive—and a much vaguer—concept. Natural rights, Jefferson maintained with Locke, are enjoyed by man in both nature and society. The idea is "quite unfounded," he wrote, that "on entering into society we give up any natural right."

Jeffersonian thought is characterized by a serious dualism as a consequence of the attempt to lay almost equal emphasis on liberty and equality, on individual welfare and the general interest.[9] Jefferson stood for absolute liberty (natural rights) as well as for equality. "The true foundation of republican government," he wrote, "is the equal right of every citizen. . . ."[10]

For Jefferson, as for Locke, government is the product of agreement among men; it remains an agent of the governed. Sovereignty resides with the people: "the mass of the citizens," according to Jefferson, "is the safest depository" of governmental power. He was convinced of the capacity of the common man to govern himself, the only requirement being that he be educated. The chief function of government is to secure and preserve liberty and equality of all citizens. When it exceeds its authority, rebellion is called for. In fact, Jefferson maintained that an occasional rebel-

9 For a discussion of some problems associated with the relationship between liberty and equality, see Chapter 1.

10 "To Samuel Kercheval," July 12, 1816. *The Writings of Thomas Jefferson,* X, collected and edited by Paul L. Ford (New York: G. P. Putnam's Sons, 1899).

lion "is a medicine necessary for the sound health of government." (The Jeffersonian ideal of "ward republic" will be discussed in Chapter 6.)

Lincoln shared with Jefferson a number of ideas crucial to the development of American democratic thought. He too consistently stressed the values of liberty and equality: democracy could only be founded on the freedom of the individual and the abolition of master-slave relationships.

Lincoln was a firm believer in the capacity of men to govern themselves. The American experiment, he thought, had established the truth of his proposition. Self-government, he argued, is "morally right and politically wise"; popular sovereignty is a "sacred right." Accordingly, he approached democracy as "government of the people, by the people, for the people."

Since unanimity is impossible, however, a legally constituted majority becomes an important element of democratic government; the alternative, Lincoln maintained, is "anarchy or despotism." Lincoln's faith in majority rule was such as to lead him to question, at least at one point, the role of the Supreme Court in the American political process. The irrevocable nature of Supreme Court decisions, he stated, means that "the people will have ceased to be their own rulers, having, to that extent, practically resigned their government into the hands of that eminent tribunal."

De Tocqueville was no particular friend of democratic government and our reason for considering him lies in the extensive commentary that he provided on American democracy. He approached democracy in terms of two basic norms —equality and popular sovereignty—and proceeded to see equality as a major threat to *his* cherished value, liberty. According to de Tocqueville, popular sovereignty must constitute the starting point in any analysis of American politics. In America, he stated, popular sovereignty "is unencumbered by those fictions that are thrown over it in other countries, and it appears in every possible form, according to the exigency of the occasion."[11] He believed that "The people reign in the American political world as the Deity does in the universe."[12]

A second distinguishing mark of American democracy, according to de Tocqueville, is equality. In fact, he wrote explicitly that "nothing struck me more forcibly than the general equality of condition among the people."[13] A main theme of de Tocqueville's work revolves around the problem of reconciling personal liberty with democratic equality. He argued that American democracy offered some possibilities for such reconciliation, but he did not see the threat to liberty as completely removed. De Tocqueville's fear of equality is understandable. In a note entitled "My Instinct, My Opinions" (November 1841), he wrote: "I am an aristocrat by instinct. . . ."

Among the institutional variables of democracy, de Tocqueville specified the following as essential: separation of powers, the federal system, local self-government, political parties, and public opinion. He was highly skeptical of majority rule and was one of the first to employ the phrase "tyranny of the majority." Majority rule, he argued, should be limited; it is oppressive and detrimental to liberty. (De Tocqueville's assessment of New England democracy will be considered in Chapter 6.)

Much of Mill's political thought was motivated by a desire to maximize liberty within the framework of representative government. He paid detailed attention to the practical requirements of democracy. In at least one place he specifically stated that "such phrases as 'self-government' and 'the power of the people over themselves' do not express

11 *Democracy in America,* 2 volumes (New York: Alfred A. Knopf, 1945), I, 57.
12 *Ibid.,* p. 58.
13 *Ibid.,* p. 3.

the true state of the case." For him, representative government signified universal suffrage, free elections, short terms of office, and popular control of government. Without liberty, however, representative institutions were meaningless.

There is, according to Mill, an intrinsic value in human personality that commands respect independently of society or government. He saw individual self-expression and freedom—particularly intellectual freedom—as means for maximizing social progress. Mill asserted the absolute character of liberty of thought and expression, the "absolute freedom of opinion." Freedom, in short, was the supreme end. Progress consisted of the development of free individuals.

Mill was no believer in equality. He wrote that although representative government means that individuals have a voice in running the government, "an equal voice is a totally different proposition." In fact, it has been sometimes argued, Mill's emphasis on the freedom of thought and expression logically culminates in the enshrinement of some sort of intellectual elitism.

SUMMARY

The historical emergence of democratic ideas confronted a series of obstacles and their firm grounding took place only in the nineteenth century. The main contributions of antiquity to democratic government consisted of the emphasis on political involvement and participation in community affairs, the belief in constitutionalism and supremacy of law, the explicit denunciation of tyranny, and the notions of natural law and natural rights.

The Middle Ages were significant for our purposes in the pervasive (albeit religious) belief in the dignity and equality of men, the infusion of natural law with a distinctly religious flavor, the belief in the relative and conditional nature of political authority, the notion that illegal government may be overthrown, the development of ideas of contractual relationships and mutual obligation, and the appearance of conceptions of consent, parliamentarianism and representation.

The modern period witnessed, in addition to the fuller elaboration of some of the foregoing ideas, a clear emphasis on individualism as a result of the coalescence of secular and religious forces, the development of concepts of governmental legitimacy, popular sovereignty, popular control, and self-government.

Having summarized the historical evolution of democratic ideas, we are now ready to proceed with the main burden of our task: an analytical treatment of the various theories of democracy in recent times. Although our primary interest lies in the twentieth-century conceptions, we shall devote some attention to the dominant features of pre-twentieth-century theories.

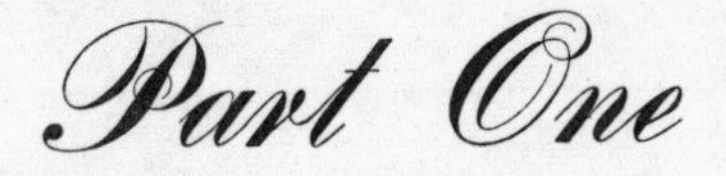

DEFINITIONS OF DEMOCRACY

1
A Typology of Definitions

It has been estimated that there may be two hundred definitions of democracy.[1] More important than specifying the mere number of definitions, however, is the development of a comprehensive typology or classification under which the various conceptions may be grouped.

Traditionally definitions of democracy have been grouped under two headings: "normative" (or "classical") and "empirical." The former definitions are primarily concerned with certain values or norms; the latter attempt to describe and explain political reality. Closer examination reveals that, as a third category, a number of definitions are neither strictly normative nor purely empirical but combine elements of the two. This group we shall designate "normative-empirical." Finally, a fourth category—"ideological"—is added to the list. It differs from the first three by placing its emphasis on a collective mental outlook, on certain shared beliefs, attitudes, and habits. Our task in this chapter is to examine each of these types in greater detail.

NORMATIVE DEFINITIONS

Normative or classical conceptions of democracy, as we have seen, are represented in the works of Locke, Rousseau, Jef-

1 Massimo Salvadori, *Liberal Democracy* (Garden City: Doubleday & Co., 1957), p. 20.

ferson, Lincoln, and Mill. From an analytical point of view, these conceptions fall into two main schools or traditions: the individualistic and the collectivistic. The former, represented in our examples by Locke, Jefferson and Mill, is concerned primarily with the welfare of the individual person. The *main* values are rights and liberties—absolute intellectual liberty for Mill; "natural," "inalienable," and "self-evident" rights for Locke and Jefferson. The collectivistic tradition, by contrast, as represented by Rousseau and Lincoln, is concerned with the welfare of the community or society as a whole. Its *main* value is equality, and it stresses such ideals as "common will" and "common good." Whereas for the individualistic tradition, equality is a secondary value, for this school, liberty is a subordinate norm. It must be stated immediately, however, that some formulations of democracy—notably those of Jefferson and Lincoln—attempted to embrace both liberty and equality, and this attempt, as we shall see, led to serious difficulties, particularly when the two values were rigidly interpreted.[2] Other norms and ideals (for example, self-government, popular sovereignty) were shared by the two varieties of classical democratic theory. Finally, all classical expressions of democracy had in common the assumption of the goodness and rationality of the ordinary individual. Without this

2 "Equality" and "liberty" have been used in a wide variety of senses in the literature of political science. Since it will not be our task to specify usage in every instance, we will clarify the principal meanings of the two concepts at this point.

"Equality" has been used in at least four principal senses: political (as in voting), legal (as before the law), economic (as in distribution of wealth or opportunity), and moral (as before God). See, for example, Sanford A. Lakoff, *Equality in Political Philosophy* (Cambridge, Mass.: Harvard University Press, 1964); J. Roland Pennock and John W. Chapman, eds., *Equality, Nomos IX* (New York: Atherton Press, 1967).

"Liberty" has had several more or less distinct usages as well: liberty as the absence of restraint, liberty as the presence of opportunity (including opportunity for self-development), and liberty as the capacity for self-exertion. See, for example, Carl J. Friedrich, ed., *Liberty, Nomos IV* (New York: Atherton Press, 1962).

assumption, all other stipulated values would lose much of their significance. What, for example, would remain of self-government or government by the people, if the "people" were not good, rational, and capable of self-rule?

The classical expressions of democracy came under heavy assault from a number of sources. Although there were other opponents, by far the most trenchant criticism of democracy was undertaken by a group of intellectuals commonly known as the elitists and including Vilfredo Pareto, Gateo Mosca, Roberto Michels, and, in a certain sense, Georges Sorel.[3] A detailed analysis of the various attacks upon the classical theory is beyond the scope of the present volume; we shall briefly outline, first, the general arguments against the classical conceptions and, then, the elitist critique.[4]

The general points raised against the classical theories of democracy may be summarized in the following terms. First, it was argued, available evidence overwhelmingly negates the notion that "government by the people" has ever been —or is ever likely to be—a reality. Men, it was pointed out, cannot—in the literal sense—rule themselves. Second, such conceptions as "common will" and "common good" are mystical, intuitive notions, incapable of demonstration and

3 Pareto's major work is *The Mind and Society,* 4 volumes (London: Jonathan Cape, 1935). For Mosca see *The Ruling Class* (New York: McGraw-Hill, 1939); and "The Final Version of the Theory of the Ruling Class," in James H. Meisel, *The Myth of the Ruling Class* (Ann Arbor: University of Michigan Press, 1958). For Michels see *Political Parties* (New York: Collier Books, 1962).

It is rather difficult to classify Sorel as an elitist. In fact, insofar as he blends aspects of Marxism, syndicalism, romanticism, etc., it is difficult to classify him at all. Relevant for our purposes are his conceptions of "myth" and "violence," as discussed in *Reflections on Violence* (New York: Collier Books, 1961).

4 For detailed treatment, see, for example: T. B. Bottomore, *Elites and Society* (London: C. A. Watts & Co., 1964); James Burnham, *The Machiavellians* (New York: John Day, 1943); Francis W. Coker, *Recent Political Thought* (New York: Appleton-Century, 1934); H. Stuart Hughes, *Consciousness and Society* (New York: Vintage Books, 1961); Meisel, *op. cit.*; Renzo Sereno, *The Rulers* (New York: Frederick A. Praeger, 1962); David Spitz, *Patterns of Anti-Democratic Thought* (New York: The Macmillan Co., 1949).

testing. There is no *one* policy, no *one* "good," that can be beneficial to every member of a society. To be sure, such "goods" as defense and education are of general benefit, but they cannot be the distinguishing marks of democracies, as they are provided by *all* states. Using these criteria, in other words, it would be impossible to sort out the democratic from the nondemocratic states. Third, "natural law" and "natural rights" are assumptions neither verifiable nor necessary to political life. There is no way in which the validity of a natural-law proposition can be tested; there is no society in which man's rights are "natural" or absolute. Fourth, liberty and equality, if interpreted in rigid and literal terms, emerge as contradictory values, incapable of attainment in any society. As George H. Sabine has put it, "the more liberty the less equality, and the more equality the less liberty."[5] Stated somewhat differently, if men are free, they are not necessarily equal; if they are forced to be equal, they are no longer free. Finally, it was suggested, the underlying premise of the classical theory—its faith in a rational political man—is untenable, particularly in the light of the findings of modern psychology.

To these general (and largely negative) criticisms of the classical theory of democracy, the elitists added a series of positive points. They maintained at the outset that to be fruitful, social and political analysis must be objective; to be objective, it must rest on observable and verifiable grounds. The raw material of social science is found in the facts of man's actual behavior in societies. The elitists insisted, under the strong influence of Freudian psychology, that the image of the rational political man held by the classical theorists was exaggerated and overdrawn. As they saw it, a significant portion of human behavior is motivated and sustained by irrational and nonlogical drives lying well below the level of consciousness. Man's conduct

5 "The Two Democratic Traditions," *The Philosophical Review,* 61 (October 1952), p. 452.

is governed as much by unconscious habit as by deliberate choice. In short, the elitist conception of human society centered on the prevalence of the nonlogical and the irrational, or to use Pareto's term, "residues."

The elitist analysis of social evolution established to their satisfaction that human society at all times has been characterized by a fundamental division between a minority that rules and a majority that is ruled, between elite and mass. They interpreted politics in terms of violent conflicts among contending groups for the ruling positions in sociey. Democratic politics, as all politics, was understood in terms of a persistent and violent struggle for power. Social change, Sorel for example argued, can only come through violence; to be effective, violence must be rationalized and justified in ideological terms.

The concept of ideology emerges as a major variable in the elitist analysis of society. Used synonymously with "myth" (Sorel) and "political formula" (Mosca), ideology was viewed as the matrix of social behavior, the guiding force in human society, and the principal means for attaining social solidarity. It was approached as an instrument for leadership manipulation and control of the masses, a means for rationalizing, legitimizing, and perpetuating a given state of affairs. (A more detailed discussion of ideology appears later in this chapter.)

Roberto Michels distinguished himself by extending the application of the elitist theme to all social organizations, large and small. A most curious phenomenon about Michels, as about the other elitists, was that they violated one of the first principles of a scientific social science on which they all insisted: they worked with limited data and generalized from a narrow empirical base. In Michels' case, empirical analysis was limited largely to the German social democratic parties.

Michels' basic arguments were that leadership is indispensable to *any* organization of whatever size; that even if initially selected through democratic processes, leadership has a tendency to become institutionalized, self-perpetuating, and oligarchical; that even though one set of leaders may replace another the rank and file never rules itself. Michels attributed the emergence of oligarchy to a number of sources, among which leadership access to organizational funds and to the media of communication were specified. He felt the most important causes of oligarchy, however, were the characteristics and needs of the followers themselves. The rank and file (and by implication, the masses), Michels argued, being generally incompetent and driven by irrational impulses, have a psychological *need* for leadership. They willingly submit to any group that is capable of making decisions for them, determining their daily routine, and simplifying their lives. In short, Michels' argument centered around the "iron law of oligarchy." The entire matter was summed up in the following line: "Who says organization, says oligarchy."[6]

To summarize to this point, the elitist arguments against the classical theories of democracy concentrated on the primacy of the irrational impulses in human life, the importance of ideology and myth, the inescapable distinction between elite and mass, the role of power and violence, and the inevitability of oligarchy. The main conclusion was that democracy is an irrational, impossible, or undesirable form of political organization; the masses are incompetent and incapable of self-government; the few will always rule.

Confronted with such an overpowering critique, and recognizing the validity of much of the argument, the modern theorists of democracy set out—ostensibly perhaps—to revise and update the classical conceptions. The net result, however, has not been mere adaptation but some basic changes in democratic theory. The principal attribute of the newer definitions is that rather than idealizing nonexistent states

6 Michels, *op. cit.*, p. 365.

of affairs, they seek to define democracy in terms of a series of propositions, practices, and institutions that can be observed and operationalized. The practical utility of metaphysical speculation and armchair philosophizing is seriously questioned. This point is well illustrated in T. D. Weldon, one of the major critics of traditional political philosophy in general. Having summarized the "metaphysical foundations of democracy," by which he means the value bases of the classical theories, he adds:

> What we really want to know however is what is the use of all this. Suppose we could accept the premises and the reasoning, should we be any better off? I think that we should not. The objection to this sort of argument is not merely that it depends for its force on . . . fallacious assumptions . . . but that the conclusions to which it leads are either vacuous or highly disputable and not at all self-evident. The position is not that the statements which go to make up the fundamental principles of democracy are false or that the basic rules of democratic legislation are bad. It is that we are mistaken in supposing that what we have to do with here are statements or rules at all. Admittedly "All men are created equal" looks like a statement and "Men are always to be treated as ends and never as means" looks like the formulation of a rule. It is natural to suppose therefore that we have here fundamental rules from which others can be deduced. . . . But it is not so. Nothing follows from these high abstractions, or if you like anything does. . . . We can derive no actual law from them and appraise no actual law by means of them. That is what I mean by saying that as foundations they are useless. They do not and cannot do what they purport to do, that is, serve as axioms from which practical conclusions can be derived.[7]

7 *The Vocabulary of Politics* (Baltimore: Penguin Books, 1953), pp. 97–98.

This point of view, needless to say, is not uniformly shared by all contemporary theorists. The group of writers whom for want of a better term we shall call "neoclassicist," seeks to maintain and perpetuate the classical tradition. Thus such contemporary writers as John H. Hallowell, J. Roland Pennock, and Austin Ranney and Willmoore Kendall continue to expound and symbolize the classical theory of democracy. Hallowell, for example, insists on the validity of "objective" moral truths that are independent of human existence and embodied in the law of nature. Natural law, he writes, "provides universally applicable principles" for all men; it is the "foundation" of democracy.[8] He persists in maintaining a view of man as a "rational, moral, and spiritual creature."[9] He argues that man's knowledge of the "good" and his capacity to choose it constitute the basis of freedom, and that freedom is the essence of democracy. This freedom, in Hallowell's view, is basically moral and religious in character.

Similarly, Pennock conceives of democracy as a "way of life" representing "the full development of the Stoic-Christian concept of the essential moral equality of men."[10] Though Pennock is aware of, and at times insistent upon, the "practicability" requirement of democratic government, this awareness is overshadowed by the normative thrust of his argument. He defines "liberal democracy" in terms of "a system of powers and a system of liberties." His analysis of the latter is essentially a reiteration of the American Bill of Rights; "the system of powers," surprisingly enough, refers to "the powers of self-government." "If democracy means anything," Pennock holds, "it means government by the people."

8 *The Moral Foundation of Democracy* (Chicago: University of Chicago Press, 1954), pp. 25, 115.
9 *Ibid.*, p. 128.
10 *Liberal Democracy: Its Merits and Prospects* (New York: Rinehart and Co., 1950), p. 17.

In Ranney and Kendall, too, the conception of democracy approaches the classical theory. Having stated categorically that "we understand the terms 'democracy' and 'self-government' to mean *exactly* the same thing,"[11] they propose a "model" of democracy embracing four principal features: popular sovereignty, political equality, popular consultation, and "absolute" majority rule. The argument for the "absolute" character of majority rule stems from the authors' belief that it is "an inescapable attribute of any model of *perfectly* democratic government," and that "any attempt to place *formal* institutional limitations upon the 'absolute' power of popular majorities logically results in the establishment of *minority* rule."

To summarize, the classical conceptions of democracy, whether individualistic or collectivistic, rest upon a series of norms and ideals lacking systematic reference to political reality. The difficulties associated with the classical theories have been amply demonstrated by their critics, particularly the elitists. Although a few writers continue to subscribe to the classical point of view, the characteristic emphasis of contemporary democratic theory is on identification and isolation of observable variables in political life. The attempt is to describe and explain rather than to idealize.

EMPIRICAL DEFINITIONS

As a rule empirical conceptions of democracy have been concerned with explicating certain behavioral or institutional variables operative in the actual working of democratic political systems. A representative sample of these conceptions may be explored in the works of E. F. M. Durbin, Joseph A. Schumpeter, Carl J. Friedrich, Robert A. Dahl, E. E. Schattschneider, and Seymour Martin Lipset.

11 *Democracy and the American Party System* (New York: Harcourt, Brace and Co., 1956), p. 2.

Durbin's work represents one of the earliest attempts to develop an operational definition of democracy.[12] He explicitly notes that "in my description of democracy, there is no reference to . . . any characteristic of the ideal society." He approaches democracy in terms of three basic variables: (1) provisions for popular selection (and dismissal) of the government; (2) existence of a viable, respected, and formal opposition; and (3) a condition of "mutual toleration" governing the relationships between the parties and groups contending for power. The role of the opposition emerges so crucial as to lead Durbin to equate democracy with "the toleration of opposition." The democratic method, he holds, is a means for reconciling competing claims and divergent interests in society.

A central theme emerging from Durbin's analysis—one that is reiterated in various forms by most of the writers represented in this volume—is the characterization of democracy as responsible and responsive government. Government is responsible to the extent to which it remains answerable to the electorate; it is responsive to the extent to which it is willing and able to meet the reasonable demands of the public. The basic feature of democratic government, in this view, is not self-rule; it is popular control of those who are selected to make the important decisions for a political society.

Schumpeter undertakes an explicit attack upon the "classical doctrine of democracy," rejecting such notions as "common good" and "common will" as unascertainable myths. He gives an alternative definition in terms of leadership and competition in a pluralistic political environment. The primary function of the people, he states, is not to decide

12 Durbin's chief interest lies in democratic socialism. Until his death in 1948, he was a ranking member of the British Labour Party and his main book is entitled *The Politics of Democratic Socialism.* However, the two concepts "democracy" and "socialism" are treated as distinctive in Durbin and they may be approached as such. In fact, he argues specifically that his definition of democracy is as applicable to capitalism as it is to socialism.

issues but "to produce a government." He writes: "the democratic method is that institutional arrangement for arriving at political decisions in which the individuals acquire the power to decide by means of a competitive struggle for the people's vote." Of particular interest in the selection reprinted from Schumpeter is his analysis of reasons for the continued existence of the classical theory of democracy.

Friedrich equates "democracy" with "constitutional democracy." The distinctive mark of "constitutionalism" is the division of powers; division makes possible a system of regularized and effective restraints upon governmental power, thereby ensuring political responsibility. Friedrich specifies two types of restraint: substantive and procedural. Substantive restraints upon political power emerge from constitutional rights specifically granted to the citizens; procedural restraints refer to the "checks and balances" regulating the day-to-day operation of government. The two types of restraint are equally important: "substantive restraints . . . rest upon a tenuous foundation unless reinforced and backed by procedural restraints. . . ." Whether substantive or procedural, however, the end is the same: production of responsible government and prevention of abuse of power.[13]

For Dahl, as for many other theorists, democracy requires, as a minimum, the existence of "processes by which ordinary citizens exert a relatively high degree of control over leaders. . . ."[14] He identifies three historical types of democracy in the United States: the Madisonian, the populistic, and the polyarchal. The first two have in common the attempt

13 In a later work Friedrich introduces a strong normative strand into his conception of constitutional democracy. In attempting to relate democratic government to certain religious and spiritual values, he specifies the Christian "self" as the all-embracing norm. Constitutionalism, Friedrich argues, came into being in the West in order "to protect the self in its dignity and worth." He writes: "the self is believed to be primary and of penultimate value." See *Transcendent Justice: The Religious Dimension of Constitutionalism* (Durham, N.C.: Duke University Press, 1964), pp. 10, 16 *et passim.*

14 *A Preface to Democratic Theory* (Chicago: University of Chicago Press, 1956), p. 3.

to maximize certain norms. The central proposition of Madisonian theory, according to Dahl, is that "If unrestrained by external checks, any given individual or group of individuals will tyrannize over others."[15] As such, the central value to be maximized is a nontyrannical government. The means are seen as majority rule, limited government, separation of powers, and checks and balances. The distinguishing feature of the populistic theory—the heart of the Jeffersonian-Jacksonian formula—is the identification of democracy with popular sovereignty, political equality, and majority rule. What is also emphasized are the inalienable and natural rights of man. (According to this interpretation, we might note, Friedrich's conception of democracy resembles the Madisonian.)

Both of these theories, as Dahl points out, rest on ethical propositions. They are concerned with logical and axiomatic relationships not necessarily consistent with the "real world." By contrast, the polyarchal theory is empirical in nature; it deals with a series of verifiable relationships. Dahl defines polyarchy in terms of eight conditions dealing essentially with pluralism, competition, bargaining, periodic elections, political participation, and the like. He is explicit that while these conditions may be approximated, they are not completely attained. Dahl's concern is not with democracy in its pure form but with the real-world approximation of democracy—that is to say, "polyarchy."[16]

Schattschneider's conception of democracy rests on somewhat different premises. Having argued the thesis that (1) the pattern of all politics is found in the "contagiousness of conflict" and (2) the primary function of democracy is the "socialization of conflict," Schattschneider defines democracy as "a competitive political system in which competing

15 *Ibid.*, p. 6.

16 It should be noted that an earlier conception of polyarchy developed by Robert A. Dahl and Charles E. Lindblom embraces explicitly normative components. See *Politics, Economics, and Welfare* (New York: Harper and Brothers, 1953), especially pp. 277–278.

leaders and organizations define the alternatives of public policy in such a way that the public can participate in the decision-making process." He specifically rejects the classical definitions, arguing that "The beginning of wisdom in democratic theory is to distinguish between the things the people can do and the things the people cannot do." Popular involvement in politics, according to Schattschneider, is not due to any specific capacity for self-rule; it is a function of the contagious nature of conflict. By overlooking this point, he maintains, the classical theorists of democracy introduced a serious gap between philosophical ideals and political reality.

For Lipset, finally, democracy consists of "a political system which supplies regular constitutional opportunities for changing the governing officials. It is a social mechanism for the resolution of the problem of societal decision-making . . . which permits the largest possible part of the population to influence these decisions through their ability to choose among alternative contenders for political office." This requires at least three groups of conditions: (1) one set of leaders in office, (2) one or more sets of leaders out of office, and (3) a "political formula" legitimizing the system as a whole.

It can be seen, then, that the contemporary empirical conceptions of democracy have fundamentally departed from the major premises of the classical theories in stipulating a set of behavior patterns, institutions, practices, and procedures that can be observed in the actual working of political societies. The core of the newer definitions may be summed up in terms of pluralism, competition, responsiveness, and responsibility.

NORMATIVE-EMPIRICAL DEFINITIONS

A third group of democratic theorists are distinguished by an endeavor to fuse aspects of the normative and empirical conceptions. Some of the more important attempts in this direction are found in the works of A. D. Lindsay, Ernest Barker, John Dewey, Robert M. MacIver, Giovanni Sartori, H. B. Mayo, and Anthony Downs.

This, to be sure, is a large group of thinkers and they differ among themselves in many respects. For our purposes, however, the important point is that they do have in common an attempt to reconcile certain traditional democratic norms with evidential variables in concrete political systems. Although taking many forms, as we shall see, the operational variables of these theories all seek to ensure governmental responsibility and popular control. The values in question can be reduced to four: liberty, equality, fraternity, and "community." The last norm is the most comprehensive and may embrace the other three.

A further word may be said about the distinction between this category of democratic theory and the classical conceptions. Two criteria have been used in distinguishing the two types of formulation: (1) the absoluteness (or relativity) with which the norms are stated, and (2) the degree of systematic attention paid to verifiable elements. These criteria are admittedly somewhat crude and arbitrary, and they may permit the intrusion of subjective elements. Nevertheless, one cannot avoid the realization that even though both Rousseau and MacIver, for example, stress the importance of "community," the two conceptions are worlds apart and cannot be lumped together. Similarly, just because both Lindsay and Locke (or Mill) emphasize the value of liberty, they do not belong in the same category.

Much of the contemporary concern with democratic theory can be traced to the work of four men: Lindsay, Barker, Dewey, and MacIver. Lindsay and Barker carry forward the tradition begun by John Stuart Mill, particularly the emphasis on liberty of thought and expression. They differ from Mill in that they impose serious qualifications on their value judgments and pay much closer attention to the operational requirements of democratic government.

Lindsay's basic ideas were set forth in a series of lectures delivered at Swarthmore College in January 1929 and subsequently published as *The Essentials of Democracy.* They were further developed in 1943 in *The Modern Democratic State.*

Lindsay is one of the earliest critics of the classical theory of democracy. He writes with specific reference to the United States that new conditions have led to "the transformation of democracy into something very different from anything Jefferson and Lincoln ever dreamed of."[17] Lindsay believes that "The democratic theory that the functions of government can all be carried on by any average citizen has done immense harm."[18] He feels that "Strictly speaking, such phrases as 'the will of the people' or 'the voice of the people' are mere mythology."

For Lindsay, the operational dimension of democracy is summed up in "government by discussion." Discussion, he notes, requires the existence of competing groups, a recognized and respected opposition, and mutual toleration. Such a system implies the importance of popular control, a concept hinted at in 1929 and developed in the 1943 volume. "The first problem of a democratic state," Lindsay writes, "is to ensure that government is kept to its proper task." He adds: "The vote at a general election is primarily a judgment on results . . . [and] an expression of approval or disapproval of what has happened." He makes an explicit distinction between "government and control," government being the function of the few and control of the many.

The normative dimension of Lindsay's work deals primarily with liberty and, to a lesser extent, with equality. Liberty is seen as the essential condition of democratic life; it is given precedence over equality. "Democracy," he writes, "assumes that each member of the community has something to contribute if it can be got out of him. It does not for a

17 *The Essentials of Democracy,* second edition (London: Oxford University Press, 1935), p. 9.
18 *Ibid.,* p. 50.

moment assume that what each member contributes is of equal value."

Barker's formulation of democracy is analogous to that of Lindsay. He too views democracy as "a method of the government of the people."[19] For him, as for Lindsay, the operational component of democracy finds expression in "government by discussion." Barker is explicit that such a government requires an informed public, a multiplicity of parties and groups, and respect for the opposition.

For Barker also, the primary value is liberty, but he sees it as the "essential condition" for the development of a moral personality. Barker is a bit more egalitarian than Lindsay. He believes that liberty "is wedded to equality," but immediately adds that this "marriage must be equal, and liberty must not be dominated or diminished by equality." He proceeds to stipulate a third value, fraternity, and defines it as "the general sense of cooperation in a national society" necessary for the "good life."

The next two writers, Dewey and MacIver, have in common the fact that they both emphasize the importance of "community," a value hinted at but not fully developed by Lindsay and Barker. Dewey's starting point is the individual and his welfare. Individuals are seen as having a multiplicity of objectives, values, and desires. These, Dewey argues, can only be realized through membership in a multiplicity of groups or "publics." A public, according to Dewey, is characterized by "conjoint" (shared, collective) action and purpose. There are as many publics as there are interests. A "community"—inescapably pluralistic in character—consists of a multiplicity of publics. It is further distinguished by common habits, norms, and customs.

The distinction between "state" and "community" emerges as crucial to Dewey's formulation of democracy. He specifically warns "against identifying the community and

19 *Reflections on Government* (New York: Oxford University Press, 1942), p. 315, note 1.

its interests with the state or the politically organized community."[20] The distinctive feature of the state is that it operates through "representative officials" having "special powers." The main problem of political life is to ensure that these officials remain responsible to the electorate. This serves to introduce the operational element in Dewey's conception of democracy: for him, democracy "denotes a mode of government, a specified practice in selecting officials and regulating their conduct as officials."[21]

Dewey, however, is skeptical of the emergence of a democratic state, primarily because such a state can only exist in the framework of the "community" and, as he sees it, the community is in "eclipse." Dewey's vision is essentially one of small-scale democracy: political relationships in close, face-to-face contexts. He sees the emergence of mass, urban, industrial society—the "Great Society," he calls it—as detrimental to his ideal: the "Great Community." He thus concludes that the Great Society must be transformed into the Great Community: democracy "is the idea of community life itself." Community is Dewey's supreme value: "Fraternity, liberty and equality isolated from communal life are hopeless abstractions. . . ."

For MacIver, as for Dewey, the conception of democracy rests on a fundamental distinction between "community" and "state." Community, MacIver believes, is the natural context of human relationships and the primary focus of man's devotion. It has its own identity, its own mores, and its own system of sanctions. State, on the other hand, refers to the structure of formal, legal, and institutional controls necessary for the ordering of community affairs. For MacIver, democracy can exist only if the state is subordinated to the community. Democracy, he states, serves to "confirm and strengthen the distinction through the establish-

20 *The Public and Its Problems* (New York: Henry Holt & Co., 1927), p. 15.
21 *Ibid.*, p. 82.

ment of constitutional forms. . . . The community establishes its formal superiority over the state." To the extent to which the community does emerge as an end in itself, it constitutes the normative dimension of MacIver's work.

But there is another, more explicit, value—and that is liberty. Although MacIver is careful to avoid rigid formulations, he does define democracy, in part, in terms of a series of freedoms, including intellectual and associational ones. The relationship between the two values, according to MacIver, is that liberty is an essential condition of community, for it is through "liberty that democracy vindicates the community against the state."

In its empirical component, MacIver views democracy as a system of responsible government characterized by popular control of officials. "Democracy," he writes, "is not a way of governing . . . but primarily a way of determining who shall govern and, broadly, to what ends." What distinguishes democracy from other forms of government is citizen participation in the selection of leaders through discussion, debate, and voting. In this sense, MacIver comes close to defining democracy as "the rule of opinion."[22] Involved in this formulation is a sense of pluralism, the existence of a multiplicity of parties and leaders from whom selection is made.

Among the more recent democratic theories of a normative-empirical character, the works of Sartori, Mayo, and Downs merit consideration.

In Sartori's formulation, the empirical dimension of democracy takes the form of "a political system in which the influence of the majority is assured by elective and competitive minorities to whom it is entrusted." In its normative aspect, democracy is equated with equality. Distinguishing between "democracy" and "liberal democracy," Sartori

22 *The Web of Government* (New York: The Macmillan Co., 1947), p. 205.

writes: "To isolate liberalism from democracy, we say that liberalism calls for liberty and democracy for equality. To unite them, we say that it is the task of liberal-democratic government to combine liberty with equality." Sartori leaves no doubt that his own point of view is "liberal-democratic." He believes that his definition "does not contradict the classical theory and does not attempt to replace it. It is rather an extension and completion of it."

An analogous conception of democracy has been developed by Mayo. Although concerned with such values as political liberty and political equality, he does stress that the most important key to democratic government is popular control of leaders. According to Mayo, "a democratic political system is one in which public policies are made, on a majority basis, by representatives subject to effective popular control at periodic elections which are conducted on the principle of political equality and under conditions of political freedom."

The inclusion of Anthony Downs in the ranks of normative-empirical theorists is based on wholly different grounds. In fact, the only reason for considering him at this point is that he reintroduces, in an explicit and vigorous fashion, the classic conception of human rationality as a working hypothesis. Otherwise, Downs' approach is strongly anti-normative; he presents a highly empirical formulation of democracy.

Downs approaches democracy from the standpoint of traditional economic theory, with self-interest and rationality as the cornerstones of the system. In its operational aspects, the democratic model developed by Downs consists of one party (or a coalition of parties) in office, one or more parties out of office, periodic elections by means of which power is transferred, provisions for popular selection and control of the governing group, and so on. Government is seen as rational: the desire for office is based on the "personal desire for income, prestige, and power." The chief function of a political party is to achieve electoral victory and perpetuate itself. To remain in office, the winning party needs to maximize public support. Hence, citizen demands must be met; policies affording concrete benefits to the majority must be sponsored. Citizens are also rational: they will support the political party that would give them the greatest benefits.[23]

In summary, the contemporary normative-empirical formulations of democracy attempt to fuse the older and newer conceptions. They are marked by a tendency to avoid dogmatic insistence on the absolute nature of the norms and by a propensity to embrace such concretely empirical propositions as those dealing with pluralism, competition, leadership, and control.

IDEOLOGICAL DEFINITIONS

It would come as no surprise to the reader if it were to be pointed out that much of our discussion up to now may be characterized as "ideology." This is particularly the case with the normative elements in the various conceptions of democracy. Such notions as "natural law," "natural rights," "popular sovereignty," "general will," properly belong to the "ideological" realm. However, the mere existence of ideological elements in definitions of democracy can be hardly interpreted as self-conscious attempts to deal with democracy from an explicitly ideological point of view. Strictly speaking, only the empirical conceptions of democracy are nonideological, since they have reference to experiential phenomena and permit verification. Our concern at this point is with those writers who have sought to approach democracy from an expressly ideological perspective and who have attempted to develop conceptions of democracy

23 Downs proceeds with an attempt to show that the equilibrium thus attained can be broken and that opposition parties can perform the seemingly unlikely task of winning an election by manipulating the electorate in certain ways.

that are distinctively ideological in nature. Before proceeding, it is necessary to clarify somewhat the meaning of "ideology."

It must be recognized at the outset that there is no universally accepted definition of "ideology," and this is one of the major difficulties that we face. The literature of ideology is vast and we cannot attempt to give it full coverage in this essay.[24] It is possible, however, to summarize briefly those characteristics of ideology that have had a tendency to recur in the literature.

At the most general level, the term "ideology" refers to a complex of beliefs that are held as a matter of habitual and routine reinforcement. These beliefs are characteristically value-laden and have a high emotional content. Moreover, ideology has a programmatic orientation: it seeks to accomplish some concrete ends. In other words, in addition to positing a set of values, ideology seeks to relate specific patterns of action to the achievement of these values. In this sense, ideology has a utopian component: it looks to a more or less ideal future state of affairs.

There is, furthermore, a degree of distortion or unreality in ideology. The proposition that ideology involves an element of "illusion" or "myth" has been stressed, since Karl Marx,[25] by most of the contributors to the literature. Thus

24 For detailed treatment, see, for example: David E. Apter, ed., *Ideology and Discontent* (New York: The Free Press, 1964); Daniel Bell, *The End of Ideology* (New York: Collier Books, 1961); G. Bergmann, "Ideology," *Ethics*, LXI (April 1951), pp. 205–218; Robert E. Lane, *Political Ideology* (New York: The Free Press, 1962); Harold D. Lasswell and Abraham Kaplan, *Power and Society* (New Haven: Yale University Press, 1950), especially pp. 116–133; Seymour Martin Lipset, *Political Man: The Social Bases of Politics* (New York: Doubleday & Co., 1960); Karl Mannheim, *Ideology and Utopia* (New York: Harcourt, Brace and Co., 1936); Edward Shils, "Ideology and Civility: On the Politics of the Intellectuals," *Sewanee Review*, LXVI (July–September 1958).

25 See especially Marx and Engels, *The German Ideology* (New York: International Publishers, 1947). They write at page 14, for example: "in all ideology men and their circumstances appear upside down as in a *camera obscura*. . . ."

Mannheim defines ideology as "more or less conscious disguises of the real nature of a situation. . . ."[26] Lasswell and Kaplan refer to ideology as "the political myth functioning to preserve the social structure. . . ."[27] Examples could be multiplied.[28]

Finally, ideology is necessarily a part of the belief system of social groups. The tenets of ideology must find acceptance and manifestation in the behavior of a political society. Moreover, the significance of ideology will vary with the social group that holds it. Thus, for example, ideology as a systematic set of propositions articulated by the political elite may be quite different from ideology as an element of mass commitment.

Not every characteristic of ideology touched upon in the foregoing paragraphs will be applicable to our discussion of democracy. The ideological formulations of democracy selected for consideration in the present volume stipulate, in general terms, the existence of certain collective beliefs, attitudes, and habits among large numbers of people. This element of belief—whether conscious or unconscious—forms the distinctive feature of the ideological formulations. A relatively small number of such definitions can be located in the literature of democracy, and the most prominent among them are those developed by Bernard Williams, Herbert McClosky and Zevedei Barbu.

Williams views ideology as a set of general and more or less integrated social and political beliefs embodying certain values as well as some principles of action. In this sense, he holds, the term "ideology" is as applicable to democracy as it is to totalitarianism—a major difference lying in the "degree of explicitness."

Williams' analysis is not particularly acute or coherent or

26 Mannheim, *op. cit.*, p. 55.
27 Lasswell and Kaplan, *op. cit.*, p. 123.
28 See, for instance: David E. Apter, "Introduction," in Apter, *op. cit.*, pp. 19–20; Raymond Aron, *The Opium of the Intellectuals* (New York: W. W. Norton & Co., 1962), *passim;* Bergmann, *op. cit.*, p. 210.

enlightening. Insofar as he largely limits his discussion of ideology to "toleration," his analysis is admittedly sketchy and incomplete. Insofar as he distinguishes between "essential" and "nonessential" toleration and then concludes by saying that nonessential toleration is in fact essential, his argument is circular. Williams' chief virtue, in fact, is that he *does* approach democracy as ideology, and this is the reason for his inclusion here.

McClosky's analysis is brief and clear. He finds that while democracy does not fully meet the requirements of ideology, "it comes close enough" to be viewed as such. He identifies among the tenets of democratic ideology "such concepts as consent, accountability, limited or constitutional government, representation, majority rule, minority rights, the principle of political opposition, freedom of thought, speech, press, and assembly, equality of opportunity, religious toleration, equality before the law, the right of juridical defense, and individual self-determination over a broad range of personal affairs." It is clear, however, that these elements are not as "integrated" as McClosky assumes. Nor are they all "ideological"—if we understand by "ideology" (at least in part) that which is a matter of belief and not of empirical verification. While it is true, for example, that freedom of thought, individual self-determination, etc., may be viewed as matters of belief, such other variables as accountability and equality before the law are empirically ascertainable.

Barbu has developed one of the most abstract and wide-ranging ideological formulations of democracy. He writes explicitly that "because democracy cannot be described in terms of a specific ideology, one cannot say that it has no specific ideological character. . . ." He questions the validity of defining democracy exclusively in terms of "popular sovereignty," "universal suffrage," "majority rule," and the like —this on the ground that apart from the ideological climate surrounding them, these conceptions are not the exclusive properties of democratic government; they may be utilized (as they have been) by totalitarian regimes. Accordingly, Barbu defines democracy in terms of "a specific frame of mind, that is, certain experiences, attitudes, prejudices and beliefs shared by . . . all, or by a large majority." Among such attitudes and beliefs, the following are included: (1) a feeling of constant change, fluidity, and adjustment; (2) a feeling of personal involvement in politics, a belief that the individual is a positive agent of change and "a maker of his own society"; (3) a rational, "individualized" attitude toward authority and the recognition of its relative and representative character; and (4) an attitude of confidence in reason as the ability to bring order to a rapidly changing environment.

These, then, are the major ideological conceptions of democracy considered in this volume. It cannot be overemphasized that a large part of the literature of democracy is, strictly speaking, ideological in character. However, we are probably justified in selecting out for specific treatment those conceptions that do self-consciously approach democracy from an explicitly ideological point of view and do emphasize shared beliefs and attitudes as the distinguishing marks of democracy.

SUMMARY

In this chapter we have been involved in a discussion of the various conceptions of democracy. Although we have by no means exhausted the subject matter, we hope to have succeeded in bringing some order and clarity to the vast literature of democratic theory by developing a fourfold typology of some of the major conceptions known to us. Our central concern has been with the twentieth-century formulations of democracy; however, as a point of departure and of comparison, some attention has been devoted to the pre-twentieth-century theories.

As we have seen, the normative or classical theorists of democracy were chiefly interested in maximization of certain values—an interest that today is shared by the neoclassicists. By contrast, the empirical theories are characterized by an attempt to describe and explain political phenomena in objective terms. The normative-empirical theories seek to reconcile these two types of democratic theory, while the ideological formulations stress the importance of certain shared attitudes and beliefs as the distinguishing feature of democracy.

We would probably agree that democratic theory has undergone something of a transformation. It has abandoned, for the most part, the basic assumptions and premises of the classical tradition. The main thrust of the contemporary conceptions of democracy is empirical. The normative and ideological formulations characteristically recognize the conditional and relativistic nature of the values with which they are concerned. The "classical" assumption of man's capacity for self-rule, the insistence on the absolute nature of certain value ideals (for example, "natural law," "natural rights"), the unwavering emphasis on homogeneity and consensus ("common will," "common good")—these and similar propositions seldom occur in contemporary democratic theory. The nexus between the classical and contemporary theories of democracy is a tenuous one.

2
Normative Definitions

SOME CLASSICAL THEORIES

∽ JOHN LOCKE

On Civil Government

THE STATE OF NATURE

To understand political power aright, and derive it from its original, we must consider what estate all men are naturally in, and that is, a state of perfect freedom to order their actions, and dispose of their possessions and persons as they think fit, within the bounds of the law of Nature, without asking leave or depending upon the will of any other man.

A state also of equality, wherein all the power and jurisdiction is reciprocal, no one having more than another, there being nothing more evident than that creatures of the same species and rank, promiscuously born to all the same advantages of Nature, and the use of the same faculties, should also be equal one amongst another, without subordination or subjection, unless the lord and master of them all should, by any manifest declaration of his will, set one

From *Two Treatises of Civil Government* by John Locke, 1690. These passages are from an edition published by E. P. Dutton & Co., New York, Everyman's Library Edition, and J. M. Dent & Sons, London, 1924, pp. 118–120, 158–159, 179–180, 164–166, 182, 184–185, 225–228.

above another, and confer on him, by an evident and clear appointment, an undoubted right to dominion and sovereignty. . . .

But though this be a state of liberty, yet it is not a state of license; though man in that state have an uncontrollable liberty to dispose of his person or possessions, yet he has not liberty to destroy himself, or so much as any creature in his possession, but where some nobler use than its bare preservation calls for. The state of Nature has a law of Nature to govern it, which obliges every one, and reason, which is that law, teaches all mankind who will but consult it, that being all equal and independent, no one ought to harm another in his life, health, liberty or possessions; for men being all the workmanship of one omnipotent and infinitely wise Maker; all the servants of one sovereign Master, sent into the world by His order and about His business; they are His property, whose workmanship they are made to last during His, not one another's pleasure. And, being furnished with like faculties, sharing all in one community of Nature, there cannot be supposed any such subordination among us that may authorize us to destroy one another, as if we were made for one another's uses, as the inferior ranks of creatures are for ours.

THE POLITICAL SOCIETY

Man being born . . . with a title to perfect freedom and uncontrollable enjoyment of all the rights and privileges of the law of Nature, equally with any other man, or number of men in the world, hath by nature a power not only to preserve his property—that is, his life, liberty, and estate, against the injuries and attempts of other men, but to judge of and punish the breaches of that law in others, as he is persuaded the offense deserves, even with death itself, in crimes where the heinousness of the fact, in his opinion, requires it. But because no political society can be, nor subsist, without having in itself the power to preserve the property, and in order thereunto punish the offenses of all those of that society, there and there only, is political society where every one of the members hath quitted this natural power, resigned it up into the hands of the community in all cases that excludes him not from appealing for protection to the law established by it. And thus all private judgment of every particular member being excluded, the community comes to be umpire, and by understanding indifferent rules and men authorized by the community for their execution, decides all the differences that may happen between any members of that society concerning any matter of right, and punishes those offenses which any member hath committed against the society with such penalties as the law has established; whereby it is easy to discern who are, and are not, in political society together. Those who are united into one body, and have a common established law and judicature to appeal to, with authority to decide controversies between them and punish offenders, are in civil society with one another; but those who have no such common appeal, I mean on earth, are still in the state of Nature, each being where there is no other, judge for himself and executioner; which is, as I have before showed it, the perfect state of Nature.

If man in the state of Nature be so free as has been said, if he be absolute lord of his own person and possessions, equal to the greatest and subject to nobody, why will he part with this freedom, this empire, and subject himself to the dominion and control of any other power? To which it is obvious to answer, that though in the state of Nature he hath such a right, yet the enjoyment of it is very uncertain and constantly exposed to the invasion of others; for all being kings as much as he, every man his equal, and the greater part no strict observers of equity and justice, the enjoyment of the property he has in this state is very unsafe, very insecure. This makes him willing to quit this condition which, however free, is full of fears and continual dangers; and it is not without reason that he seeks out and is willing to join in society with others who are already united, or have a mind to unite for the mutual preservation of their lives, liberties and estates, which I call by the general name—property.

The great and chief end, therefore, of men uniting into commonwealths, and putting themselves under government, is the preservation of their property; to which in the state of Nature there are many things wanting.

MAJORITY RULE

Men being, as has been said, by nature all free, equal, and independent, no one can be put out of this estate and subjected to the political power of another without his own consent, which is done by agreeing with other men, to join and unite into a community for their comfortable, safe, and peaceable living, one amongst another, in a secure enjoyment of their properties, and a greater security against any that are not of it. This any number of men may do, because it injures not the freedom of the rest; they are left, as they were, in the liberty of the state of Nature. When any number of men have so consented to make one community or government, they are thereby presently incorporated, and make one body politic, wherein the majority have a right to act and conclude the rest.

For, when any number of men have, by the consent of every individual, made a community, they have thereby made that community one body, with a power to act as one body, which is only by the will and determination of the majority. For that which acts any community, being only the consent of the individuals of it, and it being one body, must move one way, it is necessary the body should move that way whither the greater force carries it, which is the consent of the majority, or else it is impossible it should act or continue one body, one community, which the consent of every individual that united into it agreed that it should; and so every one is bound by that consent to be concluded by the majority. And therefore we see that in assemblies empowered to act by positive laws where no number is set by that positive law which empowers them, the act of the majority passes for the act of the whole, and of course determines as having, by the law of Nature and reason, the power of the whole.

And thus every man, by consenting with others to make one body politic under one government, puts himself under an obligation to every one of that society to submit to the determination of the majority, and to be concluded by it; or else this original compact, whereby he with others incorporates into one society, would signify nothing, and be no compact if he be left free and under no other ties than he was in before in the state of Nature. . . .

For if the consent of the majority shall not in reason be received as the act of the whole, and conclude every individual, nothing but the consent of every individual can make anything to be the act of the whole, which, considering the infirmities of health and avocations of business . . . , will necessarily keep many away from the public assembly; and the variety of opinions and contrariety of interests which unavoidably happen in all collections of men, it is next impossible ever to be had. . . . Such a constitution as this would make the mighty leviathan of a shorter duration than the feeblest creatures, and not let it outlast the day it was born in. . . . For where the majority cannot conclude the rest, there they cannot act as one body, and consequently will be immediately dissolved again. . . .

The majority having, . . . upon men's first uniting into society, the whole power of the community naturally in them, may employ all that power in making laws for the community from time to time, and executing those laws by officers of their own appointing, and then the form of the government is a perfect democracy. . . .

LEGISLATIVE POWER

Though the legislative . . . be the supreme power in every commonwealth, yet . . . it is not, nor can possibly be, absolutely arbitrary over the lives and fortunes of the people. For it being but the joint power of every member of the society given up to that person or assembly which is legislator, it can be no more than those persons had in a state of Nature before they entered into society, and gave it up to the community. For nobody can transfer to another more power than he has in himself, and nobody has an absolute arbitrary power over himself, or over any other, to destroy his own life, or take away the life or property of another. A man . . . cannot subject himself to the abitrary power of another; and having, in the state of Nature, no arbitrary power over the life, liberty, or possession of another, but only so much as the law of Nature gave him for the preservation of himself and the rest of mankind, this is all he doth, or can give up to the commonwealth, and by it to the legislative power, so that the legislative can have no more than this. Their power in the utmost bounds of it is limited to the public good of the society. It is a power that hath no other end but preservation, and therefore can never have a right to destroy, enslave, or designedly to impoverish the subjects; the obligations of the law of Nature cease not in society, but only in many cases are drawn closer, and have, by human laws, known penalties annexed to them to enforce their observation. Thus the law of Nature stands as an eternal rule to all men, legislators as well as others. The rules that they make for other men's actions must, as well as their own and other men's actions, be conformable to the law of Nature—i.e., to the will of God, of which that is a declaration, and the fundamental law of Nature being the preservation of mankind, no human sanction can be good or valid against it.

DISSOLUTION OF GOVERNMENT

Besides . . . overturning from without, governments are dissolved from within:

First, when the legislative is altered, . . . broken, or dissolved, dissolution and death follows. . . . The constitution of the legislative is the first and fundamental act of society, whereby provision is made for the continuation of their union under the direction of persons and bonds of laws, made by persons authorized thereunto, by the consent and appointment of the people, without which no one man, or number of men, amongst them can have authority of making laws that shall be binding to the rest. When any one, or more, shall take upon them to make laws whom the people have not appointed so to do, they make laws without authority, which the people are not therefore bound to obey; by which means they come again to be out of subjection, and may constitute to themselves a new legislative, as they think best, being in full liberty to resist the force of those who, without authority, would impose anything upon them. . . .

There is one way more whereby such a government may be dissolved, and that is: When he who has the supreme executive power neglects and abandons that charge, so that the laws already made can no longer be put in execution; this is demonstratively to reduce all to anarchy, and so effectively to dissolve the government. . . . Where there is no longer the administration of justice for the securing of men's rights, nor any remaining power within the community to direct the force, or provide for the necessities of the public, there certainly is no government left. Where the laws cannot be executed it is all one as if there were no laws, and a government without laws is, I suppose, a mystery in politics inconceivable to human capacity, and inconsistent with human society. . . .

There is, therefore, . . . another way whereby governments are dissolved, and that is, when the legislative, or the prince, either of them act contrary to their trust.

JEAN-JACQUES ROUSSEAU

The Social Contract

THE POLITICAL SOCIETY

Man is born free; and everywhere he is in chains. One thinks himself the master of others, and still remains a greater slave than they. How did this change come about? I do not know. What can make it legitimate? That question I think I can answer.

"The problem is to find a form of association which will defend and protect with the whole common force the person and goods of each associate, and in which each, while uniting himself with all, may still obey himself alone, and remain as free as before." This is the fundamental problem of which the *Social Contract* provides the solution.

The clauses of this contract are so determined by the nature of the act that the slightest modification would make them vain and ineffective; so that, although they have perhaps never been formally set forth, they are everywhere the same and everywhere tacitly admitted and recognized, until, on the violation of the social compact, each regains his original rights and resumes his natural liberty, while losing the conventional liberty in favor of which he renounced it.

These clauses, properly understood, may be reduced to one—the total alienation of each associate, together with all his rights, to the whole community; for, in the first place, as

From *The Social Contract* by Jean-Jacques Rousseau, 1762. These passages are from *The Social Contract and Discourses,* translated by G. D. H. Cole and published by E. P. Dutton & Co., New York, Everyman's Library Edition, and J. M. Dent & Sons, London, 1913, pp. 3, 12–15, 20–23, 26, 85, 53, 55–56.

each gives himself absolutely, the conditions are the same for all; and, this being so, no one has any interest in making them burdensome to others.

Moreover, the alienation being without reserve, the union is as perfect as it can be, and no associate has anything more to demand: for, if the individuals retained certain rights, as there would be no common superior to decide between them and the public, each, being on one point his own judge, would ask to be so on all; the state of nature would thus continue, and the association would necessarily become inoperative or tyrannical.

Finally, each man, in giving himself to all, gives himself to nobody; and as there is no associate over which he does not acquire the same right as he yields others over himself, he gains an equivalent for everything he loses, and an increase of force for the preservation of what he has.

If then we discard from the social compact what is not of its essence, we shall find that it reduces itself to the following terms:

"Each of us puts his person and all his power in common under the supreme direction of the general will, and, in our corporate capacity, we receive each member as an indivisible part of the whole."

At once, in place of the individual personality of each contracting party, this act of association creates a moral and collective body, composed of as many members as the assembly contains voters, and receiving from this act its unity, its common identity, its life, and its will.

SOVEREIGNTY AND GENERAL WILL

. . . the body politic or the Sovereign, drawing its being wholly from the sanctity of the contract, can never bind itself, even to an outsider, to do anything derogatory to the original act, for instance, to alienate any part of itself, or to submit to another Sovereign. Violation of the act by which it exists would be self-annihilation; and that which is itself nothing can create nothing.

As soon as this multitude is so united in one body, it is impossible to offend against one of the members without attacking the body, and still more to offend against the body without the members resenting it. Duty and interest therefore equally oblige the two contracting parties to give each other help; and the same men should seek to combine, in their double capacity, all the advantages dependent upon that capacity.

Again, the Sovereign, being formed wholly of the individuals who compose it, neither has nor can have any interest contrary to theirs; and consequently the sovereign power need give no guarantee to its subjects, because it is impossible for the body to wish to hurt all its members. . . . The Sovereign, merely by virtue of what it is, is always what it should be.

This, however, is not the case with the relation of the subject to the Sovereign, which, despite the common interest, would have no security that they would fulfill their undertakings, unless it found means to assure itself of their fidelity.

In fact, each individual, as a man, may have a particular will contrary or dissimilar to the general will which he has as a citizen. His particular interest may speak to him quite differently from the common interest. . . .

In order then that the social compact may not be an empty formula, it tacitly includes the undertaking, which alone can give force to the rest, that whoever refuses to obey the general will shall be compelled to do so by the whole body. This means nothing less than that he will be forced to be free. . . .

The first and most important deduction from the principles we have so far laid down is that the general will alone can direct the State according to the object for which it was instituted, i.e., the common good: for if the clashing of particular interests made the establishment of societies necessary, the agreement of these very interests made it possible. The common element in these different interests is what forms the social tie; and, were there no point of agreement between them all, no society could exist. It is solely on the basis of this common interest that every society should be governed.

I hold then that Sovereignty, being nothing less than the exercise of the general will, can never be alienated, and that the Sovereign, who is no less than a collective being, cannot be represented except by himself: the power indeed may be transmitted, but not the will. . . .

Sovereignty, for the same reason as makes it inalienable, is indivisible; for will either is, or is not, general; it is the will either of the body of the people, or only of a part of it. In the first case, the will, when declared, is an act of Sovereignty and constitutes law; in the second, it is merely a particular will, or act of magistracy—at the most a decree. . . .

It follows from what has gone before that the general will is always right and tends to the public advantage; but it does not follow that the deliberations of the people are always equally correct. Our will is always for our own good, but we do not always see what that is, the people is never corrupted, but it is often deceived, and on such occasions only does it seem to will what is bad.

There is often a great deal of difference between the will of all and the general will; the latter considers only the common interest, while the former takes private interest into account, and is no more than a sum of particular wills: but take away from these same wills the pluses and minuses that cancel one another, and the general will remains as the sum of the differences.

From whatever side we approach our principle, we reach

the same conclusion, that the social compact sets up among the citizens an equality of such a kind, that they all bind themselves to observe the same conditions and should therefore all enjoy the same rights. Thus, from the very nature of the compact, every act of Sovereignty, i.e., every authentic act of the general will, binds or favors all the citizens equally; so that the Sovereign recognizes only the body of the nation, and draws no distinction between those of whom it is made up. What, then, strictly speaking, is an act of Sovereignty? It is not a convention between a superior and an inferior, but a convention between the body and each of its members. It is legitimate, because based on the social contract, and equitable, because common to all; useful, because it can have no other object than the general good, and stable, because guaranteed by the public force and the supreme power. So long as the subjects have to submit only to conventions of this sort, they obey no one but their own will; and to ask how far the respective rights of the Sovereign and the citizens extend, is to ask up to what point the latter can enter into undertakings with themselves, each with all, and all with each.

We can see from this that the sovereign power, absolute, sacred, and inviolable as it is, does not and cannot exceed the limits of general conventions, and that every man may dispose at will of such goods and liberty as these conventions leave him; so that the Sovereign never has a right to lay more charges on one subject than on another, because, in that case, the question becomes particular, and ceases to be within its competency. . . .

As long as several men in assembly regard themselves as a single body, they have only a single will which is concerned with their common preservation and well-being. In this case, all the springs of the State are vigorous and simple and its rules clear and luminous; there are no embroilments or conflicts of interest; the common good is everywhere clearly apparent, and only good sense is needed to perceive it. . . .

When, among the happiest people in the world, bands of peasants are seen regulating affairs of State under an oak, and always acting wisely, can we help scoring the ingenious methods of other nations, which make themselves illustrious and wretched with so much art and mystery?

A State so governed needs very few laws; and, as it becomes necessary to issue new ones, the necessity is universally seen. The first man to propose them merely says what all have already felt, and there is no question of factions or intrigues or eloquence in order to secure the passage into law of what every one has already decided to do, as soon as he is sure that the rest will act with him.

ON PURE DEMOCRACY

We saw . . . what causes the various kinds or forms of government to be distinguished according to the number of the members composing them: it remains . . . to discover how the division is made.

In the first place, the Sovereign may commit the charge of the government to the whole people or to the majority of the people, so that more citizens are magistrates than are mere private individuals. This form of government is called *democracy*. . . .

If we take the term in the strict sense, there never has been a real democracy, and there never will be. It is against the natural order for the many to govern and the few to be governed. It is unimaginable that the people should remain continually assembled to devote their time to public affairs. . . .

Besides, how many conditions that are difficult to unite does such a government presuppose! First, a very small State, where the people can readily be got together and where each citizen can with ease know all the rest; secondly, great simplicity of manners, to prevent business from multiplying and raising thorny problems; next, a large measure of equality in rank and fortune, without which equality of rights and authority cannot long subsist; lastly, little or no luxury—for luxury either comes of riches or makes them necessary; it corrupts at once rich and poor, the rich by possessions and the poor by covetousness; it sells the country to softness and vanity, and takes away from the State all its citizens, to make them slaves one to another, and one and all to public opinion. . . .

Were there a people of gods, their government would be democratic. So perfect a government is not for men.

THOMAS JEFFERSON

The Meaning of "Republican" Government

NATURAL LAW AND NATURAL RIGHTS

When in the course of human events it becomes necessary for one people to dissolve the political bands which have connected them with another and to assume among the powers of the earth the separate and equal station to which the laws of nature and of nature's God entitle them, a decent respect to the opinions of mankind requires that they should declare the causes which impel them to the separation.

We hold these truths to be self-evident: that all men are created equal; that they are endowed by their creator with inherent and inalienable rights, that among these are life, liberty and the pursuit of happiness; that to secure these rights governments are instituted among men deriving their just powers from the consent of the governed; that whenever any form of government becomes destructive of these ends, it is the right of the people to alter or to abolish it, and to institute new government, laying its foundation on such principles and organizing its powers in such forms, as to them shall seem most likely to effect their happiness. Prudence indeed will dictate that governments long established should not be changed for light and transient causes; and accordingly all experience hath shown that mankind are more disposed to suffer while evils are sufferable, than to right themselves by abolishing the forms to which they are accustomed. But when a long train of abuses and usurpations

From *The Writings of Thomas Jefferson,* 10 volumes, collected and edited by Paul L. Ford. New York: G. P. Putnam's Sons, 1899.

begun at a distinguished period and pursuing invariably the same object, evinces a design to reduce them under absolute despotism, it is their right, it is their duty, to throw off such government and to provide new guards for their future security.
[From the Declaration of Independence, 1776]

. . . Our legislators are not sufficiently apprized of the rightful limits of their power: that their true office is to declare and enforce only our natural rights and duties, and to take none of them from us. No man has a natural right to commit aggression on the equal rights of another; and this is all from which the laws ought to restrain him; every man is under the natural duty of contributing to the necessities of the society; and this is all the laws should enforce on him; and, no man having a natural right to be the judge between himself and another, it is his natural duty to submit to the umpirage of an impartial third. When the laws have declared and enforced all this, they have fulfilled their functions, and the idea is quite unfounded, that on entering into society we give up any natural right. . . . Man was created for social intercourse; but social intercourse cannot be maintained without a sense of justice; then man must have been created with a sense of justice.
[From "To Francis W. Gilmer," June 7, 1816]

POPULAR SOVEREIGNTY, EQUALITY, MAJORITY RULE

. . . We of the United States, you know, are constitutionally and conscientiously democrats. We consider society as one of the natural wants with which man has been created; that he has been endowed with faculties and qualities to effect its satisfaction by concurrence of others having the same want; that when, by the exercise of these faculties, he has procured a state of society, it is one of his acquisitions which he has a right to regulate and control, jointly indeed with all those who have concurred in the procurement, whom he cannot exclude from its use or direction more than they him. We think experience has proved it safer, for the mass of individuals composing the society, to reserve to themselves personally the exercise of all rightful powers to which they are competent, and to delegate those to which they are not competent to deputies named, and removable for unfaithful conduct, by themselves immediately. . . .

But when we come to the moral principles on which the government is to be administered, we come to what is proper for all conditions of society. . . . Liberty, truth, probity, honor, are declared to be the four cardinal principles of your society. I believe with you that morality, compassion, generosity, are innate elements of the human constitution; that there exists a right independent of force; that a right to property is founded in our natural wants, in the means with which we are endowed to satisfy these wants, and the right to what we acquire by those means without violating the similar rights of other sensible beings; that no one has a right to obstruct another, exercising his faculties innocently for the relief of sensibilities made a part of his nature; that justice is the fundamental law of society; that the majority, oppressing an individual, is guilty of a crime, abuses its strength, and by acting on the law of the strongest breaks up the foundations of society; that action by the citizens in person, in affairs within their reach and competence, and in all others by representatives, chosen immediately, and removable by themselves, constitutes the essence of a republic; that all governments are more or less republican in proportion as this principle enters more or less into their composition; and that a government by representation is capable of extension over a greater surface of country than one of any other form.

[From "To P. S. Dupont de Nemours," April 24, 1816]

. . . Indeed, it must be acknowledged, that the term *republic* is of very vague application in every language. Witness the self-styled republics of Holland, Switzerland, Genoa, Venice, Poland. Were I to assign to this term a precise and definite idea, I would say, purely and simply, it means a government by citizens in mass, acting directly and personally, according to rules established by the majority; and that every other government is more or less republican, in proportion as it has in its composition more or less of this ingredient of the direct action of the citizens. Such a government is evidently restrained to very narrow limits of space and population. I doubt if it would be practicable beyond the extent of a New England township. The first shade from this pure element, which, like that of pure vital air, cannot sustain life of itself, would be where the powers of the government, being divided, should be exercised each by representatives chosen either *pro hac vice,* or for such short terms as should render secure the duty of expressing the will of their constituents. This I should consider as the nearest approach to a pure republic, which is practicable on a large scale of country or population. . . . The further the departure from direct and constant control by the citizens, the less has the government of the ingredient of republicanism; evidently none where the authorities are hereditary, as in France, Venice, etc., or self-chosen, as in Holland; and little, where for life, in proportion as the life continues in being after the act of election.

The purest republican feature in the government of our own State, is the House of Representatives. The Senate is equally so the first year, less the second, and so on. The Executive still less, because not chosen by the people directly. The Judiciary seriously anti-republican, because [appointed] for life; and the national arm wielded . . . by military leaders, irresponsible but to themselves. . . .

On this view of the import of the term republic, instead of saying, as has been said, "that it may mean anything or nothing," we may say with truth and meaning, that governments are more or less republican as they have more or less

of the element of popular election and control in their composition; and believing, as I do, that the mass of the citizens is the safest depository of their own rights, and especially, that the evils flowing from the duperies of the people, are less injurious than those from the egoism of their agents, I am a friend to that composition of government which has in it the most of this ingredient.
[From "To John Taylor," May 28, 1816]

. . . The first principle of republicanism is, that the *lex-majoris partis* is the fundamental law of every society of individuals of equal rights; to consider the will of the society enounced by the majority of a single vote, as sacred as if unanimous, is the first of all lessons in importance, yet the last which is thoroughly learnt. This law once disregarded, no other remains but that of force, which ends necessarily in military despotism.
[From "To Baron F. H. Alexander von Humboldt," June 13, 1817]

ON REBELLION

. . . I hold it that a little rebellion now and then is a good thing, and as necessary in the political world as storms in the physical. Unsuccessful rebellions indeed generally establish the encroachment on the rights of the people which have produced them. An observation of this truth should render honest republican governors so mild in their punishment of rebellions, as not to discourage them too much. It is a medicine necessary for the sound health of government.
[From "To James Madison," June 30, 1787]

ABRAHAM LINCOLN

On Self-Government

. . . That our government should have been maintained in its original form from its establishment until now, is not much to be wondered at. It had many props to support it through that period, which now are decayed, and crumbled away. Through that period, it was felt by all, to be an undecided experiment; now, it is understood to be a successful one. Then, all that sought celebrity and fame, and distinction, expected to find them in the success of that experiment. Their *all* was staked upon it; their destiny was *inseparably* linked with it. Their ambition aspired to display before an admiring world, a practical demonstration of the truth of a proposition, which had hitherto been considered, at best no better, than problematical; namely, *the capability of a people to govern themselves*. If they succeeded, they were to be immortalized; their names were to be transferred to counties and cities, and rivers and mountains; and to be revered and sung, and toasted through all time. If they failed, they were to be called knaves and fools, and fanatics for a fleeting hour; then to sink and be forgotten. They succeeded. The experiment is successful; and thousands have won their deathless names in making it so.

[From "The Perpetuation of Our Political Institutions," Address before the Young Men's Lyceum of Springfield, Illinois, January 27, 1838]

From *The Collected Works of Abraham Lincoln,* 9 volumes, edited by Roy P. Basler. New Brunswick, N.J.: Rutgers University Press, 1953.

The sacred right of self-government, rightly understood, no one appreciated more than himself. . . . The principle that men or States have the right of regulating their own affairs, is morally right and politically wise. Individuals held the sacred right to regulate their own family affairs; communities might arrange their own internal matter to suit themselves; States might make their own statutes, subject only to the Constitution of the whole country; no one disagreed with this doctrine. It had, however, no application to the question at present at issue, namely, whether slavery, a moral, social and political evil, should or should not exist in territory owned by the Government, over which the Government had control, and which looked to the Government for protection—unless it be true that a negro is not a man; if not, then it is no business of ours whether or not he is enslaved upon soil which belongs to us, any more than it is our business to trouble ourselves about the oyster-trade, cranberry-trade, or any other legitimate traffic carried on by the people in territory owned by the Government. If we admit that a negro is not a man, then it is right for the Government to own him and trade in the race, and it is right to allow the South to take their peculiar institution with them and plant it upon the virgin soil of Kansas and Nebraska. If the negro is not a man, it is consistent to apply the sacred right of popular sovereignty to the question as to whether the people of the territories shall or shall not have slavery; but if the negro, upon soil where slavery is not legalized by law and sanctioned by custom, *is* a man, then there is not even the shadow of popular sovereignty in allowing the first settlers upon such soil to decide whether it shall be right in all future time to hold men in bondage there.

[From "Speech at Bloomington, Illinois," September 26, 1854, as reported in *Peoria Weekly Republican,* October 6, 1854]

As I would not be a *slave,* so I would not be a *master.* This expresses my idea of democracy. Whatever differs from this, to the extent of the difference, is no[t] democracy. ["Definition of Democracy," August 1, 1858 (the date is conjectural)]

. . . A majority, held in restraint by constitutional checks, and limitations, and always changing easily, with deliberate changes of popular opinions and sentiments, is the only true sovereign of a free people. Whoever rejects it, does, of necessity, fly to anarchy or to despotism. Unanimity is impossible; the rule of a minority, as a permanent arrangement, is wholly inadmissible; so that, rejecting the majority principle, anarchy, or despotism in some form, is all that is left.

I do not forget the position assumed by some, that constitutional questions are to be decided by the Supreme Court; nor do I deny that such decisions must be binding in any case, upon the parties to a suit, as to the object of that suit, while they are also entitled to very high respect and consideration, in all parallel cases, by all other departments of the government. And while it is obviously possible that such decision may be erroneous in any given case, still the evil effect following it, being limited to that particular case, with the chance that it may be over-ruled, and never become a precedent for other cases, can better be borne than could the evils of a different practice. At the same time the candid citizen must confess that if the policy of the government, upon vital questions, affecting the whole people, is to be irrevocably fixed by the decisions of the Supreme Court, the instant they are made, in ordinary litigation between parties, in personal actions, the people will have ceased, to be their own rulers, having, to that extent, practically resigned their government into the hands of that eminent tribunal. . . .

This country, with its institutions, belongs to the people who inhabit it. Whenever they shall grow weary of the existing government, they can exercise their *constitutional*

right of amending it, or their *revolutionary* right to dismember, or overthrow it.
[From the First Inaugural Address, March 4, 1861]

Four score and seven years ago our fathers brought forth on this continent, a new nation, conceived in Liberty, and dedicated to the proposition that all men are created equal.

Now we are engaged in a great civil war, testing whether that nation, or any nation so conceived and so dedicated, can long endure. We are met on a great battle-field of that war. We have come to dedicate a portion of that field, as a final resting place for those who here gave their lives that that nation might live. It is altogether fitting and proper that we should do this.

But, in a larger sense, we can not dedicate—we can not consecrate—we can not hallow—this ground. The brave men, living and dead, who struggled here, have consecrated it, far above our poor power to add or detract. The world will little note, nor long remember what we say here, but it can never forget what they did here. It is for us the living, rather, to be here dedicated to the unfinished work which they who fought here have thus far so nobly advanced. It is rather for us to be here dedicated to the great task remaining before us—that from these honored dead we take increased devotion to that cause for which they gave the last full measure of devotion—that we here highly resolve that these dead shall not have died in vain—that this nation, under God, shall have a new birth of freedom—and that government of the people, by the people, for the people, shall not perish from the earth.
[The Gettysburg Address, November 18, 1863]

JOHN STUART MILL

Democracy and Liberty

REPRESENTATIVE GOVERNMENT

If we ask ourselves on what causes and conditions good government in all its senses . . . depends, we find that the principal of them, the one that transcends all others, is the qualities of the human beings composing the society over which the government is exercised.

. . . Of what avail is the most broadly popular representative system if the electors do not care to choose the best member of parliament, but choose him who will spend most money to be elected? . . . Whenever the general disposition of the people is such that each individual regards those only of his interests which are selfish, and does not dwell on . . . the general interest, in such a state of things good government is impossible. The influence of defects of intelligence in obstructing all the elements of good government requires no illustration. Government consists of acts done by human beings; and if the agents, or those who choose the agents, or those to whom the agents are responsible, or the lookers-on whose opinions ought to influence and check all these, are mere masses of ignorance, stupidity, and baleful prejudice, every operation of government will go wrong; while, in proportion as the men rise above this standard, so will the government improve in quality; up to the point of excellence, attainable but nowhere attained, where the offi-

From *Representative Government* by John Stuart Mill, 1861. These passages are from *Utilitarianism, Liberty, and Representative Government,* published by E. P. Dutton & Co., New York, Everyman's Library Edition, and J. M. Dent & Sons, London, 1951, pp. 257–259, 261–262, 278, 282, 291–292, 305, 307–308, 321, 344–345, 381.

cers of government, themselves persons of superior virtue and intellect, are surrounded by the atmosphere of a virtuous and enlightened public opinion.

The first element of good government, therefore, being the virtue and intelligence of the human beings composing the community, the most important point of excellence which any form of government can possess is to promote the virtue and intelligence of the people themselves. The first question in respect to any political institutions is, how far they tend to foster in the members of the community the various desirable qualities . . . moral, intellectual, and active. The government which does this the best has every likelihood of being the best in all other respects.

. . . A representative constitution is a means of bringing the general standard of intelligence and honesty existing in the community, and the individual intellect and virtue of its wisest members, more directly to bear upon the government, and investing them with greater influence in it, than they would in general have under any other mode of organization. . . . The greater the amount of these good qualities which the institutions of a country succeed in organizing, and the better the mode of organization, the better will be the government.

We have now, therefore, obtained a foundation for a twofold division of the merits which any set of political institutions can possess. It consists partly of the degree in which they promote the general mental advancement of the community . . . and partly of the degree of perfection with which they organize the moral, intellectual, and active worth already existing, so as to operate with the greatest effect on public affairs.

There is no difficulty in showing that the ideally best form of government is that in which the sovereignty, or supreme controlling power in the last resort, is vested in the entire aggregate of the community; every citizen not only having a voice in the exercise of that ultimate sovereignty, but being, at least occasionally, called on to take an actual part in the government, by the personal discharge of some public function, local or general. . . .

It must be acknowledged that the benefits of freedom, so far as they have hitherto been enjoyed, were obtained by the extension of its privileges to a part only of the community; and that a government in which they are extended impartially to all is a desideratum still unrealized. But though every approach to this has an independent value, . . . the participation of all in these benefits is the ideally perfect conception of free government. In proportion as any, no matter who, are excluded from it, the interests of the excluded are left without the guarantee accorded to the rest. . . .

From these accumulated considerations it is evident that the only government which can fully satisfy all the exigencies of the social state is one in which the whole people participate; that any participation, even in the smallest public function, is useful; that the participation should everywhere be as great as the general degree of improvement of the community will allow; and that nothing less can be ultimately desirable than the admission of all to a share in the sovereign power of the state. But since all cannot, in a community exceeding a single small town, participate personally in any but some very minor portion of the public business, it follows that the ideal type of a perfect government must be representative. . . .

In treating of representative government, it is above all necessary to keep in view the distinction between its idea or essence, and the particular forms in which the idea has been clothed by accidental historical development, or by the notions current at some particular period.

The meaning of representative government is, that the whole people, or some numerous portion of them, exercise through deputies periodically elected by themselves the ultimate controlling power, which, in every constitution, must reside somewhere. This ultimate power they must possess in all its completeness. They must be masters, whenever they please, of all the operations of government. . . .

But while it is essential to representative government that the practical supremacy in the state should reside in the representatives of the people, it is an open question what actual functions, what precise part in the machinery of government, shall be directly and personally discharged by the representative body. Great varieties in this respect are compatible with the essence of representative government, provided the functions are such as [to] secure to the representative body the control of everything in the last resort.

There is a radical distinction between controlling the business of government and actually doing it. The same person or body may be able to control everything, but cannot possibly do everything; and in many cases its control over everything will be more perfect the less it personally attempts to do. . . . It is one question, therefore, what a popular assembly should control, another what it should itself do. . . .

Instead of the function of governing, for which it is radically unfit, the proper office of a representative assembly is to watch and control the government; to throw the light of publicity on its acts; to compel a full exposition and justification of all of them which any one considers questionable; to censure them if found condemnable, and, if the men who compose the government abuse their trust, or fulfill it in a manner which conflicts with the deliberate sense of the nation, to expel them from office, and either expressly or virtually appoint their successors.

. . . Two very different ideas are usually confounded under the name democracy. The pure idea of democracy, according to its definition, is the government of the whole people by the whole people, equally represented. Democracy as commonly conceived and hitherto practiced is the government of the whole people by a mere majority of the people, exclusively represented. The former is synonymous with the equality of all citizens; the latter . . . is a government of privilege, in favor of the numerical majority.

. . . That the minority must yield to the majority . . . is a familiar idea. . . . In a representative body actually deliberating, the minority must of course be overruled; and in any equal democracy . . . the majority of the people, through their representatives will outvote and prevail over the minority and their representatives. But does it follow that the minority should have no representatives at all? . . . In a really equal democracy, every or any section would be represented . . . proportionately.

. . . But though every one ought to have a voice—that every one should have an equal voice is a totally different proposition. When two persons who have a joint interest in any business differ in opinion, does justice require that both opinions should be held of exactly equal value? If, with equal virtue, one is superior to the other in knowledge and intelligence—or if, with equal intelligence, one excels the other in virtue—the opinion, the judgment, of the higher moral or intellectual being is worth more than that of the inferior. . . . One of the two, as the wiser or better man, has a claim to superior weight.

ON LIBERTY

. . . The notion, that the people have no need to limit their power over themselves, might seem axiomatic, when popular government was a thing only dreamed about. . . . In time, however, a democratic republic came to occupy a large

From *On Liberty* by John Stuart Mill, 1859. These passages are from *Utilitarianism, Liberty, and Representative Government,* published by E. P. Dutton & Co., New York, and J. M. Dent & Sons, London, 1951, pp. 88–89, 95–96, 99, 104–105, 111.

portion of the earth's surface . . . and elective and responsible government became subject to the observations and criticisms which wait upon a great existing fact. It was now perceived that such phrases as "self-government," and "the power of the people over themselves," do not express the true state of the case. The "people" who exercise the power are not always the same people with those over whom it is exercised; and the "self-government" spoken of is not the government of each by himself, but of each by all the rest. The will of the people, moreover, practically means the will of the most numerous or the most active *part* of the people; the majority, or those who succeed in making themselves accepted as the majority. . . .

The object of this Essay is to assert one very simple principle, as entitled to govern absolutely the dealings of society with the individual in the way of compulsion and control, whether the means used be physical force in the form of legal penalties, or the moral coercion of public opinion. That principle is, that the sole end for which mankind are warranted, individually or collectively, in interfering with the liberty of action of any of their number, is self-protection. That the only purpose for which power can be rightfully exercised over any member of a civilized community, against his will, is to prevent harm to others.

. . . This, then, is the appropriate region of human liberty. It comprises, first, the inward domain of consciousness; demanding liberty of conscience in the most comprehensive sense; liberty of thought and feeling; absolute freedom of opinion and sentiment on all subjects, practical or speculative, scientific, moral, or theological. . . . Secondly, the principle requires liberty of taste and pursuits; of framing the plan of our life to suit our own character; of doing as we like, subject to such consequences as may follow—without impediment from our fellow creatures, so long as what we do does not harm them. . . . Thirdly, from this liberty of each individual, follows the liberty, within the same limits, of combination among individuals; freedom to unite, for any purpose not involving harm to others.

. . . If all mankind minus one were of one opinion, and only one person were of the contrary opinion, mankind would be no more justified in silencing that one person, than he, if he had the power, would be justified in silencing mankind. . . . But the peculiar evil of silencing the expression of an opinion is, that it is robbing the human race; posterity as well as the existing generation; those who dissent from the opinion, still more than those who hold it. If the opinion is right, they are deprived of the opportunity of exchanging error for truth; if wrong, they lose, what is almost as great a benefit, the clearer perception and livelier impression of truth, produced by its collision with error. . . .

. . . the opinion which it is attempted to suppress by authority may possibly be true. Those who desire to suppress it, of course deny its truth; but they are not infallible. They have no authority to decide the question for all mankind, and exclude every other person from the means of judging. To refuse a hearing to an opinion, because they are sure that it is false, is to assume that *their* certainty is the same thing as *absolute* certainty. All silencing of discussion is an assumption of infallibility.

. . . The usefulness of an opinion is itself a matter of opinion: as disputable, as open to discussion, as requiring discussion as much as the opinion itself. There is the same need of an infallible judge of opinions to decide an opinion to be noxious, as to decide it to be false, unless the opinion condemned has full opportunity of defending itself. And it will not do to say that the heretic may be allowed to maintain the utility or harmlessness of his opinion, though forbidden to maintain its truth. The truth of an opinion is part of its utility.

SOME NEOCLASSICAL THEORIES

✧ JOHN H. HALLOWELL

The Principles of Classical Realism

The dominant characteristic of the intellectual climate of our times, curiously enough, is an animus against everything intellectual. Never was the rationality of man subjected to a more sustained attack than it is today, and from all quarters, scientific, philosophical, and even theological. And this is a curious fact that we should be using the methods of science, philosophy, and theology to discredit the existence of the very thing upon which the validity of those methods depend, namely, the rationality of man and of the universe he inhabits.

That man is a rational being living in a rational universe will be the premise of my argument. And it is a premise, it seems to me, which anyone must accept if he is to argue for the truthfulness of anything. For what is the point of any intellectual discussion if it necessarily begins in irrationality and ends in irrationality? How can we hope to communicate anything meaningful to one another apart from a capacity for reasoning that is common to all? And what are we talking about if the concepts and words we use refer to no objective reality?

The attempt of many intellectuals today to *prove* that man is essentially irrational is bound to be self-defeating;

for, in the very process of assembling evidence for their contention and arguing in behalf of it, they concede, of necessity, a great deal more than they intend. For they can only hope to prove their case by using the very capacity they deny and by appealing to that capacity in others in order to win agreement. If man were essentially irrational, there would be no such thing as evidence, argument, or proof. Indeed, there would be no such concept as "irrationality." If the phrase "irrational behavior" means anything, it is because we have some understanding of what "rational behavior" means. We could have no concept or understanding of irrationality if we did not already have some understanding of rationality.

My argument will rest upon what might be called the principles of classical realism, principles that commend themselves to common sense. I am aware that there are philosophers who scorn the appeal to the common sense of man as naïve; yet the appeal to common sense, if it is not the ultimate standard of truthfulness, is not an appeal that can be ignored. . . .

The principles of classical realism might be summarized in this way. There exists a meaningful reality whose existence does not depend upon our knowledge of it. . . . The world in which we live is an orderly universe—a cosmos, not a chaos.

A second principle of classical realism is that man is endowed with a faculty which enables him, at least dimly, to grasp the meaning of this reality. . . . Knowledge does not involve the making or constructing of anything, but rather the discovery of what already exists. . . .

A third principle is that being and goodness belong together. Through knowledge of what we are, we obtain knowledge of what we ought to do. To know what man is, is to know what he should be and do. The knowledge of what man should do in order to fulfill his human nature is embodied in what has traditionally been called the "law of nature" or the "moral law." This law, though requiring positive laws to meet changing circumstances, provides universally applicable principles in terms of which we can guide our individual and social life toward the perfection of that which is distinctively human. This principle denies that there is any natural opposition between individual good and the common good; the restraints that are necessary for the development of a good man are identical with the restraints that make life in society possible.

True freedom requires both knowledge of the good and the will to choose the good when known. The denial of either is the denial of freedom, and the denial of freedom is the rejection of that moral agency in man which characterizes his humanity. . . . The preservation of freedom demands that we recover our faith both in the ability of man to know the good and in his capacity, within the limitations of historical conditioning and the defectiveness of his will, to choose the good when known. That he will inevitably fall short of knowing the good in its completeness and of acting upon it unselfishly in every instance—so much we must concede to the intellectual and moral frailty of human nature —but only in the ever constant effort to transcend his limitations with the help of God can man's freedom be preserved and enlarged. When we talk today about the preservation of democracy, what most of us, I think, are concerned about is the preservation of freedom. We realize that democratic forms and institutions find their essential and ultimate meaning in the preservation and enlargement of human freedom. They are not ends in themselves but means to an ultimate end. They are not identical with freedom but the means through which freedom may find its best political expression.

J. ROLAND PENNOCK

Democracy as Government by the People

We have sought to establish the liberal-democratic ideals of liberty, equality, and fraternity as fundamental to the best way of life. . . . It is vital that we should know in considerable detail exactly what kind of political system is required for the attainment of the liberal ideals, and that we should understand the reasons for each of the requirements.

Moreover, in dealing with political democracy, we must have regard for another point of view—that of practicability. Politics, as Aristotle remarked, is a science of the second best. The closest approximation of the ideal that is attainable is not necessarily the best practical form of government. . . . So it might be that liberal democracy in its attainable form is not the most desirable possibility. . . .

For neatness's sake, we may think of liberal democracy as composed of a system of powers and a system of liberties, although in fact either could be expressed as the converse of the other. The powers are the powers of self-government. If democracy means anything it means government by the people. Without attempting to put too fine a point on it, "the people" includes all sane adults save those criminals whose antisocial behavior has disqualified them. "Government by the people" means that the major policies of the government should be determined by the people or by their representatives freely elected at reasonably frequent inter-

From *Liberal Democracy: Its Merits and Prospects,* copyright 1950 by J. Roland Pennock. New York: Holt, Rinehart and Winston, Inc., 1950, pp. 97–100.

vals, and that the administration should be conducted by those who are accountable to the people or their representatives. In all voting each should count for one and none for more than one.

The system of liberties (historically prior to self-government) is slightly more complicated. One group has to do mainly with the realm of ideas. This category includes freedom of religious belief and observance; freedom of speech and of the press and of the access to facts; and the right of assembly and of free association. . . .

The second group of liberties may be roughly described as those which concern themselves with physical freedom. Here we have, first of all, the right to life, the right to be protected against physical violence. Here also is included a reasonable freedom of action, of movement from place to place, of choice of occupation, of contract (including the right to have others compelled to keep their contracts), and of the use and disposal of property. . . .

Finally, there is a highly important area of freedom which finds protection under the principle known as the rule of law. This principle may be defined as follows: First, no one should be detained or punished except for a violation of law. . . . Second, this law must be the same for all. . . . Third, violations of the law shall be determined only in accordance with a fixed and regular procedure designed to secure a fair and impartial judgment. . . . Fourth, punishments must bear some reasonable relationship to the enormity of the crime. . . . The fifth and last point . . . states that the legislative and administrative acts of government shall make no discrimination between persons similarly situated and that the application of the laws shall be fair and impartial.

AUSTIN RANNEY and WILLMOORE KENDALL

Democracy as Self-Government

Most writers on democracy, whatever else they may insist must be present in order for a government to be called a "democracy," are . . . committed to the view that it must exhibit the following minimum characteristics: (1) Those who hold office in it must stand ready, *in some sense,* to do whatever the people want them to do, and to refrain from doing anything the people oppose; (2) each member of the "community" for which it acts should have, *in some sense,* as good a chance as his fellows to participate in the community's decision making—no better and no worse; and (3) it must operate in terms of an understanding that when the enfranchised members of the community disagree as to what ought to be done, the last word lies, *in some sense,* with the larger number and never the smaller. . . .

One of the basic contentions . . . is that once one has committed himself to that much, he has committed himself to at least the broad outline of a highly meaningful conception of democratic government. Another is that this conception of democratic government, despite the presence of the words "in some sense" in the foregoing statements, leaves less room to move around in, and be "different," than is commonly supposed.

Anyone who carefully analyzes the above three minima will find that the conception as a whole breaks down into four, not three, principles. These are (a) popular sover-

From *Democracy and the American Party System* by Austin Ranney and Willmoore Kendall. New York: Harcourt, Brace & World, © 1956, pp. 23–25, 27–29, 37.

eignty, (b) political equality, (c) popular consultation, and (d) majority rule.

. . . the word "democracy," through most of its history and to most people, has meant "government by all.". . . "Popular sovereignty," if we mean by it sovereignty of the entire people, is undoubtedly therefore the *oldest* of the ideas associated with democracy. . . .

The doctrine of "popular sovereignty" . . . is that according to which power vests in *all* the members of the community rather than in any part of them or in any one of them. Just as sovereign power is what makes a State a State, sovereign power vested in all the community's members is what makes the State "democratic." . . . In a word, the doctrine of popular sovereignty means it when it says "sovereignty" every bit as much as when it says "popular."

We must notice at once, however, that the notion that popular sovereignty is fundamental to democracy is highly unpalatable to certain present-day writers. Of special importance in this connection are writers . . . who proclaim that in a true democracy there can be *no* unlimited power—that a State is democratic only so long as certain individual rights are entirely removed from the power of *any* governmental agency, whether popularly controlled or not. To them "limited government" or "constitutional government" is an essential attribute of democracy. . . .

The second basic principle of democracy is that of political equality. Each member of the community must have the same chance as his fellows to participate in its total decision-making process. Only thus can there be genuine popular sovereignty; for if any individual or group of individuals has *more* power . . . than the other members of the community, that group becomes a politically privileged class or elite, and popular sovereignty, as we have defined it above, cannot exist. It is for these reasons that political equality is . . . generally regarded as an essential element of democracy.

It is necessary to point out, however, that political equality involves far more than the classical slogan of "one man, one vote." If equality in voting rights were synonymous with political equality, then—on this score at least—the Communist nations' claim that they are more democratic than their Western opponents would be hard to dispute. After all, they hold elections frequently, and it is probable that a higher percentage of the population holds the suffrage than in any Western nation; and a larger proportion of the eligible voters actually go to the polls. But does this mean that therefore the Communist nations really *do* have a higher degree of political equality than the West?

The answer, we believe, can be found by analyzing the nature of the decision-making process and the part that voting plays therein. . . . the essence of making a decision is the *choice among alternatives.* And in order to make a genuine choice, each of these three conditions must obtain for the policy maker: (1) the presence of genuine alternatives before him; (2) the opportunity to find out about the nature and probable consequences of each alternative; and (3) full freedom to choose whichever of the alternatives seems to him—for whatever reasons he deems sufficient—the most desirable. In the absence of any one of these conditions he can hardly be said to be making a genuine choice. Where, then, does voting come in? At most it is a kind of machinery whereby each policy maker registers the choice he has made. In other words, voting is just one part—albeit a necessary one—of the total decision-making process, and its significance depends upon the degree to which the other parts of the process have operated *before* voting takes place. In the Communist countries the voter has only the candidates of the Communist party to choose—there are no opposition candidates. . . .

Thus political equality means not only "one man, one vote," but also an equal chance for each member of the community to participate in the total decision-making process of the community.

. . . In democratic government . . . the people must be "consulted" about the policy they wish those in power to pursue in a given matter—and the holders of office, having learned the popular desire, should proceed to do whatever the people want them to do. Thus "popular consultation" in this sense requires at least these three attributes: (1) on matters of public policy there must *be* a genuine popular will; (2) the officeholders must be aware of what that will requires; and (3) having ascertained the nature of the popular will, they must then faithfully and invariably translate it into action. . . .

Our fourth principle of democracy . . . is considerably more controversial than the other three. For we believe that a model democratic government must always be able to justify its actions on the grounds that they accord with the wishes of a majority of the enfranchised members of the community. Or, to put it another way, we believe that when there are two opinions among the members of a democratic community as to whether the government should perform any given action, the opinion of the larger group, which for most purposes we can usefully think of as one-half of the enfranchised members plus at least one, ought to prevail.

. . . we are convinced that "absolute" majority rule is an inescapable attribute of any model of *perfectly* democratic government—that it is, in short, the only decision-making principle that is consistent with the other three principles of democracy we have previously presented.

. . . any attempt to place *formal* institutional limitations upon the "absolute" power of popular majorities logically results in the establishment of *minority* rule. And from the standpoint of strict logic, "absolute" majority rule must be chosen over minority rule as a principle of ideally *democratic* government, not because there is any magical virtue or omniscience in popular majorities, but because majority rule is more nearly in accord than minority rule with the other principles of democracy that we have previously discussed.

3
Empirical Definitions

∽ E. F. M. DURBIN

The Essentials of Democracy

Democracy is an ambiguous term in political discussion. Many people use it in such a way as to make it synonymous with the phrase "the good society." A community is a "true" democracy only if all cause for sighing and weeping have passed away. Before such persons will call any society a democracy, it must be completely free from social inequalities and economic insecurity. . . . In this use the term "democracy" becomes identified with the conception of a social justice itself, and is therefore remote from the political practice of any present society.

By using the word in this way it is possible to say, quite rightly, that we have not got "democracy" in Britain, or America, or France, or Sweden. In none of these countries has inequality, or insecurity, or class antagonism, passed wholly away. Democracy, in its Utopian sense, does not yet exist within these nations. They only possess "capitalist democracy," or "*political* democracy." They do not possess "economic democracy" or "true democracy" or "real democracy."

From *The Politics of Democratic Socialism* by E. F. M. Durbin. London: Routledge & Kegan Paul, Ltd., 1940, pp. 235–243, 271–272.

Now it is perfectly open to anyone to use terms as they please. If some people choose to mean by "democracy" what other people mean by "Utopia" there is nothing to stop them doing so. The moon will still be the moon even if we call it the sun. Utopia by any other name will smell as sweet, and look as remote. But it is not in Utopia, nor in the perfect society, that I am, for the moment, interested. I wish to discuss a narrower thing, a single political habit, a method of taking political decisions, a practicable and actual condition of certain societies. In short, what I want to consider is the significance or value of what the Utopian "democrats" would call "mere political democracy.". . .

It is obvious that the institutions of "mere political democracy" must exist in some real sense, even in a capitalist society, since it is possible to distinguish "capitalist democracies" from "capitalist dictatorships." Even in his most fanatical moments the Communist has not denied the *possibility* of making the distinction, although he used to deny the *importance* of making it. There must be therefore some sense in which democracy is compatible with capitalism and consequently with economic inequality. It is with this limited form of political democracy, its meaning and value, that I am here concerned.

In what does "democracy" in this sense consist?

I believe the correct answer to this question to be that political democracy consists in the possession by any society of *three* characteristic habits or institutions:

1. The *first* and most typical of these characteristics is the ability of the people to choose a government.

Disagreement between individuals is of the very essence of human personality. As long as we are different persons, there will be some of us who like one thing and some who do not, some who desire one order of society and some another, some who believe justice to be realized in one set of circumstances and some who disagree with that judgment.

Now the course of action taken at any moment, and the

form of society thus brought slowly into existence, are determined largely by the decisions of the Government. The Government has its hands upon the controls of the "apparatus of coercion," and is therefore the *immediate* authority determining social policy. The nature of the decisions taken by the Government will depend upon the character of persons forming it. Consequently there can be no control of the form of society by us, the common people, unless it is possible to change the personnel of the Government and of the legislature. This is the first and most obvious characteristic of political democracy—the existence of a government responsible to the people, and the dependence of it and of the membership of the legislative assembly upon the free vote of the people.

In our own [British] history we have found that the essential thing to attain and preserve is the power of the people to *dismiss* a government from office. This negative power is in reality an important positive power, because ordinary men and women are moved more deeply by the disapproval of measures they dislike in practice, than by their less definite conception of what they desire in the future. Political change in democracies is more frequently induced by a slow accumulation of resentment against an existing government or institution, than by the growth of a positive idea of new social forms. Experience is more real than imagination, to unimaginative people.

Every practicing politician appreciates this fact. The enthusiasts composing the party machine through which he has to work may be animated by the clear vision of a new society; but they are, at the best, a small minority of the surrounding electoral masses, and the masses are rarely inspired by Christian's clear vision, from a great distance, of the Celestial City. This is not to say that constructive social imagination is not powerful in the affairs of men, but only that democracies proceed to realize the prophets' vision by careful processes of empirical test. By the slow testing of ideas and of institutional experiments, by rejecting all those of which they disapprove and insisting upon the gradual extension of the things they find by experience that they like, an intelligent electorate unconsciously constructs a society that in large measure contents it. Little as we reformists of the Left may like it, the absence of a reforming or revolutionary zeal in our communities is a tribute to the fundamental, and often unrecognizable, ways in which society has been adapted to suit the unconscious, but essential, requirements of the people composing it.

Of this I shall have more to say presently. For the moment I wish only to insist upon the importance of the negative power to destroy a government as a part of the broader right to choose a government. It is the continuous retention of this power that I shall call the "maintenance of democracy."

2. But the continued existence of this right implies and requires the existence of a *second,* and less obvious political institution. If liberty is to exist, if the dependence of government upon the will of the people is to be real, there must always be a real choice before the people. This implies the steady maintenance of a critical and essential institution —that of *freedom to oppose the Government of the day*. Unless the electorate has more than one possible government before it; unless there is more than one party able to place its views before the country; unless, that is to say, the opposition is free to prepare itself to take over power, and the Government to surrender it peacefully after an electoral decision against it; there is no choice before the people. . . .

This obvious reflection reveals at once the sharp absurdity of the electoral practices of modern dictatorships. Modern dictatorships pay to the institutions of democracy the sincerest form of flattery—that of imitation. They copy the device of the "General Election." But it is an empty and silly imitation—like that of an ape reading a newspaper or a baboon playing a violin. . . .

This we can see at once by asking the critical question:

What is the choice before the German or Russian electorate? There is only one party in the election. There is only one government that can be formed. There may be a choice of individuals, but there is no choice of party, no choice of government, no choice of policy. . . .

Here then is the acid test of democracy. Democracy may be defined by the toleration of opposition. In so far as it is tolerated—in so far as alternative governments are allowed to come into existence and into office—democracy, in my sense, exists. In so far as opposition is persecuted, rendered illegal or stamped out of existence, democracy is not present, and either has never existed or is in the process of being destroyed.

Obviously this is not a simple test. There are varying degrees of freedom permitted to those in opposition to the Government of the day in the various political systems of the world. In the older democracies, like our own, there is complete legal freedom for parties in opposition to the Government. Their rights in respect of political agitation are the *same* as those of the Government. From this extreme there is an almost infinite gradation of liberty [to oppose the Government]. . . . There is no precise line at which it is possible to say that all the communities on this side of it are democracies, and all on the other side of it are dictatorships. But, although the test is quantitative and complicated, it is nevertheless an acid test. The suppression of opposition, as distinct from sedition, is the proof of dictatorial ambition. It is by our judgment of that condition in society that we shall judge democracy itself.

3. But there is a *third,* and still less obvious, characteristic necessary to the existence of democracy. Both the previous characteristics—those of responsible government and of legal opposition—are the definitive properties of democracy, but they are not the causes of democracy. When these conditions are present in a society, democracy in my sense is present

also; when they are absent democracy in my sense is dead. But they do not cause democracy to become present; they simply define democracy. What then *causes* democracy to appear? What is the substantial social condition guaranteeing its existence and continuance?

Now I shall go on to argue . . . that the ultimate cause of stable democratic habits among a people is the possession by them of a certain type of emotional character. I shall argue that democracy is the epiphenomenon of a certain emotional balance in the individuals composing a nation, and I shall try to describe the kind of personality that, in my view, alone makes democracy possible. But there is a simpler and more immediate description of the *result* of the predominance of such persons in any society; and that is, in my submission, the most essential condition for the existence and maintenance of democracy. It is the existence of *an implicit undertaking between the Parties contending for power in the State not to persecute each other.* It is upon that agreement that I believe democracy can alone be securely founded. Mutual toleration is the keystone of the arch and the cornerstone of the building.

. . . Democracy requires the peaceful alternation of Parties in government. This is impossible if the Government believes that the Opposition intends to liquidate them if and when they, the Opposition, attain power. The Government is not likely in these circumstances to surrender power peacefully. Even if they did, democracy would nevertheless cease to exist, since the victorious Opposition would then proceed, by the persecution of those who disagreed with them, to the destruction of democracy itself. Political liberty or democracy, in my sense, depends, then, first and last, now and in the future, upon mutual toleration between opposing Parties.

It will be noticed that, in my description of democracy, there is no reference to social equality or distributive justice, or to any characteristic of the ideal society. It is therefore perfectly open to anyone to suggest that it is not a valuable institution.

Democracy is a *method* of taking political decisions, of compromising and reconciling conflicting interests. The method is more important, more formative of the resulting social order, than the disputes so resolved.

When individuals or groups disagree—including nations and classes and Parties within the state—the most important question is not what they disagree about, but the method or methods by which their disputes are to be resolved. If force is to be the arbiter between them, international war, civil war, cruelty and persecution are the inevitable consequences. Civilization cannot be built upon these crises of destruction.

JOSEPH A. SCHUMPETER

Competition for Political Leadership

THE CLASSICAL DOCTRINE RE-EXAMINED

The eighteenth-century philosophy of democracy may be couched in the following definition: the democratic method is that institutional arrangement for arriving at political decisions which realizes the common good by making the people itself decide issues through the election of individuals who are to assemble in order to carry out its will. Let us develop the implications of this.

It is held, then, that there exists a Common Good, the obvious beacon light of policy, which is always simple to define and which every normal person can be made to see by means of rational argument. There is hence no excuse for not seeing it and in fact no explanation for the presence of people who do not see it except ignorance—which can be removed—stupidity and anti-social interest. Moreover, this common good implies definite answers to all questions so that every social fact and every measure taken or to be taken can unequivocally be classed as "good" or "bad." All people having therefore to agree, in principle at least, there is also a Common Will of the people (= will of all reasonable individuals) that is exactly coterminous with the common good or interest or welfare or happiness. The only thing, barring stupidity and sinister interests, that can possibly bring in disagreement and account for the presence of an opposition is a difference of opinion as to the speed with which the goal, itself common to nearly all, is to be approached. Thus every member of the community, conscious of that goal, knowing his or her mind, discerning what is good and what is bad, takes part, actively and responsibly, in furthering the former and fighting the latter and all the members taken together control their public affairs.

It is true that the management of some of these affairs requires special aptitudes and techniques and will therefore have to be entrusted to specialists who have them. This does not affect the principle, however, because these specialists simply act in order to carry out the will of the people exactly as a doctor acts in order to carry out the will of the patient to get well. It is also true that in a community of any size, especially if it displays the phenomenon of division of labor, it would be highly inconvenient for every individual citizen to have to get into contact with all the other citizens on every issue in order to do his part in ruling or governing. It will be more convenient to reserve only the most important decisions for the individual citizens to pronounce upon—say by referendum—and to deal with the rest through a committee appointed by them—an assembly or parliament whose members will be elected by popular vote. This committee, or body of delegates, as we have seen, will not represent the people in a legal sense but it will do so in a less technical one—it will voice, reflect or represent the will of the electorate. . . .

As soon as we accept all the assumptions that are being made by this theory of the polity—or implied by it—democracy indeed acquires a perfectly unambiguous meaning and there is no problem in connection with it except how to bring it about. Moreover we need only to forget a few logical qualms in order to be able to add that in this case the democratic arrangement would not only be the best of all conceivable ones, but that few people would care to consider any other. It is no less obvious, however, that these assumptions are so many statements of fact every one of which would have to be proved if we are to arrive at that conclusion. And it is much easier to disprove them.

There is, first, no such thing as a uniquely determined common good that all people could agree on or be made to agree on by the force of rational argument. This is due not primarily to the fact that some people may want things other than the common good but to the much more fundamental fact that to different individuals and groups the common good is bound to mean different things. . . .

Secondly, even if a sufficiently definite common good . . . proved acceptable to all, this would not imply equally definite answers to individual issues. Opinions on these might differ to an extent important enough to produce most of the effects of "fundamental" dissension about ends themselves. . . .

But, third, as a consequence of both preceding propositions, the particular concept of the will of the people or the *volonté générale* . . . vanishes into thin air. For that concept presupposes the existence of a uniquely determined common good discernible to all. . . . And unless there is a center, the common good, toward which, in the long run at least, *all* individual wills gravitate, we shall not get that particular type of "natural" *volonté générale*. . . . Both the existence and the dignity of this kind of *volonté générale* are gone as soon as the idea of the common good fails us. And both the pillars of the classical doctrine inevitably crumble into dust.

Of course, however conclusively those arguments may tell against this particular conception of the will of the people, they do not debar us from trying to build up another and more realistic one. I do not intend to question either the reality or the importance of the socio-psychological facts we think of when speaking of the will of a nation. Their analysis is certainly the prerequisite for making headway with the problems of democracy. It would however be better not to retain the term. . . . We have every reason to be on our guard against the pitfalls that lie on the path of those defenders of democracy who while accepting, under pressure of accumulating evidence, more and more of the facts of the democratic process, yet try to anoint the results that process turns out with oil taken from eighteenth-century jars.

But though a common will or public opinion of some sort may still be said to emerge from the infinitely complex jumble of individual and group-wise situations, volitions, influences, actions and reactions of the "democratic process," the result lacks not only rational unity but also rational sanction. The former means that, although from the standpoint of analysis, the democratic process is not simply chaotic--for the analyst nothing is chaotic that can be brought within the reach of explanatory principles—yet the results would not, except by chance, be meaningful in themselves —as for instance the realization of any definite end or ideal would be. The latter means, since *that* will is no longer congruent with any "good," that in order to claim ethical dignity for the result it will now be necessary to fall back upon an unqualified confidence in democratic forms of government as such—a belief that in principle would have to be independent of the desirability of the results. As we have seen, it is not easy to place oneself on that standpoint. But even if we do so, the dropping of the . . . common good still leaves us with plenty of difficulties on our hands.

In particular, we still remain under the practical necessity of attributing to the will of the *individual* an independence and a rational quality that are altogether unrealistic. If we are to argue that the will of the citizens *per se* is a political factor entitled to respect, it must first exist. That is to say, it must be something more than an indeterminate bundle of vague impulses loosely playing about given slogans and mistaken impressions. Everyone would have to know definitely what he wants to stand for. This definite will would have to be implemented by the ability to observe and interpret correctly the facts that are directly accessible to everyone and to sift critically the information about the facts that are not. Finally, from that definite will and from these ascertained facts a clear *and prompt* conclusion as to particular issues would have to be derived according to the rules of logical inference—with so high a degree of general efficiency moreover that one man's opinion could be held, without glaring absurdity, to be roughly as good as every other man's. And all this the model citizen would have to perform for himself and independently of pressure groups and propaganda.

. . . I want to make quite sure that the reader fully appreciates another point that has been made already. I will therefore repeat that even if the opinions and desires of individual citizens were perfectly definite and independent data for the democratic process to work with, and if everyone acted on them with ideal rationality and promptitude, it would not necessarily follow that the political decisions produced by that process from the raw material of those individual volitions would represent anything that could in any convincing sense be called the will of the people. It is not only conceivable but, whenever individual wills are much divided, very likely that the political decisions produced will not conform to "what people really want."

REASONS FOR THE SURVIVAL OF THE CLASSICAL DOCTRINE

But how is it possible that a doctrine so patently contrary to fact should have survived to this day and continued to hold its place in the hearts of the people and in the official language of governments? The refuting facts are known to all; everybody admits them with perfect, frequently with cynical, frankness. The theoretical basis, utilitarian rationalism, is dead; nobody accepts it as a correct theory of the body politic. Nevertheless that question is not difficult to answer.

First of all, though the classical doctrine of collective action may not be supported by the results of empirical analysis, it is powerfully supported by . . . association with religious belief. . . . This may not be obvious at first sight. . . . But we need only cast another glance . . . in order to discover that it embodied essential features of the faith of Protestant Christianity and was in fact derived from that faith. For the intellectual who had cast off his religion the utilitarian creed provided a substitute for it. For many of those who had retained their religious belief the classical doctrine became the political complement of it.

Thus transposed into the categories of religion, this doctrine—and in consequence the kind of democratic persuasion which is based upon it—changes its very nature. There is no longer any need for logical scruples about the Common Good and Ultimate Values. All this is settled for us by the plan of the Creator whose purpose defines and sanctions everything. What seemed indefinite or unmotivated before is suddenly quite definite and convincing. The voice of the people that is the voice of God for instance. Or take Equality. Its very meaning is in doubt, and there is hardly any rational warrant for exalting it into a postulate, so long as we move in the sphere of empirical analysis. But Christianity harbors a strong equalitarian element. The Redeemer died for all: He did not differentiate between individuals of different social status. In so doing, He testified to the intrinsic value of the individual soul, of a value that admits of no gradations. . . . To be sure this interpretation does not cover the whole ground. However, so far as it goes, it seems to explain many things that otherwise would be unexplainable and in fact meaningless. In particular, it explains the believer's attitude toward criticism: again . . . fundamental dissent is looked upon not merely as error but as sin; it elicits not merely logical counterargument but also moral indignation.

We may put our problem differently and say that democracy, when motivated in this way, ceases to be a mere method that can be discussed rationally like a steam engine or a disinfectant. It actually becomes what from another standpoint I have held it incapable of becoming, viz., an ideal or rather a part of an ideal schema of things. The very word may become a flag, a symbol of all a man holds dear, of everything that he loves about his nation whether rationally contingent to it or not. On the one hand, the question how the various propositions implied in the democratic belief are related to the facts of politics will then become as irrelevant to him as is, to the believing Catholic, the question how the doings of Alexander VI tally with the supernatural halo surrounding the papal office. On the other hand, the democrat of this type, while accepting postulates carrying large implications about equality and brotherliness, will be in a position also to accept, in all sincerity, almost any amount of deviation from them that his own behavior or position may involve. That is not even illogical. Mere distance from fact is no argument against an ethical maxim or a mystical hope.

Second, there is the fact that the forms and phrases of classical democracy are for many nations associated with events and developments in their history which are enthusiastically approved by large majorities. Any opposition to an established regime is likely to use these forms and phrases whatever its meaning and social roots may be. If it prevails and if subsequent developments prove satisfactory, then these forms will take root in the national ideology.

The United States is the outstanding example. Its very existence as a sovereign state is associated with a struggle against a monarchial and aristocratic England. A minority of loyalists excepted, Americans had, at the time of the Grenville administration, probably ceased to look upon the English monarch as *their king* and the English aristocracy as *their* aristocracy. In the War of Independence they fought what in fact as well as in their feeling had become a foreign monarch and a foreign aristocracy who interfered with their political and economic interests. Yet from an early stage of the troubles they presented their case, which really was a national one, as a case of the "people" versus its "rulers," in terms of inalienable Rights of Man and in the light of the general principles of classical democracy. The wording of the Declaration of Independence and of the Constitution adopted these principles. A prodigious development followed that absorbed and satisfied most people and thereby seemed to verify the doctrine embalmed in the sacred documents of the nation. . . .

Third, it must not be forgotten that there are social patterns in which the classical doctrine will actually fit facts with a sufficient degree of approximation. As has been pointed out, this is the case with many small and primitive societies which as a matter of fact served as a prototype to the authors of that doctrine. It may be the case also with societies that are not primitive provided they are not too differentiated and do not harbor any serious problems. Switzerland is the best example. There is so little to quarrel about in a world of peasants which, excepting hotels and banks, contains no great capitalist industry, and the problems of public policy are so simple and so stable that an overwhelming majority can be expected to understand them and to agree about them. But if we can conclude that in such cases the classical doctrine approximates reality we have to add immediately that it does so not because it describes an effective mechanism of political decision but only because there are no great decisions to be made. . . .

And fourth, of course, politicians appreciate a phraseology that flatters the masses and offers an excellent opportunity not only for evading responsibility but also for crushing opponents in the name of the people.

COMPETITION FOR POLITICAL LEADERSHIP

I think that most students of politics have by now come to accept the criticisms leveled at the classical doctrine of democracy. . . . I also think that most of them agree, or will agree before long, in accepting another theory which is much truer to life and at the same time salvages much of what the sponsors of the democratic method really meant by this term. Like the classical theory, it may be put into the nutshell of a definition.

It will be remembered that our chief troubles about the classical theory centered in the proposition that "the people" hold a definite and rational opinion about every individual question and that they give effect to this opinion—in a democracy—by choosing "representatives" who will see to it that that opinion is carried out. Thus the selection of the representatives is made secondary to the primary purpose of the democratic arrangement which is to vest the power of deciding political issues in the electorate. Suppose we reverse the roles of these two elements and make the deciding of issues by the electorate secondary to the election of the men who are to do the deciding. To put it differently, we now take the view that the role of the people is to produce a government, or else an intermediate body which in turn will produce a national executive or government. And we define: the democratic method is that institutional arrangement for arriving at political decisions in which individuals acquire the power to decide by means of a competitive struggle for the people's vote.

Defense and explanation of this idea will speedily show that, as to both plausibility of assumptions and tenability of propositions, it greatly improves the theory of the democratic process.

First of all, we are provided with a reasonably efficient criterion by which to distinguish democratic governments from others. We have seen that the classical theory meets with difficulties on that score because both the will and the good of the people may be, and in many historical instances have been, served just as well or better by governments that cannot be described as democratic according to any accepted usage of the terms. Now we are in a somewhat better position partly because we are resolved to stress a *modus procedendi* the presence or absence of which it is in most cases easy to verify.

For instance, a parliamentary monarchy like the English one fulfills the requirements of the democratic method because the monarch is practically constrained to appoint to cabinet office the same people as parliament would elect. A "constitutional" monarchy does not qualify to be called democratic because the electorates and parliaments, while having all the other rights that electorates and parliaments have in parliamentary monarchies, lack the power to impose their choice as to the governing committee: the cabinet ministers are in this case servants of the monarch, in substance as well as in name, and can in principle be dismissed as well as appointed by him. Such an arrangement may satisfy the people. The electorate may reaffirm this fact by voting against any proposal for change. The monarch may be so popular as to be able to defeat any competition for the supreme office. But since no machinery is provided for making this competition effective the case does not come within our definition.

Second, the theory embodied in this definition leaves all the room we may wish to have for a proper recognition of the vital fact of leadership. The classical theory did not do this but, as we have seen, attributed to the electorate an altogether unrealistic degree of initiative which practically amounted to ignoring leadership. But collectives act almost exclusively by accepting leadership—this is the dominant mechanism of practically any collective action which is more than a reflex. Propositions about the working and the results of the democratic method that take account of this are bound to be infinitely more realistic than propositions which do not. . . .

Third, however, so far as there are genuine group-wise volitions at all—for instance the will of the unemployed to receive unemployment benefit or the will of other groups to help—our theory does not neglect them. On the contrary we are now able to insert them in exactly the role they actually play. Such volitions do not as a rule assert themselves directly. Even if strong and definite, they remain latent, often for decades, until they are called to life by some political leader who turns them into political factors. This he does, or else his agents do it for him, by organizing these volitions, by working them up and by including eventually appropriate items in his competitive offerings. The interaction between sectional interests and public opinion and the way in which they produce the pattern we call the political situation appear from this angle in a new and much clearer light.

Fourth, our theory is of course no more definite than is the concept of competition for leadership. This concept presents similar difficulties as the concept of competition in the economic sphere, with which it may be usefully compared. . . . To simplify matters we have restricted the kind of competition for leadership which is to define democracy, to free competition for a free vote. The justification for this is that democracy seems to imply a recognized method by which to conduct the competitive struggle, and that the electoral method is practically the only one available for communities of any size. But though this excludes many ways of securing leadership which should be excluded, such as competition by military insurrection, it does not exclude the cases that are strikingly analogous to the economic phenomena we label "unfair" or "fraudulent" competition or restraint of competition. And we cannot exclude them because if we did we should be left with a completely unrealistic ideal. Between this ideal case which does not exist and the cases in which all competition with the established leader is prevented by force, there is a continuous range of variation within which the democratic method of government shades off into the autocratic one by imperceptible steps. But if we wish to understand and not to philosophize, this is as it should be. The value of our criterion is not seriously impaired thereby.

Fifth, our theory seems to clarify the relation that subsists between democracy and individual freedom. If by the latter we mean the existence of a sphere of individual self-government the boundaries of which are historically variable—*no* society tolerates absolute freedom even of conscience and of speech, *no* society reduces that sphere to zero—the question clearly becomes a matter of degree. We have seen that the democratic method does not necessarily guarantee a greater amount of individual freedom than another political method would permit in similar circumstances. It may well be the other way round. But there is still a relation between the two. If, on principle at least, everyone is free to compete for political leadership by presenting himself to the electorate, this will in most cases though not in all mean a considerable amount of freedom of discussion *for all.* In particular it will normally mean a considerable amount of freedom of the press. This relation between democracy and freedom is not absolutely stringent and can be tampered with. But, from the standpoint of the intellectual, it is nevertheless very important. At the same time, it is all there is to that relation.

Sixth, it should be observed that in making the primary function of the electorate to produce a government (directly or through an intermediate body) I intend to include in this phrase also the function of evicting it. The one means simply the acceptance of a leader or a group of leaders, the other means simply the withdrawal of this acceptance. This takes care of an element the reader may have missed. He may have thought that the electorate controls as well as installs. But since electorates normally do not control their political leaders in any way except by refusing to reelect them or the parliamentary majorities that support them, it seems well to reduce our ideas about this control in the way indicated by our definition. . . .

Seventh, our theory sheds much-needed light on an old controversy. Whoever accepts the classical doctrine of democracy and in consequence believes that the democratic method is to guarantee that issues be decided and policies framed according to the will of the people must be struck by the fact that, even if that will were undeniably real and definite, decision by simple majorities would in many cases distort it rather than give effect to it. Evidently the will of the majority is the will of the majority and not the will of "the people." The latter is a mosaic that the former completely fails to "represent." To equate both by definition is not to solve the problem. Attempts at real solution have however been made by the authors of the various plans for Proportional Representation.

These plans have met with adverse criticism on practical grounds. It is in fact obvious not only that proportional representation will offer opportunities for all sorts of idiosyncracies to assert themselves but also that it may prevent democracy from producing efficient governments and thus have a danger in times of stress. But before concluding that democracy becomes unworkable if its principle is carried out consistently, it is just as well to ask ourselves whether this principle really implies proportional representation. As a matter of fact it does not. If acceptance of leadership is the true function of the electorate's vote, the case for proportional representation collapses because its premises are no longer binding. The principle of democracy then merely means that the reins of government should be handed to those who command more support than do any of the competing individuals or teams. And this in turn seems to assure the standing of the majority system within the logic of the democratic method, although we might still condemn it on grounds that lie outside of that logic.

CARL J. FRIEDRICH

Constitutional Democracy

Division of power is the basis of civilized government. It is what is meant by constitutionalism. Constitutionalism can be monarchical, or it can be democratic, and it has been both. When we in America say "democracy," we usually mean constitutional democracy. Of course, there are those who would define democracy simply as the rule of the majority, without any constitutional pattern within which such majority decisions are set. But they are utopian theorists or partisans of a particular majority, a party they happen to agree with.

. . . Constitutionalism by dividing power provides a system of effective restraints upon governmental action. In studying it, one has to explore the methods and techniques by which such restraints are established and maintained. Putting it in another, more familiar, but less exact way, it is a body of rules ensuring fair play, thus rendering the government "responsible."

. . . The definition given at the outset . . . said that to render a government constitutional required the establishment and maintenance of effective restraints upon political and more especially upon governmental action. Why should we insist that the restraints must be effective? What is this standard of effectiveness? It should be evident that the existence of formally legal restraints is in no wise an indication of the existence of a constitutional order in the political

From *Constitutional Government and Democracy* by Carl J. Friedrich. Waltham, Mass.: Blaisdell Publishing Company, A Division of Ginn and Co., 1950, pp. 5–6, 26, 123–124, 156–157, 173.

sense. . . . On the other hand, a restraint might be very effective and thoroughly regularized, without necessarily being embodied in positive law unless law is very broadly defined as including all custom. Thus, what is perhaps the most important restraint of the English constitution, namely, the alternation of government between two or three parties, is quite effective. From what has been said it can be seen that the problem of effectiveness involves a factual situation and an evaluation and existential judgment of that situation. If no one has "absolute" power, if in actual fact there exists no sovereign who holds unrestrained power in a given community, then the restraints may be said to be effective.

At this point it becomes necessary to introduce another important qualification. Unless such restraints are regularized, they cannot be said to have value as constitutionalizing factors. . . . Obviously, it is not always easy to determine what is a regularized procedure. A practice which at one time is wholly irregular, and at another fully regularized, will, for a certain period, be hard to classify. But it is enough that we can readily determine when a procedure is fully regularized. In the United States, a decision of the Supreme Court ordinarily marks the point of ultimate regularization. . . .

The political force of the [American] Constitution is particularly apparent in connection with whatever restraints a bill of rights imposes upon governmental action. Clearly, such bills of rights differ materially from institutional safeguards such as a separation of powers. If the President is given power to veto a bill passed by Congress, he is thereby enabled to restrain the action of Congress. This type of restraint, entrusted to a living human being, will be attended to by that trustee. It is a procedural restraint. But if it is provided that no person shall be deprived of his property without due process of law, that restraint depends directly upon the political force which the Constitution itself possesses. It may be converted into a procedural restraint by giving the injured party the right of appealing to a court, but primarily it is a substantive restraint. These substantive restraints embody a people's way of life.

The way of life thus safeguarded by the restraints of a bill of rights constitutes a specific pattern of freedoms. As everyone knows, the American pattern is sketched in the Constitution.

. . . the entire history of government shows that substantive restraints embodying the opinion and customs of the community, its way of life, rest upon a tenuous foundation unless reinforced and backed up by procedural restraints of one sort or another. True constitutional government does not exist unless procedural restraints are established and effectively operating. Such restraints involve some division of power; for evidently some considerable power must be vested in those who are expected to do the restraining.

ROBERT A. DAHL

Democracy as Polyarchy

Polyarchy is defined loosely as a political system in which the following conditions exist to a relatively high degree:

DURING THE VOTING PERIOD:

1. Every member of the organization performs the acts we assume to constitute an expression of preference among the scheduled alternatives, e.g., voting.
2. In tabulating these expressions (votes), the weight assigned to the choice of each individual is identical.
3. The alternative with the greatest number of votes is declared the winning choice.

DURING THE PREVOTING PERIOD:

4. Any member who perceives a set of alternatives, at least one of which he regards as preferable to any of the alternatives presently scheduled, can insert his preferred alternative(s) among those scheduled for voting.
5. All individuals possess identical information about the alternatives.

DURING THE POST VOTING PERIOD:

6. Alternatives (leaders or policies) with the greatest number of votes displace any alternatives (leaders or policies) with fewer votes.
7. The orders of elected officials are executed.

From *A Preface to Democratic Theory* by Robert A. Dahl, by permission of The University of Chicago Press,

DURING THE INTERELECTION STAGE:

8.1. Either all interelection decisions are subordinate or executory to those arrived at during the election stage, i.e., elections are in a sense controlling.

8.2. Or new decisions during the interelection period are governed by the preceding seven conditions, operating, however, under rather different institutional circumstances.

8.3. Or both.

I think it may be laid down dogmatically that no human organization—certainly none with more than a handful of people—has ever met or is ever likely to meet these eight conditions. It is true that the second, third, and sixth conditions are quite precisely met in some organizations, although in the United States corrupt practices sometimes nullify even these; the others are, at best, only crudely approximated.

As to the first, evidently in all human organizations there are significant variations in participation in political decisions—variations which in the United States appear to be functionally related to such variables as degree of concern or involvement, skill, access, socioeconomic status, education, residence, age, ethnic and religious identifications, and some little understood personality characteristics. As is well known, in national elections on the average something like half of all adults in the United States go to the polls; only a quarter do anything more than vote: write to their congressmen, for example, or contribute to campaigns, or attempt to persuade others to adopt their political views. In the 1952 election, of one nationwide sample only 11 per cent helped the political parties financially, attended party gatherings, or worked for one of the parties or candidates; only 27 per cent talked to other people to try to show them why they should vote for one of the parties or candidates.

The effective political elites, then, operate within limits often vague and broad, although occasionally narrow and well defined, set by their expectations as to the reaction of the group of politically active citizens who go to the polls. Other organizations, such as trade-unions, where political equality is prescribed in the formal charter, operate in much the same way, although the elites and the politically active members are often even a smaller proportion of the total.

In no organization of which I have any knowledge does the fourth condition exist. Perhaps the condition is most closely approximated in very small groups. Certainly in all large groups for which we have any data, control over communication is so unevenly distributed that some individuals possess considerably more influence over the designation of the alternatives scheduled for voting than do others. I do not know how to quantify this control, but if it could be quantified I suppose that it would be no exaggeration to say that Mr. Henry Luce has a thousand or ten thousand times greater control over the alternatives scheduled for debate and tentative decision at a national election than I do. Although we have here a formidable problem that so far as I know has never been adequately analyzed, it is a reasonable preliminary hypothesis that the number of individuals who exercise significant control over the alternatives scheduled is, in most organizations, only a tiny fraction of the total membership. This seems to be the case even in the most democratic organizations if the membership is at all large.

Much the same remarks apply to the fifth condition. The gap in information between the political elites and the active members—not to say the inactive members—no doubt is almost always great. In recent times the gap has been further widened in national governments by growing technical complexities and the rapid spread of security regulations. As every student of bureaucracy knows, the seventh condition is the source of serious difficulties; however, the extent to which this condition is achieved is perhaps the most puzzling of all to measure objectively.

If elections, like the market, were continuous, then we should have no need of the eighth condition. But of course elections are only periodic. It is sometimes suggested that the interelection pressures on decision processes are a kind of election, but this is at best only a deceptive metaphor. . . .

Because human organizations rarely and perhaps never reach the limit set by these eight conditions, it is necessary to interpret each of these conditions as one end of a continuum or scale along which any given organization might be measured. Unfortunately there is at present no known way of assigning meaningful weights to the eight conditions. However, even without weights, if the eight scales could each be metricized, it would be possible and perhaps useful to establish some arbitrary but not meaningless classes of which the upper chunk might be called "polyarchies."

It is perfectly evident, however, that what has just been described is no more than a program, for nothing like it has, I think, ever been attempted. I shall simply set down here, therefore, the following observations. Organizations do in fact differ markedly in the extent to which they approach the limits set by these eight conditions. Furthermore, "polyarchies" include a variety of organizations which Western political scientists would ordinarily call democratic, including certain aspects of the governments of nation states such as the United States, Great Britain, the Dominions (South Africa possibly excepted), the Scandinavian countries, Mexico, Italy, and France; states and provinces, such as the states of this country and the provinces of Canada; numerous cities and towns; some trade-unions; numerous associations such as Parent-Teachers' Associations, chapters of the League of Women Voters, and some religious groups; and some primitive societies. Thus it follows that the number of polyarchies is large. (The number of egalitarian polyarchies is probably relatively small or perhaps none exists at all.) The number of polyarchies must run well over a hundred and probably well over a thousand. Of this number, however, only a tiny handful has been exhaustively studied by political scientists, and these have been the most difficult of all, the governments of national states, and in a few instances the smaller governmental units.

E. E. SCHATTSCHNEIDER

Democracy as the Socialization of Conflict

To a great extent, the whole discussion of the role of government in modern society is at root a question of the scale of conflict. *Democratic government is the greatest single instrument for the socialization of conflict in the American community.* The controversy about democracy might be interpreted in these terms also. Government in a democracy is a great engine for expanding the scale of conflict. Government is never far away when conflict breaks out. On the other hand, if the government lacks power or resources, vast numbers of potential conflicts cannot be developed because the community is unable to do anything about them. Therefore, government thrives on conflict. The work of the government has been aided and abetted by a host of public and private agencies and organizations designed to exploit every rift in the private world. Competitiveness is intensified by the legitimation of outside interference in private conflicts. It is necessary only to mention political parties, pressure groups, the courts, congressional investigations, governmental regulatory agencies, freedom of speech and press, among others, to show the range and variety of instruments available to the government for breaking open private conflicts.

. . . The role of the people in the political system is determined largely by the conflict system, for it is conflict that

From *The Semisovereign People*, New York: Holt, Rinehart and Winston, Inc., 1960, pp. 13, 129–131, 138–142.

involves the people in politics and the nature of conflict determines the nature of the public involvement.

The idea that people are involved in politics by the contagion of conflict does not resemble the classical definition of democracy as "government by the people." The difference between the idea of popular "involvement" in conflict and the idea that people actually "govern" is great enough to invite a re-examination of the classical theory of democracy. Does the consideration of the place of conflict in a free political system open up the way for a redefinition of democracy in modern terms?

Whether we know it or not all speculation about American politics rests on some image of democracy. The literature on the subject has been so permeated by democratic and pseudodemocratic ideas that it is impossible to understand what we are talking about unless we isolate and identify these ideas and try to distinguish between the democratic and antidemocratic elements in them.

The devotion of the American public to the democratic ideal is so overwhelming that we test everything by it. It is surprising to find, therefore, that political philosophers have had remarkable difficulty in defining the word *democracy*. As a matter of fact, the failure to produce a good working definition of democracy is responsible for a great part of the confusion in the literature of politics. An examination of the problem might be worthwhile, therefore.

The classical definition of democracy as government by the people is predemocratic in its origins, based on notions about democracy developed by philosophers who never had an opportunity to see an operating democratic system. Predemocratic theorists assumed that the people would take over the conduct of public affairs in a democracy and administer the government to their own advantage as simply as landowners administer their property for their own profit. Under the historical circumstances this oversimplification is easy to understand. There is less excuse for the failure of modern scholars to re-examine the traditional definition critically in the light of modern experience.

One consequence of our reliance on old definitions is that the modern American does not look at democracy before he defines it; he defines it first and then is confused by what he sees. In spite of the fact that the ancients made some astonishing miscalculations about democracy as an operating system, their authority is so great that the traditional definition is perpetuated in the textbooks and governs our thinking in the entire area.

The confusion of ideas about democracy looks like a job for the political scientist. What we need is a modern definition of democracy explaining the facts of life of the operating political system, a definition that distinguishes between the democratic and antidemocratic elements in the developing contemporary political situation. The great deficiency of American democracy is intellectual, the lack of a good, usable definition. A good definition might shed a flood of light on modern politics; it might clarify a thousand muddy concepts and might help us to understand where we are going and what we want. It might even help us get rid of the impossible imperatives that haunt the literature of the subject and give everyone a sense of guilt. We need to re-examine the chasm between theory and practice because it is at least as likely that the ideal is wrong as it is that the reality is bad. Certainly our chances of getting democracy and keeping it would be better if we made up our minds about what it is.

The people are involved in public affairs by the conflict system. Conflicts open up questions for public intervention. Out of conflict the alternatives of public policy arise. Conflict is the occasion for political organization and leadership. In a free political system it is difficult to avoid public involvement in conflict; the ordinary, regular operations of the government give rise to controversy, and controversy is catching.

The beginning of wisdom in democratic theory is to distinguish between the things the people can do and the things the people cannot do. The worst possible disservice that can be done to the democratic cause is to attribute to the people a mystical, magical omnipotence which takes no cognizance of what very large numbers of people cannot do by the sheer weight of numbers. At this point the common definition of democracy has invited us to make fools of ourselves.

What 180 million people can do spontaneously, on their own initiative, is not much more than a locomotive can do without rails. The public is like a very rich man who is unable to supervise closely all of his enterprise. His problem is to learn how to compel his agents to define his options.

What we are saying is that conflict, competition, leadership, and organization are the essence of democratic politics. Inherent in the operation of democracy are special conditions which permit large numbers of people to function.

The problem is how to organize the political system so as to make the best possible use of the power of the public in view of its limitations. A popular decision bringing into focus the force of public support requires a tremendous effort to define the alternatives, to organize the discussion and mobilize opinion. The government and the political organizations are in the business of manufacturing this kind of alternatives.

What has been said here has not been said to belittle the power of the people but to shed some light on what it is. The power of the people is not made less by the fact that it cannot be used for trivial matters. The whole world can be run on the basis of a remarkably small number of decisions. The power of the people in a democracy depends on the *importance* of the decisions made by the electorate, not on the *number* of decisions they make. Since the adoption of the Constitution the party in power has been turned out by the opposition party fourteen times, and in about six of these instances the consequences have been so great that we could not understand American history without taking account of them.

The most important thing about any democratic regime is the *way* in which it *uses* and exploits popular sovereignty, what questions it refers to the public for decision or guidance, how it refers them to the public, how the alternatives are defined and how it respects the limitations of the public. A good democratic system protects the public against the demand that it do impossible things. The unforgivable sin of democratic politics is to dissipate the power of the public by putting it to trivial uses. What we need is a movement for the conservation of the political resources of the American people.

Above everything, *the people are powerless if the political enterprise is not competitive*. It is the competition of political organizations that provides the people with the opportunity to make a choice. Without this opportunity popular sovereignty amounts to nothing.

The common definition of democracy may be harmless if it is properly understood, but the fact is that it is very commonly misunderstood. It would be more imaginative to say that some things we now are actually doing are democratic even though they do not fit the traditional definition. Definitions of democracy since the time of Aristotle have been made on the assumption that the "many" in a democracy do the same thing that the "one" does in a monarchy and the "few" do in an aristocracy. But obviously the shift from the "one" to the "many" is more than a change in the number of people participating in power but *a change in the way the power is exercised*. The 180 million cannot do what a single ruler can do. This is not because the 180 million are stupid or ignorant but because it is physically impossible for

180 million to act the way one acts. In the interests of clarity and the survival of the political system we need a definition of democracy that recognizes the limitations that nature imposes on large numbers.

A working definition must capitalize on the limitations of the people as well as their powers. We do this when we say that liberty and leadership are the greatest of democratic concepts. *Democracy is a competitive political system in which competing leaders and organizations define the alternatives of public policy in such a way that the public can participate in the decision-making process.* The initiative in this political system is to be found largely in the government or in the opposition. The people profit by this system, but they cannot, by themselves, do the work of the system. We have already had a great deal of experience with this kind of system. Is it not about time that we begin to recognize its democratic implications?

Conflict, competition, organization, leadership and responsibility are the ingredients of a working definition of democracy. Democracy is a political system in which the people have a choice among the alternatives created by competing political organizations and leaders. The advantage of this definition over the traditional definition is that it is *operational,* it describes something that actually happens. It describes something feasible. It does not make impossible demands on the public. Moreover, it describes a going democratic concern whose achievements are tremendous.

The involvement of the public in politics is a natural outgrowth of the kind of conflict that almost inevitably arises in a free society. The exploitation of this situation by responsible political leaders and organizations is the essence of democracy; the socialization of conflict is the essential democratic process.

SEYMOUR MARTIN LIPSET

Democracy as the Peaceful "Play" of Power

. . . democracy (in a complex society) is defined as a political system which supplies regular constitutional opportunities for changing the governing officials. It is a social mechanism for the resolution of the problem of societal decision-making among conflicting interest groups which permits the largest possible part of the population to influence these decisions through their ability to choose among alternative contenders for political office. In large measure abstracted from the work of Joseph Schumpeter and Max Weber, this definition implies a number of specific conditions: (a) a "political formula," a system of beliefs, legitimizing the democratic system and specifying the institutions—parties, a free press, and so forth—which are legitimized, i.e., accepted as proper by all; (b) one set of political leaders in office; and (c) one or more sets of leaders, out of office, who act as a legitimate opposition attempting to gain office.

The need for these conditions is clear. *First,* if a political system is not characterized by a value system allowing the peaceful "play" of power—the adherence by the "outs" to decisions made by "ins" and the recognition by "ins" of the rights of the "outs"—there can be no stable democracy. This has been the problem faced by many Latin American states. *Second,* if the outcome of the political game is not the periodic awarding of effective authority to one group, a party or stable coalition, then unstable and irresponsible

From "Some Social Requisites of Democracy: Economic Development and Political Legitimacy" by Seymour Martin Lipset, *American Political Science Review,* LIII (March 1959), p. 71.

government rather than democracy will result. This state of affairs existed in pre-Fascist Italy, and for much, though not all, of the history of the Third and Fourth French Republics, which were characterized by weak coalition governments, often formed among parties which had major interest and value conflicts with each other. *Third,* if the conditions facilitating the perpetuation of an effective opposition do not exist, then the authority of officials will be maximized, and popular influence on policy will be at a minimum. This is the situation in all one-party states; and by general agreement, at least in the West, these are dictatorships.

4 Normative-Empirical Definitions

A. D. LINDSAY

Democracy as Government by Discussion

DIRECT AND REPRESENTATIVE DEMOCRACY

It is a commonplace of political theory that direct democracy became impossible when the size of the community outgrew the limits of a single public meeting. But long before that limit is reached most members of the community have ceased to take any part in the discussion or to contribute anything to the meeting. No one can really do business at a big meeting. Men can say Yes or No to cut-and-dried proposals, or compelling and spellbinding speeches may turn votes, but the real discussion and largely the real government is in the hands of the committee who prepare[s] the business.

The real point is that when a society has grown beyond the limits of a public meeting, then even the pretense of direct government has to be given up, and something has to be done about it. And that the limit of direct democracy

From *The Essentials of Democracy* by A. D. Lindsay. London: Oxford University Press, second edition, 1935, fifth impression, 1951, pp. 21–22, 30, 32–35.

was felt to be determined by the limit in the size of the public meeting, and not by the much earlier limit of the effective discussion, has been of sinister importance in the theory of democracy. It has suggested that what matters is not that the people should rule, but that they should think they rule; and it has given undue emphasis to the element of consent over the element of discussion.

. . . Strictly speaking, phrases such as "the will of the people" or "the voice of the people" are mere mythology. The great mass of the people can only consent to what government or some other organized group of people proposes to do. If the formulation of proposals or the choice of alternative candidates is not done by a responsible government organization, it will have to be done by an irresponsible organization—as a study of political parties has long made evident. The only result of insisting on the pretense that the people shall do it is to transfer the work of formulating proposals from the responsible to the irresponsible organization.

. . . Modern representative government implies an organized and official opposition. It does not only tolerate difference and criticism. It implies and demands it. It is the sense of this which is behind the oft-quoted statement that the English people dislike coalitions; or behind the curious complaints which Parliamentary governments with strong majorities often make, that the opposition is not strong or effective enough. . . . It is, I think, clear that so far from unanimous consent being the ideal of representative democracy, representative democracy would not know what to do with such a consummation. . . . We often discuss whether representative government flourishes best with two parties or with more. But no one with the least understanding of its nature would think that it could get on with one party. . . .

All this is of course a commonplace, but I am not sure that we always realize how much of the essence of democracy is contained in this insistence on a tolerated and official opposition. It implies that the business of representative government is to make articulate and get expressed different not consentaneous points of view—that democratic equality is not an equality of sameness but of difference—that we want every one to have political rights, not because and in so far as they agree with other people, but because and in so far as they have each their peculiar contribution to make. . . . democracy is based on the assumption that men can agree on common action which yet leaves each to live his own life—that if we really respect one another's personality we can find a common framework or system of rights within which the free moral life of the individual is possible.

How that can best be attained can be discovered by discussion, in which the one-sidedness of particular views can be eliminated and a principle of common action discovered which each can feel does justice to what was vital in his own contention. . . .

Now surely, if we reflect upon it, what matters most in the tiny democratic societies which we feel to be thoroughly satisfactory forms of government is what comes out of the free give and take of discussion. When men who are serving a common purpose meet to pool their experience, to air their difficulties and even their discontents, there comes about a real process of collective thinking. The narrowness and one-sidedness of each person's point of view are corrected, and something emerges which each can recognize as embodying the truth of what he stood for, and yet (or rather therefore) is seen to serve the purpose of the society better than what anyone conceived for himself. That is of course an ideal. Such perfect agreement is not often reached. But it is an ideal which is always to some extent realized when there is open and frank discussion. And anyone with experience of the effectiveness of discussion in a small democratic society must recognize how valuable is the contribution of those who are not easily convinced but can stand up resolutely for their own point of view. . . .

Observe further that the moment we take discussion seriously, we are committed to the view that we are concerned not primarily to obtain or register consent, but to find something out. . . . The root of the matter is that if the discussion is at all successful, we discover something from it which could have been discovered in no other way. . . . Democracy assumes that each member of the community has something to contribute if it can be got out of him. It does not for a moment assume that what each member contributes is of equal value.

Now if, with all this in mind, we approach the problem created by the large scale of political democracy, we shall say that what matters is not that the final decision of government should be assented to by everyone, but that everyone should have somehow made his contribution to that decision. There cannot possibly be one enormous discussion, but there may be smaller areas of discussion, and the results of these may be conveyed by the representative to a further discussion, and so on.

LIBERTY, EQUALITY, POPULAR CONTROL

Liberty is a note of a democratic society in so far as such a society believes that voluntary association, informal uncompelled relations between man and man should play a large part in society. This is only another way of saying . . . that the end of the state . . . is to serve, foster, harmonize, and strengthen the free life of the community. Freedom of speech, freedom of meeting, freedom of association—these are all necessary conditions of this general freedom.

Democratic liberty then is a means between two extremes

From *The Modern Democratic State* by A. D. Lindsay. London: Oxford University Press, 1943, pp. 265–266, 272, 281–282.

—between the extreme view that society has no need of a compulsion and that there can be no place for compulsion in a democratic society, and the other extreme that government, the organization with force behind it, should control all social activities, and that this may well be quite compatible with liberty. . . .

Democracy is a revolutionary form of government. For its aim is to find a place for continual change within government. Its law exists to foster freedom: its force exists to protect law. It is an organization to preserve, leave room for, these precious things of the spirit which in their nature cannot be organized. This may seem a high-flown statement of democracies as we know them. No doubt men and women abuse liberty and we must all be prevented from using our own liberty to destroy the liberty of others. Nevertheless the steady insistence in democratic government that there is always a strong prima facie case against interference with free associations, that there ought to be spheres of life which government does not control, is based on the conviction of the value of change and experiment and initiative.

If equality and liberty, so conceived, are the marks of a democratic community, it will be the task of the government of such a community to be sensitively aware of the conditions which are making equality and liberty hard to maintain. There are of course certain elementary minimum conditions which will have to be laid down and provided. These are the kind which can at least be defined in a list of rights—minimum legal rights and a minimum standard economic security. . . . There are some obvious and outstanding evils like widespread unemployment which can so poison the life of a community that they make equality and liberty and true democratic life impossible. The diagnosis of such evils is not difficult. But just because true equality and liberty are not mechanical conceptions and not standardized articles, a successful democratic government will, as we have said above, have to be sensitively aware of the conditions in society which prevent the community from being a community.

. . . what happens in parliamentary democracy is that the people vote for a government on the understanding that it will remedy their grievances, deal with what is most manifestly wrong, and that they judge and they alone can judge whether the grievances are remedied. The vote at a general election is primarily a judgment on results . . . [and] an expression of approval or disapproval of what has happened. This . . . does not imply . . . that the electorate are particularly intelligent. . . . It does imply that, as the end of government is to promote the free life of all its citizens, all citizens must have their say as to how that free life is actually being hindered and how far the work of government is actually removing those hindrances.

. . . In a democratic state those who have power and expert knowledge are to serve the community and be controlled by the ordinary people who have neither power nor knowledge. The first problem of a democratic state is to ensure that government is kept to its proper task. Democracy is not, properly speaking, government *by* the people. For the people . . . cannot govern.

Government involves power and organization, administration, and decision. Even a small public meeting cannot administer or organize. It can only express approval or disapproval of the persons who govern or of their general proposals. . . .

It is essential to any sound democracy to recognize what part the ordinary public can take in the government of a state and what it cannot. Experience has shown abundantly that, if in the name of democracy you ask the ordinary member of the public to do more than he can or will in fact do, the result is a sham. We must, therefore, distinguish between the various processes by which the government of a country is kept responsible to public opinion from the highly technical and specialized process of government itself. I propose to call the relation of the public to the government in a democratic country control; and keep the word government for the decisive, definite process of administering and commanding. The distinction is not always clear cut. The one function shades into the other, but the broad distinction remains and is important. There are . . . some forms of control of government, which are quite unlike commanding or governing, which are apt to be overlooked if we think of democracy as government by the people. If . . . the task of democracy is to make the organized power which is government subservient and sensitive to the whole complex common life of society, the expression of general approval or disapproval conveyed in votes will be sure to be only one among several ways of ensuring this control.

ERNEST BARKER

Practical and Moral Dimensions of Democracy

The word democracy, in its etymological significance, means government by the people. It is thus synonymous with Popular Government. The principle which underlies such government is often stated in the words, "The will of the people must prevail." Without, for the moment, challenging that principle, we have to remark that the will of the people is not a single will. There are some who will one thing, and some who will another. "In that case," the answer comes, "let us count heads: let us discover the majority. . . ." But why, we may ask, should the will of a part, however numerous, be identified with the will of the whole? The answer generally given to that question is an answer which rests on the argument of force. "We count heads instead of breaking them: the majority would win the day if it came to an actual struggle. . . ." This reduces the proposition that "the will of the people must prevail" to the simpler but less attractive proposition that "the force of the majority of the people must prevail, because, if it were challenged, it would prevail." In a word, the basis of democracy becomes force—not actual force, but hypothetical force. . . .

Democracy which rests merely on the will of numbers rests merely on force. If we keep the name and idea of democracy, we must find some other basis. . . . We have to discover a system of government which squares with, and

From *Reflections on Government* by Ernest Barker. Oxford: The Clarendon Press, 1942, pp. 35–38, 15–16, 417–420.

is based upon, the free and full development of human personality—not in some, or even in many, but in all. From this point of view it is not the people, as a people, that matters. It is not the majority, as a majority, that matters. It is each human being, as such. The form of government we have to find is one which elicits and enlists . . . the thought, the will, and the general capacity of every member. It must be a government depending on mutual interchange of ideas, on mutual criticism of the ideas interchanged, and on the common and agreed choice of the idea which emerges triumphant from the ordeal of interchange and criticism. A government depending on such a process can enlist in itself and its own operation the self of every member. . . .

That process is, in a word, discussion—discussion of competing ideas, leading to a compromise in which all the ideas are reconciled and which can be accepted by all because it bears the imprint of all. . . .

The great States of our modern world, with populations which run to tens and even hundreds of millions, seem precluded by their very size from acting as circles of discussion. Looking at their magnitude, we might despair of our principle. . . . But we need despair only if we make the assumption that discussion must proceed immediately and solely from the whole civic body. That is an assumption at once unnecessary and untrue to life. Discussion . . . in modern States . . . proceeds in a number of stages and moves in a series of concentric circles. It begins on the circumference, with general issues; it moves inwards toward the center, and ends in concrete decision. . . . We speak of democracy or popular government. But we also speak of the parliamentary system or representative institutions. . . . We also speak of responsible government or the cabinet system. . . .

A system of government by discussion proceeds through four main stages—first of party, next of the electorate, then of parliament, and finally of cabinet. These stages have not developed historically in that sequence. . . . But if we look at the logic of modern life rather than the sequence of history, we may say that the process of political discussion begins originally with the action of political parties, which debate and formulate their programs as the issues for electoral discussion, and then proceed to select and propose their candidates as the exponents of those programs. Discussion is then carried forward to the electorate, which chooses between the programs, after the grand debate of a general election, by the simple act of choosing between the candidates and thus constituting a majority in favor of one of the programs. It is next carried forward to parliament, in which the majority, subject to the condition of constant debate with the minority, seeks to give legislative force to the measures. . . . Finally, the process of discussion is carried forward to the cabinet, a body of colleagues, selected by the accredited leader of the majority, who discuss and settle . . . the legislative measure to be submitted to parliament and the general lines of administrative action to be taken.

. . . The assumption is that in our human world, and under God, the individual personality of man alone has intrinsic and ultimate worth, and having also the capacity of development has also an intrinsic and ultimate claim to the essential condition of its development. Liberty will then be that essential condition; and the essence of liberty will be that it is a condition, or status, or quality, which individual personality must possess in order that it may translate itself from what it is to what it has the capacity of becoming.

The personality which has this capacity of development . . . is moral personality. . . . The liberty which such a personality claims is therefore a moral liberty. It is a liberty which consists in possessing the status or condition or quality of determining one's own action by one's own conception of the good. The essential ground for claiming such liberty is that personality only develops, and disengages its intrinsic worth, if it determines itself by its own conceptions in the process of that development. . . . Moral personality can only develop through the moral liberty of a personal will which wills for itself the conceptions which it has itself embraced. . . .

If democracy is wedded to liberty, liberty, in its turn, is wedded to equality. If men share a common liberty of thought and action, they are already, in that respect, the equals of one another. But the equal possession of liberty of thought and action is not the whole of equality. . . . Equality in liberty of thought, if it is to have substance and content, must mean a large measure of equality in the education of mental capacity. Equality in liberty of action, if it too is to have substance and content, must mean some measure of equality in the possession of what we call "means," and this for the obvious reason that "means" are means and conditions of action, and that inadequate "means" prevent free and liberal activity in the pursuit of ends. . . . If equality is wedded to liberty, the marriage must be equal, and liberty must not be dominated or diminished by equality. The compulsory institution of a system of pure equality would freeze the springs of initiative and reduce the variety of a living society to a static and dead uniformity. If a new and broader conception of equality is needed, it must not be purchased at the cost of surrendering our old conception of liberty. Each new approach to equality must be made by the methods of liberty, and it must also be consistent with the retention of liberty.

. . . There remains the cause of fraternity. . . Fraternity is an old and vague term, which may almost seem to have been given vogue in 1789 for the simple purpose of rounding a triad. But it is possible to find a sense for the term which gives it a large and substantive value. Fraternity is the general sense of cooperation in a national society which impels its members to create, in the spirit of a family, the common framework or equipment, both material and mental, which is the necessary condition of the good life of the society and of each and all of its members. . . . On the material side it runs through a whole ascending gamut, from the provision of roads for the movement of the community to the promotion of its health, the development of its soil, and the preservation of all its amenities. . . . On the mental side it begins with the provision of schools, . . . galleries, museums, libraries, . . . national theaters, concert-halls, and opera-houses. . . .

Fraternity of this order, serving to provide a common stock and equal facilities for a common and equal enjoyment, and thus allying itself readily with a new and broader conception of equality, will enable the democratic State to meet and direct the movements impinging on its life.

JOHN DEWEY

Democracy and the Great Community

. . . Conjoint, combined, associated action is a universal trait of the behavior of things. Such action has results. Some of the results of human collective action are perceived, that is, they are noted in such ways that they are taken account of. Then there arise purposes, plans, measures and means, to secure consequences which are liked and eliminate those which are found obnoxious. Thus perception generates a common interest; that is, those affected by the consequences are perforce concerned in conduct of all those who along with themselves share in bringing about the results. Sometimes the consequences are confined to those who directly share in the transaction which produces them. In other cases they extend far beyond those immediately engaged in producing them. Thus two kinds of interests and of measures of regulation of acts in view of consequences are generated. In the first, interest and control are limited to those directly engaged; in the second, they extend to those who do not directly share in the performance of acts.

. . . Those indirectly and seriously affected for good or for evil form a group distinctive enough to require recognition and a name. The name selected is The Public. This public is organized and made effective by means of representatives who as guardians of custom, as legislators, as executives, judges, etc., care for its special interests by methods intended to regulate the conjoint actions of individuals and groups. Then and in so far, association adds to itself

From *The Public and Its Problems* by John Dewey. Henry Holt & Co., 1927, pp. 34–35, 111, 113–115, 116–118, 141–142, 146–150.

political organization, and something which may be government comes into being: the public is a political state.

American democratic polity was developed out of genuine community life, that is, association in local and small centers where industry was mainly agricultural and where production was carried on mainly with hand tools. . . . The township or some not much larger area was the political unit, the town meeting the political medium, and roads, schools, the peace of the community, were the political objectives. . . . The imagination of the founders did not travel far beyond what could be accomplished and understood in a congeries of self-governing communities. . . .

We have inherited, in short, local town-meeting practices and ideas. But we live and act and have our being in a continental national state. . . . The notion of maintaining a unified state, even nominally self-governing, over a country as extended as the United States and consisting of a large and racially diversified population would once have seemed the wildest of fancies. It was assumed that such a state could be found only in territories hardly larger than a city-state and with a homogeneous population. It seemed almost self-evident to Plato—as to Rousseau later—that a genuine state could hardly be larger than the number of persons capable of personal acquaintance with one another. Our modern state-unity is due to the consequences of technology employed so as to facilitate the rapid and easy circulation of opinions and information, and so as to generate constant and intricate interaction far beyond the limits of face-to-face communities. Political and legal forms have only piecemeal and haltingly, with great lag, accommodated themselves to the industrial transformation. The elimination of distance . . . has called into being the new form of political association. . . .

In spite of attained integration, or rather perhaps because of its nature, the Public seems to be lost; it is certainly bewildered. The government, officials and their activities, are plainly with us. Legislatures make laws with luxurious abandon; subordinate officials engage in a losing struggle to enforce some of them; judges on the bench deal as best they can with the steadily mounting pile of disputes that come before them. But where is the public which these officials are supposed to represent? How much more is it than geographical names and official titles? The United States, the state of Ohio or New York, the county of this and the city of that? . . . If a public exists, it is surely . . . uncertain about its own whereabouts. . . The number of voters who take advantage of their majestic right is steadily decreasing in proportion to those who might use it. The ratio of actual to eligible voters is now about one-half. In spite of somewhat frantic appeals and organized effort, the endeavor to bring voters to a sense of their privileges and duties has so far been noted for failure. . . .

The new era of human relationships in which we live is one marked by mass production for remote markets, by cable and telephone, by cheap printing, by railways and steam navigation. Only geographically did Columbus discover a new world. The actual new world has been generated in the last hundred years. . . . There are those who lay the blame for all the evils of our lives on steam, electricity and machinery. It is always convenient to have a devil as well as a savior to bear the responsibilities of humanity. In reality, the trouble springs rather from the ideas and absence of ideas in connection with which technological factors operate. Mental and moral beliefs and ideals change more slowly than outward conditions. . . . Since the aims, desires and purposes created by a machine age do not connect with tradition, there are two sets of rival ideals. . . . Because the two are rivals and because the older ones retain their glamor and sentimental prestige in literature and religion, the newer ones are perforce harsh and narrow. For the older symbols of ideal life still engage thought and command loyalty. Conditions have changed, but every aspect of life, from religion and education to property and trade, shows that nothing approaching a transformation has taken place in ideas and ideals. Symbols control sentiment and thought, and the new age has no symbols consonant with its activities. . . . We have the physical tools of communication as never before. The thoughts and aspirations congruous with them are not communicated, and hence are not common. Without such communication the public will remain shadowy and formless, seeking spasmodically for itself, but seizing and holding its shadow rather than its substance. Till the Great Society is converted into a Great Community, the Public will remain in eclipse. Communication can alone create a great community. Our Babel is not one of tongues but of the signs and symbols without which shared experience is impossible.

. . . That government exists to serve its community, and that this purpose cannot be achieved unless the community itself shares in selecting its governors and determining its policies, are a deposit of fact left, as far as we can see, permanently. . . . We have every reason to think that whatever changes may take place in existing democratic machinery, they will be of a sort to make the interest of the public a more supreme guide and criterion of governmental activity, and to enable the public to form and manifest its purposes still more authoritatively. In this sense the cure for the ailments of democracy is more democracy. The prime difficulty, as we have seen, is that of discovering the means by which a scattered, mobile and manifold public may so recognize itself as to define and express its interests. This discovery is necessarily precedent to any fundamental change in the machinery. We are not concerned therefore to set forth counsels as to advisable improvements in the political forms of democracy. . . . The problem lies deeper; it is in the first instance an intellectual problem: the search for conditions under which the Great Society may become the Great Community. . . .

In a search for the conditions under which the inchoate public now extant may function democratically, we may proceed from a statement of the nature of the democratic idea in its generic social sense. From the standpoint of the individual, it consists in having a responsible share according to capacity in forming and directing the activities of the groups to which one belongs and in participating according to need in the values which the groups sustain. From the standpoint of the group, it demands liberation of the potentialities of members of a group in harmony with the interests and goods which are common. Since every individual is a member of many groups, this specification cannot be fulfilled except when different groups interact flexibly and fully in connection with other groups. . . .

Regarded as an idea, democracy is not an alternative to other principles of associated life. It is the idea of community life itself. It is an ideal in the only intelligible sense of an ideal: namely, the tendency and movement of some thing which exists carried to its final limit, viewed as completed, perfected. Since things do not attain such fulfillment but are in actuality distracted and interfered with, democracy in this sense is not a fact and never will be. But neither in this sense is there or has there ever been anything which is a community in its full measure, a community unalloyed by alien elements. . . . The clear consciousness of a communal life, in all its implications, constitutes the idea of democracy.

Only when we start from a community as a fact, grasp the fact in thought so as to clarify and enhance its constituent elements, can we reach an idea of democracy which is not utopian. The conceptions and shibboleths which are traditionally associated with the idea of democracy take on a veridical and directive meaning only when they are construed as marks and traits of an association which realizes the defining characteristics of a community. Fraternity, liberty and equality isolated from communal life are hopeless abstractions. . . . In its just connection with communal experience, fraternity is another name for the consciously appreciated goods which accrue from an association in which all share, and which give direction to the conduct of each. Liberty is that secure release and fulfillment of personal potentialities which take place only in rich and manifold association with others: the power to be an individualized self making a distinctive contribution and enjoying in its own way the fruits of association. Equality denotes the unhampered share which each individual member of the community has in the consequences of associated action.

ROBERT M. MacIVER

Democracy, Community, State

We live in communities; we do not live *in* states. We do not move and have our being in states, they are not integral things like communities. The nation, the great community, is not identical with the state; in the national state the boundaries of state and nation tend to coincide, and then the state becomes the political organization of the nation, a system of controls and institutional devices through which the nation, in some sense, governs itself. . . .

Yet the distinction, once it is brought to our attention, is surely obvious. Everywhere men weave a web of relationships with their fellows, as they buy and sell, as they worship, as they rejoice and mourn. This greater web of relationships is society, and a community is a delimited area of society. Within this web of community are generated many controls that are not governmental controls, many associations that are not political associations, many usages and standards of behavior that are in no sense the creation of the state. In the community develops the law behind law, the multi-sanctioned law that existed before governments began and that the law of government can never supersede. Without the prior laws of the community all the laws of the state would be empty formulas. Custom, the first "king of men," still rules. The *mores* still prescribe. Manners and modes still flourish. The laws made by governments cannot rescind them, cannot long defy them or deeply invade them. . . .

From *The Web of Government* by Robert M. MacIver. New York: The Macmillan Co., 1947, pp. 193, 196–199, 201–202.

If the distinction between the community and the state exists everywhere, how then is it related to the form of democracy? The answer is simple. Democracy, and democracy alone, gives a constitutional sanction to the universal principle. In most other forms of state the distinction between community and state is implicitly admitted—only under totalitarianism is it explicitly denied. In the old empires, for example, the customs of the people and not the decrees of government regulated the greater part of the everyday life. The folkways were dominant. Government intruded here and there, collected taxes, trained soldiers, fought wars, undertook public works, enriched itself with spoils, administered justice of some kind. But the kin and the countryside bred its own usages, maintained its own order, came to terms with the issues of life and death. That is community in being.

What the coming of democracy does is to confirm and to strengthen the distinction through the establishment of constitutional forms. . . . Under the democratic system government becomes an agent and the people the principal who holds it to account. The community establishes its formal superiority over the state. There are difficulties in the actual assertion of this superiority. Some areas, and particularly the area of foreign relations, are hard to bring under control. The control of the community is general rather than specific, is sporadic rather than continuous. But always the community sets determinate limits to the power of government. Always, even if belatedly, the community exerts its authority over its government.

Now when we say that the community or the people controls the government we should never imply that the people are a unity in any matter of policy. The people are always divided on any program of action. The government always represents or at least is backed by some portion of the people. Even the most tyrannous government must be approved by some of its subjects. . . . Does democracy then mean that the majority on every occasion, instead of some minority, gives effect to its will? Any such description of the nature of democracy would be grossly mistaken. A despotic government may have the majority of the people behind it. A majority, even if it attained control by the most approved devices of democracy, could still flagrantly abuse and even overthrow the democratic principle. Sometimes a demagogue or a ruthless totalitarian wins out in the contest for votes, and then destroys the democratic institutions through which he rose to power. Even if he does so with the consensus of the majority he has brought an end to democracy.

Democracy, then, cannot mean the rule of the majority or the rule of the masses. . . . Democracy is not a way of governing, whether by majority or otherwise, but primarily a way of determining who shall govern and, broadly, to what ends. The only way in which the people, *all the people,* can determine who shall govern is by referring the question to public opinion and accepting on each occasion the verdict of the polls. Apart from this activity of the people there is no way of distinguishing democracy from other forms of government. Any kind of government can claim to rest on "the will of the people," whether it be oligarchy or dictatorship or monarchy. One kind of government alone rests on the constitutional exercise of the will of the people. Every other kind prevents the minority—or the majority—from freely expressing opinion concerning the policies of government, or at least from making that opinion the free determinant of government. . . .

The growth of democracy has always been associated with the free discussion of political issues, with the right to differ concerning them, and with the settlement of the differences, not by *force majeure* but by resort to the counting of votes. . . . The right to differ did not end with the victory of the majority but was inherent in the system. It was a necessary condition of democracy everywhere that opposing doctrines remained free to express themselves, to seek converts, to form organizations, and so to compete for success before the tribunal of public opinion. Any major trend of opinion could thus register itself in the character and the policies of government.

On this principle democracy is founded. Only through the operation of this principle does the community become the master of government, thus making the political system responsive to its dominant desires. In effect this principle asserts that the state, the political system in its entirety, is *one* form of the organization of the community, limited to the ends that meet with major approval within it. It is the meaning of democracy that force is never directed against opinion as such. . . .

Democracy is founded in the free responsiveness of the state to the community. The community is sanctioned against any attempt of government to overpower it. The primary sanction is the constitutional provision for the free organization of conflicting opinions and doctrines. This is the democratic liberty *against* government. It is further provided that the prevalence of opinion, as measured by a system of elections, shall determine the choice of government and the general direction of governmental policy. This is democratic liberty to make and unmake government. These are the peculiar liberties of democracy, by which it differs from all other forms of government. Whatever other liberties co-exist with these, unless they are the direct corollaries and consequences of these fundamental ones, depend on the disposition of the democracy. Every system involves restraints as well as liberties, and we merely confuse the issue if we seek to identify democracy as such with certain particular liberties of another order. . . . How far certain other liberties are upheld by democracies depends on their changing conditions and changing needs. At all times men must choose between liberties. There is no sacred totality called "the liberty of the individual," for men are bound together in such a network of relations that in many respects the greater liberty of one is the lesser liberty of another. In the last resort it is a question of which liberties men prize the most—in a democracy a question of the liberties most prized by the majority of men, according to their degree of enlightenment or their mode of indoctrination.

Nevertheless the particular liberties assured by democracy constitute the central area of human liberty. If a man is not denied the right to communicate his thoughts and give free range to his opinions, if he can associate freely with those who share his values and his aims, if at the same time he is a citizen whose opinion counts, or at least is counted, equally with that of everyone else, then his personality is protected against the worst repressions. What he needs beyond is rather more opportunities than more liberties—he needs the equipment, economic and educational, by means of which he can more fully utilize the form of freedom he already possesses. . . . Men have other important needs besides liberty against oppression, but this liberty is primary liberty. It means in effect the liberty of the whole realm of culture, of all the creative arts and of most of the ways of living.

It is by the establishment of this central area of liberty that democracy vindicates the community against the state. Government, the great regulative agency of the community, is barred from doing certain things, from enacting certain kinds of law. Definite limits are set to the use of coercive power—it must refrain from over-riding the rights that go with the expression of opinion.

GIOVANNI SARTORI

Democracy and Liberal Democracy

The term democracy . . . has not only a descriptive or denotative function, but also a normative and a persuasive function. Consequently, the problem of defining democracy is twofold, requiring both a descriptive and a prescriptive definition. One cannot exist without the other and, at the same time, one cannot be replaced by the other. So, to avoid starting out on the wrong foot we must keep in mind three points: first, that a firm distinction has to be made between the *ought* and the *is* of democracy; second, that this distinction must not be misunderstood, because, clearly, ideals and reality interact (without its ideals a democracy cannot materialize and, consequently, without a basis of fact the democratic prescription is self-denying); third, that although complementary, the prescriptive and the descriptive definitions of democracy must not be confused, because the democratic ideal does not define the democratic reality, and vice versa, a real democracy is not, and cannot be, the same as an ideal one.

Politics is, and always will be, the output of the politically active. Thus democracy is, and can only be, the political system in which the power resides in the active *demos*. Of course, looking at the figures, we shall discover that the active demos is only a *minor pars*: but this discovery should not be taken with dismay. Even if the *demos* turns out to be a numerical minority or rather a constellation of mi-

From *Democratic Theory* by Giovanni Sartori. Detroit, Mich.: Wayne State University Press, 1962, pp. 4–5, 90–91, 126–127, 367–369.

norities, the principle remains intact as long as the rule is respected that opportunities are offered to all without exception. The foregoing definition can be implemented accordingly by saying that democracy is the power of active democratic minorities, the word "democratic" meaning that the recruitment of these minorities must be open, and that they must compete according to the rules of a multi-party system. . . .

I have said that democracy *can* only mean that the power resides in the active people. Let me add that this is right; I mean, this is also what it *should* mean. For if we do not accept this conclusion as valid, there are two possibilities. Either we ask that political apathy be met by coercion, or that those who are politically active be penalized in favor of the politically inert. And these solutions are both absurd. . . .

Let me sum up. Prescriptively—and therefore potentially —democracy is "equal power for everybody." Actually, democracy is "the power of the active *demos,*" which amounts to saying that power resides in those who avail themselves of it.

According to the main argument developed [regarding the role of leadership] . . . our definition of democracy can be reformulated as follows: democracy is a political system in which *the influence of the majority is assured by elective and competitive minorities to whom it is entrusted.* This definition . . . has the virtue of bringing out the vital role of leadership, as it implies that minorities are a *sine qua non* condition of the system.

The above definition, however, is only descriptive, in that it does not bring out the requisite conditions for the good functioning of the system. Electoral competition does not assure the quality of the results but only their democratic character. The rest—the worth of the output, so to speak—depends on the quality of leadership. So if we are considering specifically the qualitative aspect of the problem, our definition will have to be rephrased as follows: democracy should be *a polyarchy of elected elites.* We may also put it in this way: democracy ought to be *a selective system of competing elected minorities.* . . .

Do my conclusions add up to "another theory" of democracy? At first sight it may seem so. It has been said that there are two theories of democracy, the mandate theory, which is the orthodox one, and the competitive theory. . . . I have undoubtedly been working along these lines. Yet, I am unwilling to accept the so-called new theory as another theory. For I by no means reject the mandate theory; I have only said that it has a prescriptive validity. And if I have followed the competitive theory, I have done so stating that it is the descriptive theory. Therefore the definition that has been suggested in this chapter does not contradict the classical theory and does not attempt to replace it. It is rather an extension and completion of it. For the fault of the classical doctrine is that it stops midway and does not go to the end of the road.

In other words, the inadequacy of the orthodox theory of democracy does not imply that it should be replaced . . . but that it should be developed to its complete extent. The classical conception is simply an unfinished picture, and my point is that the time has come to finish it.

The framework of the basic relationship between liberalism and democracy can be outlined simply by referring to Tocqueville's classic distinction. To isolate liberalism from democracy, we say that liberalism calls for liberty and democracy for equality. To unite them, we say that it is the task of liberal-democratic systems to combine liberty with equality.

That liberty and equality can converge is shown by the very fact that our systems are both liberal and democratic. And how they can cooperate is just what we have been examining for some time. Actually it is not that liberalism is wholly a matter of liberty and democracy wholly a matter of equality. Rather, it is that there are freedoms which are not appreciated, or appreciated enough, by the democratic viewpoint, just as there are equalities which fall outside the range of liberal sensibility. As I have already stressed, all the equalities are not democratic acquisitions, just as the over-all question of liberty cannot be reduced to its liberal formulation. If, then, liberty and equality mark the line of demarcation between liberalism and democracy it is because of a different underlying basic logic. And it is in this light that liberal democracy can be viewed as a skein with two ends. As long as the skein is not touched, all is well, but if we begin to pull the ends and unravel it, we see that it is made up of two different-colored threads.

If we pull the liberal thread, not every form of equality disappears; but liberal equality, as such, is above all intended to promote, by way of liberty, qualitative aristocracies. Liberalism per se is wary of granting more than juridico-political equality because it distrusts and opposes any equality gratuitously bestowed from above. . . .

If, on the other hand, we start to pull on the democratic thread, we find an equality which neutralizes every spontaneous process of differentiation. . . .

In the final analysis, equality has a horizontal urge whereas liberty has a vertical impetus. Democracy is concerned with social cohesion and levelling, liberalism esteems prominence and innovation. Equality desires to integrate and to attune, liberty is troubled, wasteful, and disordered. The fundamental difference is that liberalism pivots on the individual, and democracy on society.

H. B. MAYO

The Distinguishing Principles of Democracy

Popular control of policy-makers is . . . the basic feature or principle, and political systems can be classified as more or less democratic according to a number of criteria associated with popular control and designed to make it effective; only if a particular system meets the tests of a substantial number of these criteria do we, by common consent, agree to call it democratic. But although the existence of democracy then becomes a matter of degree, the distinction is valid enough as we shall see, and the criteria will enable us to say in what respects and to what extent a system is democratic.

It must now be our purpose to try to make this somewhat vague language more precise. Accordingly I shall . . . sketch what I take to be a consistent and coherent theory of democracy in the form of the minimum number of distinguishing principles. At the same time, the outline will be reasonably close to contemporary usage, and is recognizably approximated by a number of existing democracies. . . .

1. *Popular control of policy-makers* . . . is our first and most general principle. The one institutional embodiment of the principle universally regarded as indispensable in modern democracies is that of choosing the policy-makers (representatives) at elections held at more or less regular intervals. . . .

Three riders must be added to our general principle at the outset in order to avoid misunderstanding:

From *An Introduction to Democratic Theory* by H. B. Mayo. New York: Oxford University Press, 1960, pp. 60–70.

a. On the whole, no democratic system operates on the principle that voters directly decide public policies at elections. The control over policy is much more indirect—through the representatives. . . .

b. The popular influence upon policies, as distinct from control over policy-makers, goes on all the time and may take many institutionalized and legitimate forms. The extent of such influence, however, cannot be reduced to any public test which can be incorporated at the present time into a general theory. The reason is that popular influence and consultation take such an infinity of forms—of which interest or pressure groups are perhaps the best known—that hardly any general principle can as yet be enunciated. What gives popular influence its sanction is that it can affect the chances of a representative at election time, or, more accurately, the representative's estimate of his chances.

c. Popular control by means of modern elections has only a faint resemblance to the old principle that, in some sense, authority stems from the people, and to old practices such as an elective monarchy. . . .

2. The second principle of democracy is that of *political equality*, which in turn is institutionalized as the equality of all adult citizens in voting. . . . There is, of course, more to citizenship than voting, and hence other ways in which political equality or inequality can prevail, but it is not debatable today that in any democracy the principle of equality of voting is taken for granted. . . .

Political equality is complex, like all general principles, and may be broken down into several elements, consisting at least of the following:

a. Every adult should have the vote—the familiar device of the universal adult suffrage. . . .

b. One person should have one vote—that is, there should be no plural voting.

c. Each vote should count equally—that is, votes are not weighted in any way. . . .

d. If every vote is to count equally, the corollary follows that the number of representatives elected should be directly proportional to the number of votes cast for them. If we assume, for simplicity of argument, a two-party system, then the number of representatives elected from each party will be proportional to the number of votes cast for that party. . . .

A little reflection will show that equality of voting, even if followed to the letter, is not enough of itself to distinguish a democratic system from an elected dictatorship. The belief and indeed the practice of equal voting are both official in the Soviet Union. Equality of voting, with its corollary, may thus be regarded as a necessary, but not a sufficient, principle of democracy. Is there, then, anything else about political equality and the franchise to distinguish a democratic political system? The answer must lie in the fact that voting alone does not ensure the reality of popular control; the mechanism may be manipulated to prevent such control.

3. The third principle may be stated either in terms of the *effectiveness of the popular control* or in terms of *political freedoms.*

Again, it makes little difference whether we regard "effectiveness" as part of the first principle (popular control) or as specifying the conditions of effective control. Can one set of decision-makers be turned out of office at elections and another set installed? Is there a free choice among alternatives, whether independent candidates or parties? That is, is the voting merely ritual, or does it effectively (freely) control the decision-makers? . . .

The effectiveness of popular control . . . entails a range of political freedoms. Among them are certainly the freedoms of speech, assembly, and organization, as well as the freedom to run for office. . . .

Among those political freedoms, that of organization leads almost inevitably . . . to the formation of political parties, with different sets of candidates and sometimes with different outlooks and policy alternatives. . . .

The existence and extent of these political liberties, as manifested above all in political opposition, is perhaps the most crucial test of the extent of democracy within the country. They are often summed up in the single concept "freedom to oppose." The touchstone of a democratic system is political freedoms, opposition, and parties. . . .

The result of political activity taking place within these rules—equality of voting and political liberties—is to enable the effective choice of representatives to take place, i.e., to ensure the popular control of decision-makers at election time, and to keep the channels open to legitimate influence at all times. From the viewpoint of the individual voter, the vote is the formal means by which he takes his share in political power. . . .

Although equality of voting within the context of political freedoms is a basic part of a democratic system, it is not all. Another essential part, already implicit, is that the policy decisions are made by the elected representatives, since only these are susceptible to popular control. . . .

It is plain that we cannot expect the representatives to be unanimous, any more than we can expect the electorate to be so. Political systems are devised *because* there is conflict and disagreement. There must, then, be a principle or rule according to which decisions are made among the representatives themselves.

4. The fourth principle is that *when the representatives are divided, the decision of the majority prevails.*

This is, in fact, the nearly universal rule for decision-making in all legislatures. Let us be clear how it links with the previous principles. Equality of voting, in a context of political freedoms, turns up representatives who are authorized to make the policies for the time being. This may be loosely called "consent of the governed" in the sense that there is a choice and one set of representatives rather than another is chosen. But "consent" is a slippery term, and it is better to think of election results as authorizing the successful candidates to make decisions, or in other words, as investing the government and its policies with legitimacy.

The common assumption is that with an electoral system based on equality of voting a majority of the representatives have been chosen by a majority of the voters, and hence the majority rule in the legislature yields decisions as legitimate "as if" they had been made directly by a majority of the voters, and indeed by a majority of all the adult citizens. That is why this fourth principle is sometimes called "majority rule." In fact, however, if governments depended for their legitimacy on this strict relation of votes to representatives, half the democratic governments of the world could at times claim no rightful authority from the "people.". . .

From this method of policy-making there follow certain implications, which may be called the rules of the game for representatives.

First, the majority of the representatives makes the policy decisions within the framework of the political freedoms mentioned earlier. These freedoms are taken as given, as part of the formal principles or essential conditions of democracy. Whatever else the majority may do . . . it does not shut up the opposition, the critics, the dissenters, whether these are within or without the legislature. Opponents may be coerced into obedience to law, but not abolished or silenced or shorn of their political liberties: this is the one inhibition upon the majority decisions so long as a democracy exists. When the political liberties and the legitimate opposition are gone, so, too, is democracy.

Second, the minority of representatives and their supporters among the public obey even though under protest, while working either to alter the policy to which they object or to dislodge the government and if possible to become a majority—by all peaceful political means, but only by these. . . .

Third, when the opposition in its turn has grown into a majority and attains office, the play begins all over again with different actors in the roles of government and opposition. The minority also agrees beforehand that they, too, will extend the same political freedoms and follow the same rules of the game should they arrive in the seats of office. . . .

The foregoing is a simplified, formal, abstract sketch of a democratic political system—its essential principles of operation for political policy-making. It concentrates upon how the binding decisions, related to government and arising from conflict and disputes, are made in the context of political freedoms. In other terms, the outline concentrates upon the ways in which policy-makers get their power and authorization—their legitimacy, always a prime concern to any political theory. The principles are close enough to common usage, and to some political systems in existence, to warrant the description democratic.

Each of the principles can be cast in operational terms. This has the great advantage of giving us practical tests which, taken together, enable us to distinguish democratic from non-democratic systems, and also to identify democracies empirically as more or less democratic, in this or that respect. . . .

Each of the principles can also be cast in normative (moral) terms—for example, that political equality *should* prevail—and in this form they constitute the moral justification of a theory of democracy. They are moral beliefs for which a case can be made. . . .

A working definition may be constructed from the above: a democratic political system is one in which public policies are made, on a majority basis, by representatives subject to effective popular control at periodic elections which are conducted on the principle of political equality and under conditions of political freedom.

ANTHONY DOWNS

Democracy and Rationality

THE MEANING OF RATIONALITY

Economic theorists have nearly always looked at decisions as though they were made by rational minds. Some such simplification is necessary for the prediction of behavior, because decisions made at random, or without any relation to each other, do not fall into any pattern. Yet only if human actions form some pattern can they ever be forecast or the relations between them subject to analysis. Therefore economists must assume an ordering of behavior takes place.

There is no *a priori* reason to suppose that this ordering is rational, i.e., reasonably directed toward the achievement of conscious goals. Nevertheless, economic theory has been erected upon the supposition that conscious rationality prevails, in spite of acid assertions to the contrary by men like Thorstein Veblen and John Maurice Clark. Since our model is *ex definitione* one concerning rational behavior, we also make this assumption.

As a result, the traditional methods of prediction and analysis are applicable to our model. If a theorist knows the ends of some decision-maker, he can predict what actions will be taken to achieve them as follows: (1) he calculates the most reasonable way for the decision-maker to reach his goals, and (2) he assumes this way will actually be chosen because the decision-maker is rational. . . .

In such analysis, the term *rational* is never applied to an agent's ends, but only to his means. This follows from the definition of *rational* as efficient, i.e., maximizing output for a given input, or minimizing input for a given output. Thus, whenever economists refer to a "rational man" they are not designating a man whose thought processes consist exclusively of logical propositions, or a man without prejudices, or a man whose emotions are inoperative. In normal usage all of these could be considered rational men. But the economic definition refers solely to a man who moves toward his goals in a way which, to the best of his knowledge, uses the least possible input of scarce resources per unit of valued output. . . .

Economic rationality can also be formally defined in another manner. A rational man is one who behaves as follows: (1) he can always make a decision when confronted with a range of alternatives; (2) he ranks all the alternatives facing him in order of his preference in such a way that each is either preferred to, indifferent to, or inferior to each other; (3) his preference ranking is transitive; (4) he always chooses from among the possible alternatives that which ranks highest in his preference ordering; and (5) he always makes the same decision each time he is confronted with the same alternatives. All rational decision-makers in our model—including political parties, interest groups, and governments—exhibit the same qualities.

Rationality thus defined refers to processes of action, not to their ends or even to their success at reaching desired ends. . . . since behavior in our model cannot be tested by its results, we apply the term *rational* or *irrational* only to processes of action, i.e., to means. Of course, some intermediate ends are themselves means to ultimate goals. The rationality of the former we can judge, but evaluation of the latter is beyond our scope. . . .

Thus we do not take into consideration the whole personality of each individual when we discuss what behavior is rational for him. We do not allow for the rich diversity of ends served by each of his acts, the complexity of his motives, the way in which every part of his life is intimately related to his emotional needs. Rather we borrow from traditional economic theory the idea of the rational consumer. Corresponding to the infamous *homo economicus* which Veblen and others have excoriated, our *homo politicus* is the "average man" in the electorate, the "rational citizen" of our model democracy.

RATIONALITY AND DEMOCRACY

To avoid ethical premises, we define democratic government descriptively, i.e., by enumerating certain characteristics which in practice distinguish this form of government from others. A government is democratic if it exists in a society where the following conditions prevail:

1. A single party (or coalition of parties) is chosen by popular election to run the governing apparatus.
2. Such elections are held within periodic intervals, the duration of which cannot be altered by the party in power acting alone.
3. All adults who are permanent residents of the society, are sane, and abide by the laws of the land are eligible to vote in each such election.
4. Each voter may cast one and only one vote in each election.
5. Any party (or coalition) receiving the support of a majority of those voting is entitled to take over the powers of government until the next election.
6. The losing parties in an election never try by force or any illegal means to prevent the winning party (or parties) from taking office.
7. The party in power never attempts to restrict the political activities of any citizens or other parties as long as they make no attempt to overthrow the government by force.
8. There are two or more parties competing for control of the governing apparatus in every election. . . .

An important conclusion can be drawn from the above definition: the central purpose of elections in a democracy is to select a government. Therefore any citizen is rational in regard to elections if his actions enable him to play his part in selecting a government efficiently. This specific definition of rationality underlies much of our later analysis.

The preceding discussion shows what an important role political parties play in democratic government. To demonstrate how that role is carried out in our model, we next examine the nature, motives, and operation of parties. . . .

A party is a team of individuals seeking to control the governing apparatus by gaining office in an election. Its function in the division of labor is to formulate and carry out government policies whenever it succeeds in getting into power. However, its members are motivated by their personal desire for the income, prestige, and power which come from holding office. Thus, carrying out their social function is to them a means of achieving their private ambitions. Though this arrangement may seem odd, it is found throughout the division of labor because of the prevalence of self-interest in human action.

Since none of the appurtenances of office can be obtained without being elected, the main goal of every party is the winning of elections. Thus all its actions are aimed at maximizing votes, and it treats policies merely as means towards this end.

Though our model is a purely positive one, it can be used to test the rationality of behavior prescribed in normative political models. In descriptive science, it (1) advances the vote-maximizing hypothesis as an explanation of democratic political behavior and (2) constructs a positive norm by which to distinguish between rational and irrational behavior in politics.

In a world where he is furnished with complete, costless information, the rational citizen makes his voting decision in the following way:

1. By comparing the stream of utility income [i.e., benefits] from government activity he has received under the present government (adjusted for trends) with those streams he believes he would have received if the various opposition parties had been in office, the voter finds his current party differentials. They establish his preference among the competing parties.

2. In a two-party system, the voter then votes for the party he prefers. In a multi-party system, he estimates what he believes are the preferences of other voters; then he acts as follows:

   a. If his favorite party seems to have a reasonable chance of winning, he votes for it.
   b. If his favorite party seems to have almost no chance of winning, he votes for some other party that has a reasonable chance in order to keep the party he least favors from winning.
   c. If he is a future-oriented voter, he may vote for his favorite party even if it seems to have almost no chance of winning in order to improve the alternatives open to him in future elections.

3. If the voter cannot establish a preference among parties because at least one opposition party is tied with the incumbents for first place in his preference ordering, he then acts as follows:

   a. If the parties are deadlocked even though they have differing platforms or current policies or both, he abstains.
   b. If the parties are deadlocked because they have identical platforms and current policies, he compares the performance ratings of the incumbent party with those of its predecessors in office. If the incumbents have done a good job, he votes for them; if they have done a bad job, he votes against them; and if their performance is neither good nor bad, he abstains.

5
Ideological Definitions

☙ BERNARD WILLIAMS

Democracy and Ideology

The term "ideology" is not in very good odor in serious political discussion in this country, except in purely historical or descriptive connections. The grounds of the distaste for the term center round the feeling, perhaps, that an ideology is something inherently totalitarian in tendency, or at least involves an uncompromising fanaticism inappropriate to liberal democracy of the British type. This feeling is fortified, on the whole, by experience of the outlooks and methods of argument of those who have proclaimed either the existence of, or (more characteristically) the need for, "an ideology of Western values" and so forth; in their case, . . . the aim of the discussion is often patently that of finding an emotional or intellectual engine that can be neatly fitted into the pre-existing capitalist chassis.

However, it may well be that these qualms attach to the term because it is narrowly or superficially understood. In its broadest sense, I take the term "ideology" to stand for a system of political and social beliefs that does two things.

From "Democracy and Ideology" by Bernard Williams, *The Political Quarterly*, 32 (October–December 1961), pp. 374–375, 378–384.

First, it embodies some set of values or ideals, and, consequently, some principles of action: though such principles will be of necessity very general, and in some cases mainly negative, being concerned more with limitations on political action, for instance, rather than with an overall aim of it. Secondly, an ideology connects with its values and principles of action some set of very general theoretical beliefs which give the values and principles some sort of backing or justification. The generality of these beliefs must, moreover, be of a special kind, if we are to speak of "an ideology": they must, I think, be general beliefs about man, society, and the state, and not merely about some aspect of man in society. For instance, a belief in Free Trade or federalism, even though supported by general economic or political reasons, could not by itself constitute an ideology. The distinguishing mark of an ideology is that its general beliefs concern man and society as such, and hence concern things that are presupposed in any political or social situation whatsoever.

If this represents fairly accurately what is involved in the notion of an ideology, it will be clear that a totalitarian ideology will be only one sort of ideology; on this account, there can as well be ideologies of liberalism as of totalitarianism, just as there can be conservative as well as revolutionary ideologies, democratic as well as absolutist ones. It may be, also, that ideologies differ in their degree of explicitness. One's normal picture of an ideology, it is true, is of a body of fairly well-articulated beliefs, explicitly formulated and constituting in the limiting case a form of creed, inculcated by authorities and developed by casuists. But once again, this may be one sort of ideology, to be found at one end of the scale; at the other end, there may be systems of beliefs far less explicitly formulated, and correspondingly less openly inculcated, but which may nevertheless exist implicitly in a society or group, and perform much the same function as the noisier form of ideology, directing and shaping political discussion and action. That they do perform the same function will be the justification for applying to such systems of belief the term "ideology"; an application which may have the merit of encouraging the search for such tacit systems of presuppositions, and the attempt to make them more explicit. It must be worth while to make them more explicit, if they exist: for one thing, that which is less openly inculcated is more liable to evade criticism.

It seems, then, at least worth asking whether such tacit ideologies exist in cases of political beliefs that lack the more explicit or creed-like ideology; and this I shall attempt to do in this article—I am afraid, very sketchily—in respect of liberal democracy.

We may . . . ask whether we can identify any system of beliefs, however tacit and latent, which might be called an ideology of liberal democracy. By "liberal democracy" I mean a system of government characterized by a universal and secret suffrage, for a choice of different rulers; an independent press and freedom of expression; and by what may generally be called the rule of law, which includes the requirement of a fair trial for any alleged offense, limitations on the powers of the police, etc. . . .

The very rough characterization of liberal democracy just given is given in primarily institutional terms; but it must, of course, be understood that the actual existence and functioning of such a system implies the existence of more than a set of institutions. For institutions of this type will in fact function only if they have certain kinds of social foundation, e.g., of an electorate not too radically and violently divided on vital issues; so that in thinking of liberal democracy as a going concern, one must think not only of certain institutions, but of certain attitudes which are the precondition of those institutions functioning.

One attitude that is, in this sense, a precondition of the institutions functioning, is a measure of *toleration*. To be more precise, one has to add one further condition of toleration being necessary, namely, that there should be attitudes and groups to which people *need* to be tolerant; for presumably if a people were spontaneously entirely unanimous on important issues, the democratic machine would function excellently without any need for toleration. However, this condition scarcely needs, for any real situation, to be spelled out; and indeed, even at the theoretical level, one might well wonder whether, if there were no need for toleration, there would really be much need for democracy, since there would be no requirement of choice between policies or social attitudes, but only between persons to administer the state. This might be sufficient to keep the democratic machine going, but certainly not in any very full-blooded way.

We may say, then, that one precondition of liberal democracy's working is toleration: sufficient toleration of rival groups, with different attitudes, to allow one to foresee—if not with equanimity, at least without fundamental despair—their coming to power, or otherwise influencing the governmental process. However, this kind of toleration, the kind which is a precondition of the democratic machine working at all, is toleration directed only towards certain groups: namely, those groups who are, in effect, the alternative government, or potentially alternative government. This we may call *essential* toleration: essential, that is to say, to the working of the democratic machine. It is essential toleration that is directed in this country [England] at the moment by the Conservative and Labour parties towards each other.

There is, however, another kind of toleration that is always, and rightly, regarded as part of the liberal democratic outlook, and for which, perhaps, the word "toleration" is most characteristically used: this is the toleration of minorities, racial, religious, and so on. Such toleration is not essential to the working of the machine in the way that the sort just discussed is. For if all the major power groups were united, say, in anti-Semitism, anti-Semitic persecution could flourish without jeopardy to the actual workings of the democratic process. This we may call non-essential toleration; where "non-essential" is to be understood, of course, in the technical sense just discussed, and not as meaning that such toleration can be dispensed with if convenient.

Much needs to be said about this distinction between essential and non-essential toleration, if it is to be properly worked out. In particular, it is clear that the characterization of the two sorts of toleration merely in terms of what sorts of groups they are directed towards is too crude. If, for instance, one has a healthy public opinion passionately engaged in the defense of minorities, what seems to be non-essential toleration might turn out to be essential; for persecution of a minority might have the effect of so incensing public opinion that the government was overthrown by force, and the democratic process brought to a halt. Of such a case, however, it can be noted that in describing it, one has to posit a public *belief in* non-essential toleration, so that it does not really break down the distinction. . . .

However it should be refined, the distinction between two sorts of, or two operations of, toleration seems to correspond to something real. Corresponding to it, there is a possible distinction between the general attitudes that underlie toleration. For essential toleration will be underwritten by any belief that underwrites the democratic system itself: this follows merely from its being essential. But of non-essential toleration this will not necessarily be true, since I might have the firmest belief in the democratic process, and hence in the toleration of anything necessary to its workings, but no *general* belief in toleration at all.

This, at least, is a theoretical possibility; and one may be able to find actual examples of such attitudes. For instance, it may be that there are in the United States at the present time at least some groups whose attitudes are a genuine combination of a belief in the operation of the democratic, two-party, machine, and a strong desire for general conformity—and, indeed, for the enforcement of conformity—in all matters that do not directly abut on the political struggle. However, it must be said that such a combination is at least not very common. More common, of course, is the combination of a belief in the democratic system with a lack of tolerance for some particular groups; but this is really a different matter, since the persons who have such attitudes usually accept, or claim to accept, the principles of non-essential toleration in general, but make a particular exception to them against certain groups, on special grounds or merely irrationally. What would be interesting from the ideological point of view would be the combination of a belief in democracy with no belief in non-essential toleration at all; and this combination certainly seems to be at least rare.

It is not hard to see why such a combination should be rare. For it seems that there could only be two sorts of grounds on which an opposition to non-essential toleration in general can rest. Either the opponent of such toleration believes that he possesses *certainty* on the matters of belief, conduct, etc., on which the minority groups hold divergent views, and moreover thinks that it is the right or duty of the state to impose the truth in such matters; or else, while he does not claim certainty on such matters, he thinks that society should be strongly unified round some set of beliefs or other, and so will not tolerate the divergent opinions—not, like the first man, because he believes them to be false, but merely because he sees them to be divergent. Any opposition to non-essential toleration will, I think, be found in the end to rest on one of these two sorts of grounds. But either of these grounds is also a sufficient ground for being opposed to essential toleration, and so to liberal democracy itself. The first man cannot be in favor of free competition at the governmental level of policies and social views, at least one of which he must regard as absolutely false; while the second man will obviously recognize an opposition between liberal democracy and the highly unified and closed society which is his aim.

If this line of argument is correct, it would seem that the grounds of belief in liberal democracy are closely bound up with the grounds of belief in toleration in general; and both involve the rejection of both of the attitudes just described as grounds of opposition to non-essential toleration. The liberal democrat cannot put a very high price, at least, on the ideal of a community highly unified in belief; and he must be one who either does not claim certainty in the matters about which divergent views are to be found in society, or, if he does claim such certainty, must believe that the state has no right to impose what he regards as the truth on those who do not believe in it.

Corresponding to these last two alternatives, two strains of democratic thought can be identified. Corresponding to the first, there is the strain of *skepticism;* corresponding to the second, the strain of belief in *individual rights.* The first broadly takes the line that since we do not, and perhaps cannot, possess any certainty about political, moral, and religious matters, the safest course for society is to allow a free competition of opinions and attitudes. There tends to go with this a skeptical or at least minimalist attitude to democracy itself: namely, that it is the best system yet devised for running a society, though no more absolute claim can be made for it. The second, individual rights, type of thought is slightly more ambitious. This would claim that it was certain that democracy was the ideal form of government, since it is the only form that truly represents the relations of man to the state; which are, that the state is an instrument for maintaining the rights and the welfare of an assemblage of individual men. If this is what a state is, then it is certain that the correct way of running a state must be that which allows the translation of the views and preferences of individual men into political action; while preserving, however, the rights of those involved in society who do not agree with the majority of it.

Neither of these strains of democratic thought can, of course, be taken quite by itself. On the one hand, skepticism alone could not constitute a basis for any political outlook: it has to be fortified by some view on what is worth pursuing or avoiding. . . . The skepticism that leads to democracy has to be supplemented by some elements of the individual rights doctrine: it has to start with a presumption in favor of individual men choosing their own way. It has to be a skepticism which is at least as suspicious of any inherited authority or caste privilege as it is of Utopian or millennialist aspirations.

Just as the skeptical approach needs some help from the individual rights doctrine, if it is to lead to democracy, so conversely. The curious dialectic of Rousseau's *Social Contract,* and still more of the uses to which that work was put after its author's death, illustrates the possibility of moving from an individualist position, which regards democracy as certainly the only justified form of government, to an interpretation of democracy in which a mystical General Will . . . perversely takes the place of the original liberal conception of individual rights. Here it seems that it is some measure of the skepticism of the first approach that is needed to discourage the excessive detachment of the rights of man from what men would normally and unmetaphysically regard as their rights.

Does this set of ideas that has very roughly been sketched constitute any sort of tacit ideology of liberal democracy? . . .

In general, I think it might be said that the liberal democratic outlook does constitute a tacit ideology, but that it is a peculiar example of that species, in being the *smallest* ideology that can actually survive. It offers some practical proposals, and backs them up with some views on man, society, and the state. Where, however, its larger relatives offer large-scale explanations of history and human life, it offers for the most part a program of empirical inquiry; and where they offer large-scale predictions and hopes, it offers few predictions and a good number of warnings. This small-scaleness may not be entirely a disadvantage. It may be that ideologies are like dinosaurs; the small ones no doubt came off worst in a contest of roaring or clawing, but when the big ones started to collapse under their own weight, the small ones turned out to have been better endowed for survival.

HERBERT McCLOSKY

Elements of Democratic Ideology

Whether a word like ideology can properly be employed in the American context depends, in part, on which of its many connotations one chooses to emphasize. Agreement on the meaning of the term is far from universal, but a tendency can be discerned among contemporary writers to regard ideologies as *systems* of belief that are elaborate, integrated, and coherent, that justify the exercise of power, explain and judge historical events, identify political right and wrong, set forth the interconnections (causal and moral) between politics and other spheres of activity, and furnish guides for action. While liberal democracy does not fulfill perfectly the terms of this definition, it comes close enough, in my opinion, to be considered an ideology. The elements of liberal democratic thought are not nearly so vague as they are sometimes made out to be, and their coalescence into a single body of belief is by no means fortuitous. American democratic "ideology" possesses an elaborately defined theory, a body of interrelated assumptions, axioms, and principles, and a set of ideals that serve as guides for action. Its tenets, postulates, sentiments, and values inspired the great revolutions of the seventeenth and eighteenth centuries, and have been repeatedly and explicitly set forth in fundamental documents, such as the Constitution, the Declaration, and the Federalist Papers. They have been restated with remarkable unanimity in the messages of Presidents, in political speeches, in the pronouncements of

From "Consensus and Ideology in American Politics" by Herbert McClosky, *American Political Science Review*, LVIII (June 1964), pp. 362–363.

judges and constitutional commentators, and in the writings of political theorists, historians, and publicists. They are so familiar that we are likely to see them not as a coherent union of ideas and principles embodying a well-defined tendency, but as a miscellany of slogans and noble sentiments to be trotted out on ceremonial occasions.

Although scholars or Supreme Court justices might argue over fine points of interpretation, they would uniformly recognize as elements of American democratic ideology such concepts as consent, accountability, limited or constitutional government, representation, majority rule, minority rights, the principle of political opposition, freedom of thought, speech, press, and assembly, equality of opportunity, religious toleration, equality before the law, the rights of juridical defense, and individual self-determination over a broad range of personal affairs. How widely such elements of American liberal democracy are approved, by whom and with what measure of understanding, is another question. . . . But that they form an integrated body of ideas which has become part of the American inheritance seems scarcely open to debate.

∽ ZEVEDEI BARBU

Democracy as a Frame of Mind

The current use of the term ideology shows that it implies not only an abstract intellectual, but also a practical order, a body of ideas which determines in the mind of the individual a particular type of social action and a particular way of life. The concept of ideology, used in this sense, is opposed to the basic tenets of democracy.

But, because democracy cannot be described in terms of a specific ideology, one cannot say that it has no specific ideological character, or that ideas and theories are to it no more than the straw which it used for its bed. It would, however, be necessary to state from the very beginning that what is characteristic of democracy is not a specific idea or theory, but a specific cultural climate. In what follows we shall describe certain motives of thought and certain intellectual attitudes which are, in our opinion, inherent in a democratic way of life.

Democracy as a political concept can be described in terms of methods or techniques of government. . . . Formulae such as government of, by, and for the people, the sovereignty of the people, universal suffrage, popular and responsible government, and others are often used for the description of democracy.

But in spite of this rich and colorful collection of formulae, anyone attempting to define democracy has an almost impossible task. The reason for this lies in the fact that the validity of all fundamental concepts normally involved in such a definition has been seriously challenged by the various historical conditions in which democracy has been realized. Even Aristotle, while agreeing that the main feature of democracy consists in "the election of magistrates by all, out of all," becomes involved in a discussion about the meaning of the concept of "the many." Finally he has to specify that the many who rule in a democracy "are also poor," while the rich, who govern in aristocracy, are "at the same time few in number."

Today it would be easy to prove that decisions taken by "the many"—who are also poor—are not necessarily democratic. During the last century some absolutist monarchs were in favor of extending the right to vote to the propertyless classes in the hope that they would be more conservative, i.e., more in favor of the absolutist regime, than the well-to-do classes.

The results of a series of modern "plebiscites" lead inevitably to the conclusion that universal suffrage, or decisions taken by majorities, are but political instruments which can serve democracy as well as other forms of government. One has therefore to take into account a number of factors influencing the behavior of the people in political matters in order to specify under what conditions the majority act democratically. Thus one has to specify first of all that the concept of majority enters into the definition of democracy only to the extent to which the many possess, and know how to make use of, political power in the community. This obviously means something more than a simple political equality contained in the formula "one man one vote."

Self-government is undoubtedly an essential feature of democracy. Alexis de Tocqueville, amongst others, lays particular stress on this. In the people's interest and participation in the life of their community, in their wish and capacity to conduct their own affairs, he sees not only the spring, but also the main guarantee of democracy. On this point he goes so far as to distinguish between self-government and good government, i.e., government carried on by an enlightened group in the best interest of the people. A democratic reform, or democratic action in general, has to "be brought about not only with the assent of the people, but by their hand."

Now this is obviously true, but it requires certain qualifications. In order to make their society "by their hand" the members of a group have to possess considerable experience in, and knowledge of, public administration. They need also certain institutions which allow them to take a share in the making of their society. But they need something more than this; they need a specific *frame of mind,* that is, certain experiences, attitudes, prejudices, and beliefs shared by them all, or by a large majority.

1. One of the basic traits of the democratic frame of mind can be described as the feeling of change. The feeling shared by the members of a community that their personal and their communal life as well are in a state of permanent transformation and readjustment forms, so to speak, the first category of the democratic frame of mind. Owing to this the individual regards his society as an *open* structure, ready to keep pace with the process of general change, and with the changes taking place in its members in the first place. We classify this trait of the democratic frame of mind as a feeling, because of its general and undifferentiated nature. Considering its origins one can call it also a habit of mind, that particular habit of mind, shared by the majority of the members of a group, to adjust themselves, and to adjust the structure of their society, to the ever-changing conditions of life. . . .

On the social plane the feeling of change is articulated in the conviction, and in the social behavior resulting from it, that society is an open structure in a state of permanent readiness for change. . . .

2. The feeling of change cannot be regarded as an iso-

lated trait; the social and cultural behavior generated by it is molded by other categories of the democratic frame of mind. Thus, the feeling of change and any other category of the democratic frame of mind are parts of a whole.

The individuals who create or live in a democracy not only hold the belief that their society is in perpetual change, but also that this change is the direct result of their own activities. Consequently the feeling that society grows from within, by the activity of its members, individuals and corporate bodies, can be considered as another category of the democratic frame of mind. . . .

It is not too difficult to find how the belief that society is a matter of co-operation originated in the mind of modern man. The need for, and the experience of co-operation among various social groups, divided and antagonized by a system of privileges, against an autocratic monarch formed in fact an important feature in the rise of modern societies and states. . . . The conviction that each individual is a maker of his own society constitutes a basic trait of a democratic frame of mind.

At the cultural level, this trait is articulated in various forms. In the feeling that each individual is, in his own way, an agent in the making of his society lies the seed of both the doctrine of equality and that of freedom. With regard to the former, we are only too aware that, in its most radical form as total equality, it is not necessarily a feature of democratic society. We cannot, however, help noticing that certain equalitarian conceptions arose in the culture-pattern of every community in the process of democratization. . . .

As for the doctrine of freedom one can say that it can be found in every democratic culture-pattern. Its origins lie, as stated before, in the conviction that the structure of society is not based on a permanent and fixed order, and that, on the contrary, it results from the activity of each of its members, from their common experiences, from their interactions, deliberations and agreements. . . .

3. From what has been said so far one can easily infer that a democratic frame of mind contains also a specific attitude towards authority, as one of its categories. To start with, one can say that the basic element of this attitude consists in a feeling of the instability and relativity of power and authority. This aspect of the democratic frame of mind would perhaps be better understood if it were described as the awareness, present in various degrees in the members of a certain community, that the holding of power and authority implies the concession made by one part to another part of the community. In other words it implies a process of delegation. . . .

But . . . this is only one aspect—the negative one—of the democratic attitude towards authority. The social experience leading towards the rise of modern democracies shows clearly that the attitude towards authority could not be exclusively negative. The authority based on absolute power was undoubtedly negated, but another type of authority took its place. This is the internal authority of reason and conscience. One can speak in this case about a displacement of authority which is characteristic of modern man; the confidence in and reliance on external and divine authority was gradually transformed into confidence in and reliance on the powers of human reason and conscience.

But human reason and conscience are not social authority in themselves. Here comes an important point in the formation of that aspect of the democratic frame of mind which refers to the nature of social authority. The experiences in self-government, in building up new social forms and groups, characteristic of some modern Western communities, implanted in the individual the conviction that the authority based on the principles of the human mind—logical and moral—can be imparted to other individuals by deliberation. The same experiences implanted also the conviction that the authority founded on the individual's reason can be concentrated by an act of common will, and conferred as such upon a man, a party, or an institution. In other words, authority can be represented.

Therefore, the essence of the democratic attitude towards authority consists in the concept of inner and individualized authority. This authority can be concentrated by agreement and conferred upon a representative. Hence the social order is a representative order. . . .

4. The last category of the democratic frame of mind can be described as an attitude of confidence in reason. . . .

. . . For the action of a free individual in a flexible society is always carried out on the deep—often unconscious—presupposition that this action will be finally adjusted to an harmonious social pattern based on reason. This is what we mean here by the feeling of confidence in reason.

. . . the feeling of confidence in reason is necessary as a balancing factor in the mind of the individual who has to adjust himself to a world of change and novelty; it is necessary for this individual to develop the belief that there is an order and stability behind the change, and that there are certain regulative principles which put a check upon change. . . .

Individuals living in a world of rapid change, and in a dynamic social structure in particular, develop, apart from the feeling of confidence in a fundamental order, habits of mind which facilitate an adequate adjustment to a changeable environment. This is another important source of the need for reason in modern man. For reason is that complex of mental functions or habits by which the individual is able to grasp the unity in diversity, and the order in change. Reason presupposes a high degree of mental flexibility which enables the individual to compare things, to establish differences and identities, and finally to compromise.

New events demand new relations, and consequently readjustment.

At the root of this type of adjustment one can certainly find the belief that there is a certain order in the nature of things. . . . On the other hand, this type of adjustment would hardly have been possible without the feeling of confidence in the ability of humankind, and without a strong feeling of security, both individual and collective.

PRECONDITIONS OF DEMOCRACY

6
A Typology of Preconditions

The preceding chapters have illustrated and documented some major changes in democratic theory. Current theories of democracy, as we have seen, have succeeded in revamping the premises and assumptions of the classical definitions.

All this, however, has not exhausted our discussion of democratic theory. Not satisfied with mere definition, the contemporary theorists of democracy have proceeded to stipulate an array of preconditions as essential to democratic political life. A host of prerequisites—some superficial and others plausible—have been regularly associated with the emergence and survival of democracy. The particular cluster of variables that presumably accounts for the emergence and flourishing of democracy is by no means clear. What *is* patently clear is that these stipulations have further transformed "democracy" by placing, as will be seen, serious constraints upon the kind of environment in which it can emerge and flourish. The preconditions in question may be grouped under five principal headings: physical, religious, socioeconomic, political, and psychocultural. In this typology a degree of arbitrariness is inescapable.

PHYSICAL PRECONDITIONS

The question of scale—in terms of both land mass and population—has often appeared in discussions of democracy as well as of totalitarianism. Quite frequently, totalitarianism has been associated with largeness in magnitude, whereas democracy has been correlated with smallness in size.

Two explicit and thoroughgoing statements praising and defending small-scale (or grass-roots) democracy are found in Jefferson and de Tocqueville. Ideally, Jefferson maintained, the political organization of American society should find expression at four levels: federal, state, county, and ward. The "ward republics" were to be sufficiently small to permit personal participation of every individual in the affairs of the community. They were looked upon by Jefferson as "the wisest invention ever devised by the wit of man for the perfect exercise of self-government, and for its preservation."

De Tocqueville's praise for small-scale democracy was similarly lavish. The town, he wrote, "seems to come directly from the hand of God." It is the place where the people exercise "their power" most directly and immediately. The town is characterized by a high degree of "spirit" and "excite[s] the warmest of human affections without arousing the ambitious passions. . . ."

The notion of grass-roots democracy, we may say in general, rests on the assumption that small political units, being close to the people, make possible the purest expression of self-government. Thus, the town has often been considered the "natural" home of democracy. De Tocqueville, for example, regarded the town as the "only association" that is "perfectly natural." A contemporary writer states that "democracy is more likely to survive, other things being equal, in small states."[1]

The belief in the criterion of smallness has been seriously challenged, and the finding has repeatedly been made that even the New England town meetings (highly praised

1 Ernest S. Griffith, "Cultural Prerequisites to a Successfully Functioning Democracy: A Symposium," *American Political Science Review,* L (March 1956), p. 102.

by both Jefferson and de Tocqueville) were dominated by minority interests. One of the most comprehensive critiques of small-scale democracy has been provided by Roscoe C. Martin. His examination of the "folklore" surrounding the grass-roots concept reveals that the correlation of democracy with size is not supported by evidence. Martin holds that "smallness in size . . . provide[s] neither a guarantee of the existence nor a standard for measuring the effectiveness of local democracy." He shows in some detail that grass-roots democracy is neither particularly virtuous, nor particularly representative, nor particularly motivated by "democratic spirit," nor particularly "productive of democratic results." Similarly, E. E. Schattschneider points out that the crisis of grass-roots democracy is a purely theoretical one, that is to say, it is a consequence of some conceptual illusions entertained by the classical theorists.

We may conclude that empirical evidence seems to suggest that large-scale democracy is as feasible as small-scale totalitarianism. The reader can easily identify contemporary states that fit each category.

RELIGIOUS PRECONDITIONS

Attempts have been made repeatedly to correlate democracy with Christianity, to establish logical and historical connections between the two. The point of departure, as we saw in the opening chapter of this book, is usually the Reformation. The argument is that there was an "elective affinity"—to use Max Weber's apt terminology[2]—between the Protestant ethic and the spirit of capitalism, and that capitalism was conducive to the emergence and flourishing of democracy. Appearing within the framework of Protes-

2 See H. H. Gerth and C. Wright Mills, eds., *From Max Weber: Essays in Sociology* (New York: Oxford University Press, 1958), pp. 62–63, 284–285; Max Weber, *The Protestant Ethic and the Spirit of Capitalism,* translated by Talcott Parsons with a Foreword by R. H. Tawney (New York: Charles Scribner's Sons, 1958).

tant societies, it is stated, capitalism created a middle class whose existence was a necessary condition for democracy. Instructive in this regard is R. H. Tawney's argument that Calvin did for the sixteenth-century middle class what Marx was to do for the nineteenth-century proletariat.[3]

A clear statement of the position seeking to establish a firm nexus between Christianity and democracy is found in Reinhold Niebuhr. Niebuhr's basic argument, as stated explicitly in *The Children of Light and the Children of Darkness* (1945), is that democratic theory must necessarily rest on a "realistic"—i.e., Protestant—conception of the nature of man as a being capable of both good and evil. Excessively optimistic conceptions lead to unmitigated individualism, he argues, and excessively pessimistic notions, to absolutist government. According to Niebuhr, the correct Christian point of view as it relates to political democracy is this: "Man's capacity for justice makes democracy possible; but man's inclination to injustice makes democracy necessary." Democratic government, he believes, must rest on a firm and lasting reconciliation of man's self-interest with the general interest. The "children of light"—those "who believe that self-interest should be brought under the discipline of a higher law"—must come to terms with the "children of darkness"—those who "know no law beyond the self."

Such a conception of the nature of man, Niebuhr holds, is an indispensable contribution of "profound religion" to democracy. Other important contributions include the Protestant precepts of toleration and humility. "The real point of contact between democracy and profound religion," Niebuhr writes, "is in the spirit of humility which democracy requires and which must be one of the fruits of religion." He adds: "Historically the highest form of democratic toleration is based upon . . . religious insights."

3 *Religion and the Rise of Capitalism* (New York: The New American Library, 1947), p. 99.

In a later work, Niebuhr appears to modify his view by arguing that both Christian and secular precepts are essential to democratic political life. The basic points, however, remain unchanged and there is the same emphasis on the Protestant conceptions of the nature of man, toleration, and humility.[4]

The Catholic counterpart of the Niebuhr position is set forth by Jacques Maritain. "Not only does the democratic state of mind proceed from the inspiration of the Gospel," he writes, "but it cannot exist without it." A democratic society ("a society of free men") is essentially religious in character: "civil society is organically linked to religion." Specifically, Maritain identifies the following religious beliefs as the foundations of democracy: belief in the dignity of the individual; belief in equality, liberty, justice, and neighborly love; and "respect for authority." According to Maritain, moreover, a democratic society is distinguished by three important features, all having strong religious overtones: "personalism," "communalism," and "pluralism." The first refers to the moral and ethical emphasis on the value of the human person, without which "perfect spiritual liberty" is unattainable. "Communalism" addresses itself to the value of collective life to which all men aspire, and the "common good" which all men are called upon to set before their personal interests. "Pluralism" refers to the value of independent sociopolitical associations. It rests on the assumption that the full development of human personality can be accomplished only through a multiplicity of organizations and groups, of which the family and the Church are considered to be the most important.

An analogous point of view is developed by Ernest S. Griffith, in whose conviction the Judaeo-Christian tradition provides "a powerful matrix" and a "cluster of basic attitudes or mores" without which democracy is inconceivable.

4 See *Christian Realism and Political Problems* (New York: Charles Scribner's Sons, 1953), especially pp. 101–103.

Christian beliefs, he argues, supply "a common denominator, an ultimate sustainer" of attitudes essential for democratic political life. Among such attitudes, the following are included: belief in, and respect for, the individual; a sense of civic obligation and a concern for the general welfare; "integrity in discussion"; the channeling of passion into "constructive ends." Each of these, Griffith holds, is "best based upon" Christian precepts. In fact, he insists, only Christianity can give to these attitudes the character of "absolutes" which is "necessary for democratic survival."

A number of writers, including John Plamenatz and Currin V. Shields, have taken serious exception to this line of argument, pointing out that there is no necessary connection between democracy and Christianity.[5] Christianity and democracy are systems of belief, principle, and practice that have no particular relation to one another. In Plamenatz's words, in themselves Christianity and democracy "neither exclude nor suppose one another." A democrat, it would seem, may embrace any religion: "a good Christian need not be a democrat, nor a good democrat a Christian." Nor, as Shields points out, is the notion of a "higher law" necessary to democracy: "In fact, for the democrat any appeal to a higher moral law to resolve questions of political value is both unnecessary and futile." Democracy, he adds, consists of "a set of purely secular beliefs." It can have no religious or antireligious bias.

SOCIOECONOMIC PRECONDITIONS

The socioeconomic prerequisites of democracy embrace a host of variables, among which the following are included: wealth, urbanization, industrialization, literacy, participation, and the media of communication. Also stipulated is

5. Although Shields' immediate concern is with the relationship between Catholicism and democracy, his analyses and conclusions are clearly of broader significance.

the existence of a middle class and a network of voluntary groups and associations.

"Economic development" is perhaps the most widely discussed precondition of democratic government. The general proposition, as developed by Seymour Martin Lipset, for example, is that only in a relatively prosperous society in which some reasonably fair distribution of the national wealth has taken place can there develop the popular self-confidence necessary for resisting authoritarian and dictatorial tendencies. Only in a society that provides the necessary leisure and information can intelligent political participation take place. Lipset's empirical analyses establish a positive correlation between wealth, urbanization, industrialization, and literacy, on the one hand, and democratic government, on the other. Employing a series of economic indices, Lipset finds that the more developed countries consistently rate as the "more democratic" on every index. The most important single variable, however, turns out to be education. "The higher one's education," Lipset writes, "the more likely one is to believe in democratic values and support democratic practices."

To Daniel Lerner, democracy is "a crowning institution of the participant society."[6] A democratic society is above all one in which the people participate in public affairs, and in which the practice of participation is institutionalized in voting, elections, and the like. The evolution of the participant society, according to Lerner, is contingent on the sequential development of three interrelated variables: urbanization, literacy, and media of communication. Urbanization makes possible the transfer of rural populations to the cities; city life requires a degree of literacy and communication; literacy encourages and facilitates political participation.

Although a number of writers have viewed citizen in-

6 *The Passing of Traditional Society* (New York: The Free Press, 1958), p. 64.

terest and participation as essential preconditions of democracy, it should not go unnoticed that considerable attention has also been devoted to the role of apathy in democratic societies. W. H. Morris-Jones has argued, for example, that a degree of apathy may be the sign of a healthy democracy and that compulsory participation ("the Duty to Vote") is a feature of totalitarian regimes. As he sees it, while widespread political participation may exist in small communities, it cannot be duplicated in contemporary mass society. A degree of apathy—(and no writer specifies what degree)—is seen as no particular cause for concern, and not a sign of democratic decay. On the contrary, according to Morris-Jones, apathy may be an indication of democratic permissiveness, tolerance, and flexibility. A complete "cure" for apathy, he concludes, can only be found in totalitarian states.

The question of causes and determinants of political apathy has been treated clearly and succinctly by Morris Rosenberg. He identifies the following causes (actual or potential) as particularly important for apathy: (1) fear that political activity may entail unpleasant consequences, such as alienating friends or jeopardizing economic gain; (2) belief in the futility of political activity and loss of faith in the effectiveness of political participation; and (3) absence of motivating forces and "shining examples" in the community. The last factor, according to Rosenberg, tends to relieve any sense of guilt that may be associated with nonparticipation. Thus apathy becomes self-reinforcing: one man's nonparticipation finds satisfaction and rationalization in the nonparticipation of others.

Rosenberg notes a number of other factors accounting for apathy, and we might do well to mention them here: contentment with things as they are, a feeling that all is well; faith in the democratic process and in one's representatives; inability to see sharp differences between the major parties;

and "mental laziness" and even "phobia toward serious thought."

The relationship between the middle class and political democracy has been briefly touched upon. The basic propositions are that (1) historically this class has acted as a buffer between the extremes of poverty and wealth, and (2) the interests of this class can be maintained only in a political environment in which a degree of permissiveness prevails. Perhaps the earliest analysis of the relation of the middle class to political democracy was undertaken by Aristotle. Consistent with his doctrine of moderation, Aristotle viewed the middle class as the least violent, the most secure and therefore the most conducive to political stability. The middle class, he thought, is open to reason and free from envy, pettiness, and overambition—all potentially disruptive.[7]

Since Aristotle's time, the importance of the middle class for political democracy has been a recurring theme in political theory. Thus Lipset notes, for example, that "A large middle class plays a mitigating role in moderating conflict since it is able to reward moderate and democratic parties and penalize extremist groups."

The importance of a network of voluntary groups and associations (social pluralism) for democratic politics has been emphasized by numerous writers. The general point is that, acting as structures of power and authority in their own right, groups help prevent concentration of power in the state. Robert A. Dahl and Charles E. Lindblom, for example, see social pluralism as an essential precondition of "polyarchy." (For a discussion of "polyarchy" see Chapter 1.) The basic reason is that pluralism, by promoting a condition in which power is diffused and distributed among

7 See *The Politics of Aristotle*, translated by Ernest Barker (New York: Oxford University Press, 1958), Book IV, Chapter XI.

a host of contending parties and groups, creates a system of mutual controls and reciprocal relations, facilitates popular control, and prevents monopoly of power in governmental hands.

POLITICAL PRECONDITIONS

Among the more distinctively political prerequisites of democracy, the following are often included: legitimacy, effectiveness, an effective political opposition, and agreement (or disagreement) on "fundamentals."

Democratic government, it is often argued, is effective in realizing certain goals and maintaining itself through widespread popular support and confidence. According to Lipset, for example, effectiveness refers to the ability of the system to perform the basic functions of government and provide the necessary services. Legitimacy is viewed as the capacity of the system to promote and maintain popular support for the existing state of affairs. The relationship between the two is reciprocal: legitimacy enhances effectiveness, effectiveness reinforces legitimacy. Together, they ensure political stability.

The existence of effective opposition parties is frequently regarded as a crucial criterion of democratic government. "Practice and acceptance of opposition" is treated by Edward Shils as a major variable in distinguishing democratic and nondemocratic systems.[8] As Dahl notes, historically *coercion* has been the method of dealing with political opponents. The emergence of a legal and respected opposition has been a fairly recent phenomenon and exists in relatively few states. In fact, Dahl regards political opposition as "very nearly the most distinctive characteristic of democracy." Its absence is taken as an indication of the absence of democratic government.

8 *Political Development in the New States* (The Hague: Mouton & Co., 1962), p. 54 *et passim.*

Agreement on "fundamental principles" or "rules of the game" has long been a point of contention between those who continue to insist on its essentiality as a precondition of democracy and those who maintain that democracy implies agreement to disagree. J. Roland Pennock, for example, identifies agreement on fundamentals as "a prerequisite of any form of government, not just for democracy."[9] Similarly, much of David B. Truman's analysis of American politics is conducted in the matrix of consensus on the "rules of the game."[10] He repeatedly insists that the executive, the legislature, the judiciary, the parties, etc.—all must play their roles so as to comply with the "rules." Any serious disturbance of the rules, Truman believes, brings forth explicit demand for conformity.

This point of view, however, appears to be untenable. As early as 1942, Carl J. Friedrich argued that consensus on "fundamentals" is not only unnecessary, but may even be undesirable.[11] In fact, he suggested, any demand for such agreement would tend to be antidemocratic. A democratic society, Friedrich held, requires diversity and dissent. "In spite of all the theorizing," he wrote, "democracy in action has functioned in communities divided by disagreement on fundamentals." He concluded that consensus cannot be a precondition of democracy "because it cannot be assumed that there will be any agreement upon what is fundamental."[12]

Some years later, James W. Prothro and Charles M. Grigg sought empirical verification of Friedrich's proposition. Concluding their study of the attitudes of voters in two communities, they noted that while consensus on fundamental

9 *Liberal Democracy: Its Merits and Prospects* (New York: Rinehart and Co., 1950), p. 213.

10 *The Governmental Process* (New York: Alfred A. Knopf, 1951), pp. 512–524 *et passim.*

11 *The New Belief in the Common Man* (Boston: Little, Brown and Co., 1942).

12 *Ibid.,* pp. 171, 173.

principles may exist at the most general and abstract level, when tested on specific precepts of democratic government, "the voters in both communities were closer to complete discord than to complete consensus. . . ."

Similarly, Herbert McClosky has found that while a degree of consensus and awareness may exist among the political activists and the political influentials, the same cannot be said of the general public. The electorate, McClosky notes, appears to agree on the value of "freedom in the abstract" but is sharply divided on every other democratic principle.

It is not clear, in McClosky's view, that consensus even among the activists is a prerequisite of democracy. Agreement, according to him, may be required at times of political crisis and instability but not at other times. He writes: "so long as conditions remain stable, consensus is not required." He concludes that as a factor in democratic stability, agreement has been "over-valued." American democracy, according to McClosky, "survives and even flourishes" under conditions of widespread public disagreement.

PSYCHOCULTURAL PRECONDITIONS

A host of personality requirements has regularly been associated with the democratic style of life. The psychocultural approach has sought to identify a "national character" or "modal personality" as a distinctive feature of democratic societies.[13] Although in the discussion that follows, our principal concern is with the democratic character and personality, references to, and comparisons with, the "authoritarian personality" will be inescapable.

13 "National character" has been defined as "relatively enduring personality characteristics and patterns that are modal among the adult members of a society." See Alex Inkeles, "National Character and Modern Political Systems," in Francis L. K. Hsu, ed., *Psychological Anthropology: Approaches to Culture and Personality* (Homewood, Ill.: Dorsey Press, 1961), p. 173.

One of the earliest formulations of the "democratic personality" as ideal type is found in the work of Karl Mannheim. The key to Mannheim's conception is the notion of "integrative behavior," which he views as "the archetype of democratic behavior." "Integrative behavior," according to Mannheim, is underscored by receptivity to divergent points of view—this in contrast to authoritarian behavior, which is marked by intolerance of variety and a corresponding attempt to superimpose one's own views upon others. Democratic behavior is characterized by openness to change, itself resting on a feeling of security on the part of the individual; authoritarian behavior is marked by rigidity and insecurity associated with status-ridden personalities. Mannheim believes that much of the behavior of the authoritarian personality is a reaction to the constant fear of losing face and status. Democratic behavior, by contrast, rests on a belief in "partnership" which gives rise to a desire to integrate divergent interests, values, and goals. Through such "creative integration," the democratic personality expands his perspective and enriches his life. Authoritarian behavior, by contrast, rejects integration; it is guided by a system of rituals and roles.

In the discussion of the relation of the democratic personality to democratic society, Mannheim's analysis becomes circular. On the one hand, he holds, democratic behavior presupposes democratic personality and democratic personality is a product of democratic society; on the other, he argues, democratic society rests on democratic personality. It is not clear, in other words, whether a democratic society creates a democratic personality or is created by it. Perhaps the question is not answerable. According to Mannheim, at any rate, the democratic personality is characterized by security, tolerance, openness, spontaneity, adaptiveness, and cooperation; the authoritarian personality is marked by insecurity, intolerance, rigidity, and unfailing conformity.

The most far-reaching and controversial study of the

authoritarian personality to date has been undertaken by T. W. Adorno and his associates (hereafter simply referred to as "Adorno").[14] Writing immediately after World War II, Adorno's main concern is identification of the "potentially fascist" personality. The major hypothesis is that "the political, economic, and social convictions of an individual often form a broad and coherent pattern . . . and that this pattern is an expression of deep-lying trends in his personality."[15] The approach is psychoanalytic and based on Freudian personality theory. Although a detailed discussion of this theory is beyond our concern, some grasp of its essentials is indispensable to an understanding of the findings of the Adorno study.[16]

The Freudian personality system is conceived in terms of three interrelated and interacting variables: the id, the superego, and the ego. The id is the realm of instincts, and instincts take two major forms: the Eros (life forces) and the Thanatos (destructive impulses). The id operates in accordance with the pleasure principle: it seeks instinctual excitation and gratification. The id does not "think," it merely wishes or acts.

The superego is the moral aspect of personality, the realm of virtue. Although initially representing the child's internalization and assimilation of parental norms and values, the superego undergoes modification as the child grows and

14 T. W. Adorno, Else Frenkel-Brunswik, Daniel J. Levinson, and R. Nevitt Sanford, *The Authoritarian Personality* (New York: Harper and Brothers, 1950).

15 *Ibid.*, p. 1.

16 The best source for the original statement of psychoanalytic theory is Sigmund Freud himself. See *The Standard Edition of the Complete Psychological Works of Sigmund Freud,* 21 volumes, translated under the general editorship of James Strachey in collaboration with Anna Freud (London: The Hogarth Press and the Institute of Psychoanalysis, 1953–1961). Some of the most important of Freud's works are available in *The Basic Writings of Sigmund Freud,* translated by A. A. Brill (New York: The Modern Library, 1938). A short and clear introduction is Calvin S. Hall, *A Primer of Freudian Psychology* (New York: The New American Library, 1955).

acquires new experience. The superego operates in accordance with ideal standards and strives for perfection.

The ego comprises the rational component of personality. It acts as an intermediary between the id and the superego, between the individual and the external world. Before the individual can satisfy the id, it is necessary to take into account the external environment, social mores, and social sanctions. The ego, in other words, operates in accordance with the reality principle: it does not say that pleasure should not be pursued but that it must be pursued in socially appropriate ways.

A "normal" personality, according to psychoanalytic theory, is characterized by balance, harmony, and integration so far as these three variables are concerned. The id must not be so strong as to come into conflict with the superego; the superego must not, as a result of guilt feelings perhaps, become "punitive" toward the id; and the ego must be sufficiently strong to perform the function of mediating successfully between the id and the superego when temporary conflicts arise.

We are now in a position to look at the findings of the Adorno study. The "authoritarian syndrome" as sketched by Adorno may be summarized in the following terms: the id has become unusually strong and highly ambivalent in tendencies; the superego, ridden by a guilt complex and highly punitive, seeks to deny material gratification to the id, an attempt which in turn forces the id to become increasingly rebellious and unwieldy; and the ego is too weak to mediate between the id and the superego.[17] Consequently, the authoritarian personality is characterized by serious imbalance and disharmony, by such pronounced ambivalent tendencies as sadism-masochism and mania-depression. He is highly compulsive, as manifested, for example, in the rigid

17 Adorno *et al., op. cit.,* especially pp. 753, 759–762.

organization of all aspects of life. The compulsiveness is partly a consequence of deep feelings of insecurity. The authoritarian personality "is driven by the fear of being weak,"[18] for which he compensates through overidentification with people of high status. Finally—and this finding has been repeated in some other studies—the authoritarian personality is authoritarian and submissive at the same time. He is violently assertive toward those whom he judges to be his inferiors and highly submissive vis-à-vis those considered his superiors. The authoritarian personality, in other words, takes pleasure in both assertiveness and obedience—another ambivalent characteristic. What all this amounts to, according to Adorno, is that the authoritarian personality tends to be open to external control and susceptible to totalitarian movements and ideologies, particularly of the fascist type. By extension, we might note, the democratic personality would be characterized by security, openness, and tolerance—traits similar to those Mannheim identified.

The Adorno study has been criticized on a number of grounds; the following are among the more important objections: (1) Freudian personality theory is nonempirical—even antiempirical—since there is no way in which the actual existence of the id, ego, and superego can be verified; (2) the psychoanalytic scheme sets up a closed system and fails to take into account social and cultural variations; and (3) the Adorno study, concerned exclusively with the "potentially fascist" personality, leaves out altogether the communist variety.[19]

18 *Ibid.*, p. 753.

19 See, for example: Richard Christie and Marie Jahoda, eds., *Studies in the Scope and Method of "The Authoritarian Personality": Continuities in Social Research* (New York: The Free Press, 1954); Morris Janowitz and Dwaine Marvick, "Authoritarianism and Political Behavior," *Public Opinion Quarterly,* 17 (Summer 1953), pp. 185–201; Arthur W. Kornhauser, Harold L. Sheppard, and Albert J. Mayer, *When Labor Votes: A Study of the Auto Workers* (New York: University Books, 1956), especially pp. 146–200; Robert E.

Among other important studies of the democratic personality, those of Harold D. Lasswell, Daniel Lerner, and Alex Inkeles should be briefly considered. Lasswell's conception of democratic character embraces four principal components: (1) the "democrat" has an "open ego" and a "warm" personality; (2) he is multi-valued and value-sharing (rather than single-valued and value-monopolizing); (3) he has confidence in human potentialities; and (4) he enjoys relative freedom from anxiety.

Lerner identifies the unique feature of the democratic personality as "empathy," denoting "psychic mobility" or "the capacity to see oneself in the other fellow's situation," whether favorably or unfavorably. A "mobile" personality is flexible and adaptive: empathy, Lerner writes, refers to "a high capacity for rearranging the self-system on short notice." The democratic order, he believes, requires "an expansive and adaptive self-system, ready to incorporate new roles and to identify personal values with public issues." Moreover, the democratic personality is characteristically participant. The capacity for empathy, Lerner states, is associated with a "personal style . . . which is distinctively industrial, urban, literate and *participant.*" In short, the distinctive mark of the democratic society is the "participant style"; the distinctive personality mechanism of the participant style is empathy.

A systematic attempt to relate national character to political systems is undertaken by Inkeles, in whose view there is "substantial and rather compelling evidence" of a direct and regular relationship between personality structure and political behavior.[20] According to Inkeles, "political ex-

---

Lane, "Political Personality and Electoral Choice," *American Political Science Review,* XLIX (March 1955), pp. 173–190; Don Stewart and Thomas Hoult, "A Social-Psychological Theory of the Authoritarian Personality," *American Journal of Sociology,* 65 (November 1959), pp. 274–279.

20 Inkeles, *op. cit.,* p. 193. This article provides an excellent review of much of the recent literature on national character, and the interested reader is urged to consult it in its entirety.

tremism" and authoritarian behavior are characterized by dogmatism and rigidity, intolerance of diversity, suspicion and distrust of others, xenophobia and the hatred of the outsider, idolization of the powerful leader, and a sense of guilt and alienation. The democratic personality, by contrast, is marked by openness to new ideas and experience, tolerance of diversity and differences, belief in the dignity of others, aloof and distant attitude toward authority, and so on.

So far in this section we have discussed "national character" as if it were a matter of universal acceptance and agreement. But, in fact, the debate over the subject matter is by no means closed. The proponents of the approach continue to insist that there are regular and intimate connections between personality and political attitude, between psychology and political activity. By contrast, Ralph Linton has argued, for example, that it is virtually impossible to isolate and study national character in contemporary mass society. Modern society, he holds, is too large, too complex, and too heterogeneous to permit identification of a single modal personality. He writes: "The sheer labor required to establish the existence or otherwise of national character norms by scientifically valid techniques would be staggering."[21] He does agree, however, that personality studies may be feasible in small, homogeneous communities.

Among a host of other criticisms voiced against the psychocultural approach, the following are particularly important: (1) absence of an operational definition of "national character"; (2) need for clarification of determinants of national character; (3) need for clarification of the relationship between the personality of the "modal individual" and that

21 "The Concept of National Character," in Alfred H. Stanton and Stewart E. Perry, eds., *Personality and Political Crisis* (New York: The Free Press, 1951), p. 140.

of the leader; (4) absence of systematic sampling and testing techniques; and (5) operation of Western biases in approaching non-Western societies.[22]

A recent attempt to clarify and surmount some of these difficulties was made by Gabriel A. Almond and Sidney Verba in their quest for a verifiable theory of "political culture." "Political culture" is preferred to "national character" and "modal personality," Almond and Verba state, because it affords precision, specificity, and interdisciplinary endeavor. It is interesting to note, however, that: (1) the Almond-Verba concern is not with culture as such, but with the individual and his interaction with the political environment; and (2) the study of national character has always been interdisciplinary. In any case, relying heavily on Talcott Parsons and Edward Shils, Almond and Verba define "political culture" in terms of three interrelated "patterns of orientation": (1) "cognitive orientation," or the individual's *knowledge* of the various aspects of the political system; (2) "affective orientation," or the individual's *feelings* toward the political system; and (3) "evaluational orientation," or the individual's *assessment* of, and judgment about, the political system.[23]

Proceeding on this basis, and armed with the results of a five-country survey involving some five thousand questionnaires and interviews, Almond and Verba construct a threefold typology of political cultures: "participant," "subject," and "parochial." A "participant" political culture is defined as one in which "cognition," "affect" and "evaluation" are all high and positive. The individual is aware of both the "inputs" and the "outputs" of the political sys-

22 See, for example: Inkeles, *op. cit.*; Linton, *op. cit.*; Alfred R. Lindesmith and Anselm L. Strauss, "A Critique of Culture-Personality Writings," *American Sociological Review,* 15 (October 1950), pp. 587–600.

23 Gabriel A. Almond and Sidney Verba, *The Civic Culture* (Princeton: Princeton University Press, 1963), p. 15. Cf. Talcott Parsons and Edward Shils, *Toward A General Theory of Action* (Cambridge, Mass.: Harvard University Press, 1951), especially p. 163.

tem.[24] He is both "active" and "responsive." A "parochial" political culture, by contrast, is one in which the individual is aware neither of the inputs nor of the outputs of the political system. In the "subject" variety, on the other hand, there is orientation toward the outputs of the political system (insofar as the individual may be affected by political decisions), but none toward the inputs or toward the self as an active participant.

An important insight of Almond and Verba lies in their insistence on the "mixed," "ambivalent" or "dualistic" character of political cultures. Almond writes: "No political system, however modern, ever fully eliminates intermittency and traditionality."[25] The suggested typology, Almond and Verba recognize, is one of "ideal types" or "pure forms." The three actual types of "systemically mixed" political cultures include the "parochial-subject," "subject-participant," and "parochial-participant." Accordingly, the "civic culture"—that is, the distinctively democratic culture of the Anglo-American tradition—represents a fusion of "participant," "subject," and "parochial," with a preponderance of the first. Almond and Verba write: "the most striking characteristic of the civic culture . . . is its mixed quality."

A central point of the Almond–Verba study is that the civic culture is one that contributes to democratic stability and survival. "It is not," they recognize, "the only form of democratic political culture, but it seems to be the one

24 Almond has identified four input or "political" functions and three output or "governmental" functions of political systems. The former include political socialization and recruitment, interest articulation, interest aggregation, and political communication; the latter consist of rule making, rule application, and rule adjudication. See Almond, "Introduction: A Functional Approach to Comparative Politics," in Almond and James S. Coleman, eds., *The Politics of the Developing Areas* (Princeton: Princeton University Press, 1960), pp. 3–64; Almond and Verba, *op. cit.*; Almond and G. Bingham Powell, Jr., *Comparative Politics: A Developmental Approach* (Boston: Little, Brown and Co., 1966).

25 Almond, "Introduction . . . ," *op. cit.*, p. 16.

most congruent with a stable, democratic system.[26] In a word, where political system is consonant with political culture, political stability is the outcome.

We have identified a number of studies that seek to shed light on the psychocultural requirements of political life. Although they differ in many respects, there appears to be general agreement that the "democratic personality" is characterized by security, receptivity, openness, tolerance, permissiveness, adaptiveness, and flexibility, whereas the "authoritarian personality" is marked by insecurity, inflexibility, intolerance, distrust, and suspicion.

SUMMARY

In this chapter we have discussed some preconditions deemed essential for democratic political life. A few of these impress us as superficial and we are obliged to reject them. In this category such variables as size and religion may be included, although we recognize that the latter is far more controversial. A second group of preconditions appear plausible but evidence supporting them is inconclusive. In this group the personality requirements of democracy may fall. Finally, evidence in support of the validity of some of the preconditions appears to be of a substantial nature and we are inclined to accept them on a provisional basis, that is, until they are refuted by more conclusive evidence. In this category some of the socioeconomic and political prerequisites of democracy may be listed. In general, the more conclusively supported by empirical evidence, the greater the likelihood that we will accept a precondition; the more abstract and intuitive, the more skeptical we would tend to be.

26 Almond and Verba, *op. cit.*, p. 498.

7
Physical Preconditions

THOMAS JEFFERSON

The Ward Republic

The organization of our county administrations may be thought more difficult. But follow principle, and the knot unties itself. Divide the counties into wards of such size as that every citizen can attend, when called on, and act in person. Ascribe to them the government of their wards in all things relating to themselves exclusively. A justice, chosen by themselves, in each, a constable, a military company, a patrol, a school, the care of their own poor, their own portion of public roads, the choice of one or more jurors to serve in some court, and the delivery, within their own wards, of their own votes for all elective officers of higher sphere, will relieve the county administration of nearly all its business, will have it better done, and by making every citizen an acting member of the government, and in the offices nearest and most interesting to him, will attach him by his strongest feelings to the independence of his country, and its republican constitution. The justices

From "To Samuel Kercheval," July 12, 1816. *The Writings of Thomas Jefferson,* X, collected and edited by Paul L. Ford. New York: G. P. Putnam's Sons, 1899.

thus chosen by every ward, would constitute the county court, would do its judiciary business, direct roads and bridges, levy county and poor rates, and administer all the matters of common interest to the whole county. These wards, called townships in New England, are the vital principle of their governments, and have proved themselves the wisest invention ever devised by the wit of man for the perfect exercise of self-government, and for its preservation. We should thus marshal our government into: (1) the general federal republic, for all concerns foreign and federal; (2) that of the State, for what relates to our own citizens exclusively; (3) the county republics, for the duties and concerns of the county; and (4) the ward republics, for the small, and yet numerous and interesting concerns of the neighborhood; and in government, as well as in every other business of life, it is by division and subdivision of duties alone, that all matters, great and small, can be managed to perfection. And the whole is cemented by giving to every citizen, personally, a part in the administration of the public affairs.

. . . The mayor of every ward, on a question, . . . would call his ward together, take the simple yea or nay of its members, convey these to the county court, who would hand on those of all its wards to the proper general authority; and the voice of the whole people would be thus fairly, fully, and peaceably expressed, discussed, and decided by the common reason of the society. If this avenue be shut to the call of sufferance, it will make itself heard through that of force, and we shall go on, as other nations are doing, in the endless circle of oppression, rebellion, reformation; and oppression, rebellion, reformation, again; and so on forever.

ALEXIS DE TOCQUEVILLE

The New England Town

It is not without intention that I begin this subject with the township. The village or township is the only association which is so perfectly natural that, wherever a number of men are collected, it seems to constitute itself.

The town or tithing, then, exists in all nations, whatever their laws and customs may be: it is man who makes monarchies and establishes republics, but the township seems to come directly from the hand of God. . . . Town meetings are to liberty what primary schools are to science; they bring it within the people's reach, they teach men how to use and how to enjoy it. A nation may establish a free government, but without municipal institutions it cannot have the spirit of liberty. . . .

The township of New England holds a middle place between the *commune* and the *canton* of France. Its average population is from two to three thousand, so that it is not so large, on the one hand, that the interests of its inhabitants would be likely to conflict, and not so small, on the other, but that men capable of conducting its affairs may always be found among its citizens.

In the township, as well as everywhere else, the people are the source of power; but nowhere do they exercise their power more immediately. In America the people form a master who must be obeyed to the utmost limits of possibility.

In New England the majority acts by representatives in

From *Democracy in America* by Alexis de Tocqueville, the Henry Reeve text, as revised by Francis Bowen and further edited by Phillips Bradley. New York: Alfred A. Knopf, Inc., 1945, Vol. I, pp. 60–62, 66–68.

conducting the general business of the state. It is necessary that it should be so. But in the townships, where the legislative and administrative action of the government is nearer to the governed, the system of representation is not adopted. There is no municipal council; but the body of voters, after having chosen its magistrates, directs them in everything that exceeds the simple and ordinary execution of the laws of the state.

In America not only do municipal bodies exist, but they are kept alive and supported by town spirit. The township of New England possesses two advantages which strongly excite the interest of mankind: namely, independence and authority. Its sphere is limited, indeed; but within that sphere its action is unrestrained. This independence alone gives it a real importance, which its extent and population would not ensure.

. . . The New Englander is attached to his township not so much because he was born in it, but because it is a free and strong community, of which he is a member, and which deserves the care spent in managing it. . . . Another important fact is that the township of New England is so constituted as to excite the warmest of human affections without arousing the ambitious passions of the heart of man. . . . the township, at the center of the ordinary relations of life, serves as a field for the desire of public esteem, the want of exciting interest, and the taste for authority and popularity; and the passions that commonly embroil society change their character when they find a vent so near the domestic hearth and the family circle.

In the American townships power has been distributed with admirable skill, for the purpose of interesting the greatest possible number of persons in the common weal. Independently of the voters, who are from time to time called into action, the power is divided among innumerable functionaries and officers, who all, in their several spheres, represent the powerful community in whose name they act. The local administration thus affords an unfailing source of profit and interest to a vast number of individuals. . . .

The existence of the townships of New England is, in general, a happy one. Their government is suited to their tastes, and chosen by themselves. In the midst of the profound peace and general comfort that reign in America, the commotions of municipal life are infrequent. The conduct of local business is easy. The political education of the people has long been complete; say rather that it was complete when the people first set foot upon the soil. In New England no tradition exists of a distinction of rank; no portion of the community is tempted to oppress the remainder; and the wrongs that may injure isolated individuals are forgotten in the general contentment that prevails. . . .

The native of New England is attached to his township because it is independent and free: his co-operation in its affairs ensures his attachment to its interests; the well-being it affords him secures his affection; and its welfare is the aim of his ambition and of his future exertions. He takes a part in every occurrence in the place; he practices the art of government in the small sphere within his reach; he accustoms himself to those forms without which liberty can only advance by revolutions; he imbibes their spirit; he acquires a taste for order, comprehends the balance of powers, and collects clear practical notions on the nature of his duties and the extent of his rights.

ROSCOE C. MARTIN

Grass-Roots Democracy Re-examined

An analysis of grass roots in its more responsible employment will suggest that it has at least five significant facets. First, it is usually employed in connection with government. In the general area of public affairs it may be used in reference to administrative decentralization, for example, or to the representativeness of the legislative organ, or to political action "at the branchhead." Obviously not all such references have scientific validity or content; but we will pass by this demurrer for the present in favor of a general bounding of the term.

Second, the concept appears normally to have a geographical import. In this sense, a place which partakes of the grass roots is non-metropolitan, even non-urban, in character. . . .

Third, grass roots is frequently employed to symbolize a spirit of community independence. The basic problems of government, the argument goes, are local in character, and should be dealt with by local initiative. Stated positively, this view leads logically to the doctrine of local self-government and home-rule. . . .

Fourth, in one of its important aspects the term has a personal or individual meaning. Thus a view held by an individual is *ipso facto* a grass-roots view, an expression of personal opinion, a grass-roots judgment. In this sense, the concept is not limited geographically but has application wherever people are found, although its validity is always greater when it is applied to a rural setting. In this sense,

From *Grass Roots* by Roscoe C. Martin. University, Ala.: University of Alabama Press, 1957, pp. 3–5, 56–64.

too, grass roots is an expression of belief in the worth of the individual, of confidence in personal judgment.

Fifth, and as a direct corollary to the above, grass roots is almost invariably equated with democracy. . . . Grass roots would appear to be a peculiarly American phenomenon ultimately connected with the expression of popular judgment on public questions. It is in fact an important symbol of American democracy. It provides, in a sense, a court of last appeal, since in democratic doctrine there is no tribunal above or beyond the people. In final analysis, grass roots serves as a fundamental article of the democratic faith, for it carries the indelible impression of the sovereign individual.

. . . One of the things most needed to permit a reasoned judgment of the grass-roots practice of democracy is an examination of the folklore enveloping the subject.

It will prove useful to begin with an analysis of the tacit (sometimes the explicit) assumption of the devotees of agrarian democracy that Lilliputian government is more democratic *per se* than big government. The argument runs thus: government to be democratic must be close to the people; little government is close to the people, and the smaller it is the closer it is; therefore the smaller the units of government and the larger their number the greater the degree of democracy. A companion line holds that little government tends to be more democratic than big government because it lacks the incentive, the resources, and the power to be otherwise; it is democratic, so to speak, by default. . . .

It must be concluded that smallness in size and multiplicity in number of rural governments provide neither a guarantee of the existence nor a standard for measuring the effectiveness of local democracy. There are other and more meaningful criteria, among them the nature of popular participation, the representativeness of policy-making bodies, and the kind and efficacy of the control exercised over administrative officials. The relationship between the degree of democracy and the complexity of local governmental machinery is much more likely to be inverse than direct.

Second among the hallowed articles of faith is the tradition that the local community serves as the "school for democracy." As a writer in a recent issue of the *National Municipal Review* put it, "The value of democracy is not open to question in this discussion. Assuming its virtue, there is little doubt that the most effective training ground for democracy lies in the field of local self-government." Here is the doctrine, naked and unadorned. It is worthy of analysis.

The author makes two basic assumptions. The first, that democracy is virtuous, few will wish to challenge; but the second, concerning the effectiveness of local self-government as a training ground for democracy, may be open to question. The assumption is that the citizen learns about democracy from participation in the affairs of local government. But what does he learn and how does he learn it? What is the curriculum offered? Who are the faculty? What are the teaching and learning materials? To answer some of these questions, let it be noted that the citizen learns only about local affairs—that is, provincial and parochial affairs, that his teachers are small-time politicians and part-time functionaries, and that the courses of study are village pump politics and strictly amateur administration. The value of this kind of knowledge imparted in this fashion to the students of democracy is doubtful. . . .

An important aspect of the "training ground" argument is found in the notion that persons trained in the rural arena go on to achieve renown on larger stages and before greater audiences. This assumption may be valid up to a point: it may well be that large numbers of state legislators gain their initial experience in public life from local office.

Of the 31 state governors listed in *Who's Who* in 1954, however, only eleven confessed to previous local experience. Two-thirds therefore came to the gubernatorial office through other than local channels. Of the 96 United States senators in 1955, more than two-thirds (67) reported no experience in local government. Among the members of the House of Representatives, 71 per cent had no experience as local office-holders. These figures do not dispose of the onward-and-upward argument, but they do suggest that the assumption on which the point rests deserves to be questioned. . . .

Yet another phase of the myth concerns citizen participation in local affairs, both as candidate for public office and as voter. It appears to be generally assumed that non-participation poses no problem at the grass roots. . . . The New England town has played a prominent role in song and story for more than three centuries as America's chief exemplar of local democracy. Yet even in colonial times some of the towns found cause to question the presumed warmth of local patriotism. Boston, as a single example, was driven to levy a fine of ten pounds on any person who without good cause refused, having been elected, to serve as constable. In latter days, the problem of non-participation in town affairs has in many instances been acute. A credible reporter describes a town meeting which, with 700 adult citizens qualified to take part, was attended by 110 citizens who came and stayed most of the day. That is a participation figure of 15.7 per cent. An additional ninety citizens dropped by during the day to cast a vote on this or that issue and, having voted, went away. If these ninety are added to the original 110, total participation comes to 29 per cent; but were the ninety casual droppers-by participants in town affairs in any real sense? They were instead special pleaders who came in to vote on a single issue; their concern was a particular, fragmental one, and it may be argued with some logic that the cause of town government would have been better served and a consensus of citizen opinion more accurately recorded had these ninety remained at home with their special interests and left the decisions to those who came and stayed through the day. . . .

Another cause for concern over democracy as it is practiced in rural government arises from the representative system, and on two principal counts. First, the legislative bodies are not representative; and second, the procedures are neither democratic themselves nor productive of democratic results. As to the first, most legislative bodies, local and otherwise, consist of representatives elected by districts. This is true, for example, of the typical rural county court (or board of commissioners or supervisors). . . . This means that county problems are viewed through myopic local eyes. It means, for example, that bridges must be scattered about the county in accordance with the residence of the commissioners; it means that roads are parceled out the same way; it means that a commissioner will seize "his" road machinery with a firm grasp and refuse to allow it to be used outside his own district. It means finally, and of course most importantly, that the interests of the county are lost in those of the individual election districts. . . .

Yet another aspect of the representative system which is worthy of note concerns the procedures employed in the legislatures. In South Carolina, to cite a single example, the state legislature is dominated by the various county delegations, as it is, indeed, in most states where the county is an important unit. In South Carolina, however, the hold of the counties on their representatives and of the county delegations in turn on the legislature appears to be particularly strong. As evidence, it may be noted that most of the measures passed by the legislature are local in import: of all bills passed over a period of 24 years recently ended, 83.9 per cent were local measures. Friday is the day set aside during a legislative session for consideration of local and uncontested matters. The question of a quorum by general agreement is never raised on that day, and a mere handful in each house proceeds to enact local measures. According to a recent count of a number of Friday meetings, the median meeting time for the House was six minutes. The Senate normally met for somewhat longer, though there was no effort in either house to give local bills any real consideration. They were passed by courtesy at the request of local delegations. . . .

How democratic is a government whose legislative body is palpably unrepresentative in any real sense and whose practice is deliberately designed to serve the desires of ward and district delegates? Such a body is in fact more a congress of ambassadors than a legislative assembly. The system operates on the unspoken premise that what the five (or 25) county commissioners desire individually will add up to what is best for the county as a whole, that the 46 particularistic programs of the several county delegations in the aggregate will constitute a sound general legislative program for the state. It is not clear where responsibility for the welfare of the county or the state as a whole lies under this theory of representative government, but clearly it does not reside in any real sense in the representative body.

E. E. SCHATTSCHNEIDER

Illusion and Reality

Primitive democratic theorists never tire of telling us that democracy was designed to work in New England town meetings, not in a modern national state. The analysis is fatuous. We might as well attempt to return to a handicraft economy. The crisis is a purely theoretical one because operating democratic political systems have in fact already accomplished what is theoretically impossible and are doing it every day. It is only the theory that has broken down. The problem of modern democracy is the problem of learning to live in the modern world.

We can find our way through the maze if we learn to distinguish between different kinds of knowledge, between what amateurs know and what professionals know, between what generalists know and what specialists know. The problem is not how 180 million Aristotles can run a democracy, but how we can organize a political community of 180 million ordinary people so that it remains sensitive to their needs. This is a problem of *leadership, organization, alternatives and systems of responsibility and confidence.* The emphasis is on the role of leadership and organization in a democracy, not on the spontaneous generation of something at the grass roots. If we approach the problem from this side, it does not look impossible. The achievements of the American regime are tremendous, but they have been brought about in spite of the theoretical illusions under which we have labored.

From *The Semisovereign People* by E. E. Schattschneider. New York: Holt, Rinehart and Winston, Inc., 1960, p. 138.

8
Religious Preconditions

REINHOLD NIEBUHR

The Protestant Foundation of Democracy

The thesis of this volume grew out of my conviction that democracy has a more compelling justification and requires a more realistic vindication than is given it by the liberal culture with which it has been associated in modern history. The excessively optimistic estimates of human nature and of human history with which the democratic credo has been historically associated are a source of peril to democratic society; for contemporary experience is refuting this optimism and there is danger that it will seem to refute the democratic ideal as well.

A free society requires some confidence in the ability of men to reach tentative and tolerable adjustments between their competing interests and to arrive at some common notions of justice which transcend all partial interests. A consistent pessimism in regard to man's rational capacity for justice invariably leads to absolutistic political theories; for they prompt the conviction that only preponderant

From *The Children of Light and the Children of Darkness* by Reinhold Niebuhr. New York: Charles Scribner's Sons, and London: James Nisbet & Co., Ltd., 1945, pp. x–xiii, 9–11, 40–41, 150–152, 135–136.

power can coerce the various vitalities of a community into a working harmony. But a too consistent optimism in regard to man's ability and inclination to grant justice to his fellows obscures the perils of chaos which perennially confront every society, including a free society. In one sense a democratic society is particularly exposed to the dangers of confusion. If these perils are not appreciated they may overtake a free society and invite the alternative evil of tyranny.

But modern democracy requires a more realistic philosophical and religious basis, not only in order to anticipate and understand the perils to which it is exposed; but also to give it more persuasive justification. Man's capacity for justice makes democracy possible; but man's inclination to injustice makes democracy necessary. In all non-democratic political theories the state or the ruler is invested with uncontrolled power for the sake of achieving order and unity in the community. But the pessimism which prompts and justifies this policy is not consistent; for it is not applied, as it should be, to the ruler. If men are inclined to deal unjustly with their fellows, the possession of power aggravates this inclination. That is why irresponsible and uncontrolled power is the greatest source of injustice.

The democratic techniques of a free society place checks upon the power of the ruler and administrator and thus prevent it from becoming vexatious. The perils of uncontrolled power are perennial reminders of the virtues of a democratic society; particularly if a society should become inclined to impatience with the dangers of freedom and should be tempted to choose the advantages of coerced unity at the price of freedom.

The consistent optimism of our liberal culture has prevented modern democratic societies both from gauging the perils of freedom accurately and from appreciating democracy fully as the only alternative to injustice and oppression. When this optimism is not qualified to accord with the real and complex facts of human nature and history, there is always a danger that sentimentality will give way to despair and that a too consistent optimism will alternate with a too consistent pessimism.

I have not sought to elaborate the religious and theological convictions upon which the political philosophy of the following pages rests. It will be apparent, however, that they are informed by the belief that a Christian view of human nature is more adequate for the development of a democratic society than either the optimism with which democracy has become historically associated or the moral cynicism which inclines human communities to tyrannical political strategies.

In illumining this important distinction [between self-interest and the general interest] more fully, we may well designate the moral cynics, who know no law beyond their will and interest, with the scriptural designation of "children of this world" or "children of darkness." Those who believe that self-interest should be brought under the discipline of the higher law could then be termed "the children of light." This is no mere arbitrary device; for evil is always the assertion of some self-interest without regard to the whole, whether the whole be conceived as the immediate community, or the total community of mankind, or the total order of the world. . . . The "children of light" may thus be defined as those who seek to bring self-interest under the discipline of a more universal law and in harmony with a more universal good.

According to the scripture "the children of this world are in their generation wiser than the children of light." This observation fits the modern situation. Our democratic civilization has been built, not by children of darkness but by foolish children of light. It has been under attack by the children of darkness, by the moral cynics, who declare that a strong nation need acknowledge no law beyond its strength. It has come close to complete disaster under this attack . . . because it underestimated the power of self-interest, both individual and collective, in modern society. The children of light have not been as wise as the children of darkness.

The children of darkness are evil because they know no law beyond the self. They are wise, though evil, because they understand the power of self-interest. The children of light are virtuous because they have some conception of a higher law than their own will. They are usually foolish because they do not know the power of self-will. They underestimate the peril of anarchy in both the national and the international community. . . .

It must be understood that the children of light are foolish not merely because they underestimate the power of self-interest among the children of darkness. They underestimate this power among themselves. The democratic world came so close to disaster not merely because it never believed that Nazism possessed the demonic fury which it avowed. Civilization refused to recognize the power of class interest in its own communities. . . .

The preservation of a democratic civilization requires the wisdom of the serpent and the harmlessness of the dove. The children of light must be armed with the wisdom of the children of darkness but remain free from their malice. They must know the power of self-interest in human society without giving it moral justification. They must have this wisdom in order that they may beguile, deflect, harness and restrain self-interest, individual and collective, for the sake of the community.

. . . Religious idealists usually insist that the primary contribution of religion to democratic life is the cultivation of a moral idealism which inculcates concern for the other rather than the self. But this is only part of the contribution which a profound religion can make. Consistent egotists would, of course, wreck any democratic process; for it requires some decent consideration of the needs of others. But some of the greatest perils to democracy arise from the fanaticism of moral idealists who are not conscious of the corruption of self-interest in their professed ideals. Democracy therefore requires something more than a religious devotion to moral ideals. It requires religious humility. Every absolute devotion to relative political ends (and all political ends are relative) is a threat to communal peace. But religious humility is no simple moral or political achievement. It springs only from the depth of a religion which confronts the individual with a more ultimate majesty and purity than all human majesties and values, and persuades him to confess: "Why callest thou me good? there is none good but one, that is, God."

The real point of contact between democracy and profound religion is in the spirit of humility which democracy requires and which must be one of the fruits of religion. Democratic life requires a spirit of tolerant cooperation between individuals and groups which can be achieved by neither moral cynics, who know no law beyond their own interest, nor by moral idealists, who acknowledge such a law but are unconscious of the corruption which insinuates itself into the statement of it by even the most disinterested idealists. Democracy may be challenged from without by the force of barbarism and the creed of cynicism. But its internal peril lies in the conflict of various schools and classes of idealists, who profess different ideals but exhibit a common conviction that their own ideals are perfect. . . .

Religious humility is in perfect accord with the presuppositions of a democratic society. Profound religion must recognize the difference between divine majesty and human creatureliness; between the unconditioned character of the divine and the conditioned character of all human enterprise. According to the Christian faith the pride, which seeks to hide the conditioned and finite character of all human endeavor, is the very quintessence of sin. Religious faith ought therefore to be a constant fount of humility; for it ought to encourage men to moderate their natural pride and to achieve some decent consciousness of the relativity of their own statement of even the most ultimate truth. . . .

Historically the highest form of democratic toleration is based upon these very religious insights. The real foundation of Anglo-Saxon toleration lies in the religious experience of seventeenth-century England. In the religious conflicts of the Cromwellian period there were religious fanatics who were anxious to secure religious monopoly for their particular version of the Christian faith. There were also some secularists who hoped for toleration through the decay of religion. But the victory for toleration was really won by various groups of Christians, among which were the Independents and the Levellers, certain types of moderate Anglicans touched with Renaissance-humanistic perspectives and some individuals in other sectarian groups.

JACQUES MARITAIN

The Catholic Foundation of Democracy

THE INSPIRATION OF THE GOSPEL

Not only does the democratic state of mind proceed from the inspiration of the Gospel, but it cannot exist without it. To keep faith in the forward march of humanity despite all the temptations to despair of man that are furnished by history, and particularly contemporary history; to have faith in the dignity of the person and of common humanity, in human rights and in justice—that is, in essentially spiritual values; to have, not in formulas but in reality, the sense of and respect for the dignity of the people, which is a spiritual dignity and is revealed to whoever knows how to love it; to sustain and revive the sense of equality without sinking into a levelling equalitarianism; to respect authority, knowing that its wielders are only men, like those they rule, and derive their trust from the consent or the will of the people whose vicars or representatives they are; to believe in the sanctity of law and in the efficacious virtue . . . of political justice in face of the scandalous triumphs of falsehood and violence; to have faith in liberty and in fraternity, an heroical inspiration and an heroical belief are needed which fortify and vivify reason, and which none other than Jesus of Nazareth brought forth in the world.

From *Christianity and Democracy* by Jacques Maritain. New York: Charles Scribner's Sons, and London: Geoffrey Bles, Ltd., 1945, pp. 39–40.

A SOCIETY OF FREE MEN

We see that the conception of society which I have just outlined may be characterized by the following features: it is *personalist,* because it considers society to be a whole composed of persons whose dignity is anterior to society and who, however indigent they may be, contain within their very being a root of independence and aspire to ever greater degrees of independence until they achieve that perfect spiritual liberty which no human society has within its gift.

This conception is, in the second place, *communal,* because it recognizes the fact that the person tends naturally towards society and communion, in particular towards the political community, and because, in the specifically political sphere and to the extent that man is a part of political society, it considers the common good superior to that of individuals.

In the third place this conception is *pluralist,* because it assumes that the development of the human person normally requires a plurality of autonomous communities which have their own rights, liberties and authority; among these communities there are some of a rank inferior to the political state, which arise either from the fundamental exigencies of nature (as in the case of the family community) or else from the will of persons freely coming together to form diverse groups. Other communities are of a rank superior to the state, as is above all the Church in the mind of Christians, and as would also be, in the temporal realm, that organized international community towards which we aspire today.

Finally the conception of society we are describing is *theist* or *Christian,* not in the sense that it would require every member of society to believe in God and to be Chris-

From *The Rights of Man and Natural Law* by Jacques Maritain. New York: Charles Scribner's Sons, and London: Geoffrey Bles, Ltd., 1943, pp. 20–22.

tian, but in the sense that it recognizes that in the reality of things, God, principle and end of the human person and prime source of natural law, is by the same token the prime source of political society and authority among men; and in the sense that it recognizes that the currents of liberty and fraternity released by the Gospel, the virtues of justice and friendship sanctioned by it, the practical respect for the human person proclaimed by it, the feeling of responsibility before God required by it, as much from him who exercises the authority as from him who is subject to it, are the internal energy which civilization needs to achieve its fulfillment. As for those who do not believe in God or who do not profess Christianity, if they do, however, believe in the dignity of the human person, in justice, in liberty, in neighborly love, they also can cooperate in the realization of such a conception of society, and cooperate in the common good, even though they cannot trace their practical convictions to basic principles, or even though they seek to base these convictions on defective principles. In this conception civil society is organically linked to religion and turns consciously towards the source of its being by invoking divine assistance and the divine name as its members know it. Independent in its own temporal sphere, it has above it the kingdom of things that are not Caesar's, and it must cooperate with religion, not by any kind of theocracy or clericalism, nor by exercising any sort of pressure in religious matters, but by respecting and facilitating, on the basis of the rights and liberties of each of us, the spiritual activity of the Church and of the diverse religious families which are grouped within the temporal community.

ERNEST S. GRIFFITH

The Case for Religion Restated

It is my hypothesis that the Christian and Hebrew faiths constitute a powerful matrix, a common denominator of those attitudes most essential to a flourishing democracy. Moreover, it would appear that it is these faiths, and especially the Christian faith, that perhaps alone can cloak such attitudes with the character of "absolutes"—a character which is not only desirable, but perhaps even necessary to democratic survival. . . .

I suggest at the outset an examination of a cluster of basic attitudes or *mores* which, to the degree that they have been present, are apparently closely associated with democratic success. Each of these will be considered in turn. It will be my objective not merely to indicate the relevance of these attitudes in the matter of the survival and flourishing of democratic institutions (which for the most part would be agreed upon), but also to probe still more deeply to discover whether the hypothesis of religious belief as a common denominator, an ultimate sustainer, of these attitudes is the correct one. It will be my further contention that in a pragmatic sense it is in the strength of such faiths that the most serious dilemma facing contemporary free society may best be resolved. This is the dilemma between individualism and civic or social obligation. . . .

In preliminary fashion, one may note how the absence of certain attitudes contributed to the collapse of the more

From "Cultural Prerequisites to a Successfully Functioning Democracy: A Symposium" by Ernest S. Griffith, John Plamenatz, and J. Roland Pennock, *American Political Science Review,* L (March 1956), pp. 103–113.

fragile democracies. Surely lack of respect for the individual was a factor in the collapse of democratic institutions in Germany, Italy, and Japan, and in their failure to take root in Russia. Lack of integrity and dedication to the public interest cost the Kuomintang of China its existence. Lack of a strong sense of the basic unity necessary for an integrated political economy characterized Pre-Hitlerite Germany and casts serious doubt upon the viability of the democratic constitution of contemporary France--though the latter's love of freedom is more deeply rooted that Germany's. The *mores* of Japan included a sense of civic obligation but without respect for the individual; those of France involved individualism without the necessary concomitant of civic loyalty. . . .

Let us now consider affirmatively each attitude of the series I propose as prerequisites [for democratic government]. . . .

It is not accidental that I give first place to the value placed upon individual personality, or rather the view of the nature of the individual as being end and not means. The heart of freedom as a hallmark of democracy consists in a formal or informal constitutional allocation to the individual of certain areas of action which no government . . . may touch. . . . Jefferson spoke of the inalienable rights of "life, liberty, and the pursuit of happiness," and gave them a theological grounding. . . .

I do not claim that only among those who profess and practice the Christian and Jewish faiths is such a value placed upon individual personality. I do call attention to the valiant witness of many thousands of churchmen against Hitler and his ilk, and against communism. I do point out that it is the church that is the vanguard of contemporary responsible Southern leadership in working out a constructive program of racial integration in the schools. "Thus saith the Lord" resounds from a thousand pulpits against violations of the intrinsic dignity of man. It is an "absolute" in the creeds and doctrines of these faiths that men everywhere can find this dignity best in a society of the free—a society in which men are able to think and act spontaneously and responsibly. More and more the spiritual leaders are urging that practice conform to doctrine. As political scientists, we may at least observe the effect on attitude of regarding a man—any man—as a child of God. It provides a norm by which political and economic conduct is to be judged. There are things, if you will, which one who regards himself as a child of God just does not do to another child of God. One does not exploit him, for example; nor does one terrorize or cheat or deceive him; nor irrationally and arbitrarily coerce him. Conversely and affirmatively it leads staight to a conviction of the importance of justice for the individual. It also defines justice by providing norms. . . .

In the second place, a democracy withers away if its people lose interest in its institutions and their constructive use for the general welfare. This is a much wider matter than merely voting or not voting, though this latter is certainly a relevant barometer. Its importance extends to every form of responsible citizen participation in community life: to business and industry, social work, religious activity, as well as to formal government. In government it also means alertness, and the communication of alertness, between elections. Willingness to accept or even to seek office must be sufficiently widespread among the civic minded to assure a measure of disinterested service. Careers in public administration must have attached to them a prestige and an appeal equal to those of other professions. . . .

I am speaking here of the need for responsible participation. By this I mean an affirmative attitude toward society, an attitude that places obligations at least on a par with rights; that in blunt and governmental terms expects to pay taxes in return for services; that in larger terms accepts and welcomes the opportunity to expend effort in behalf of the general welfare or the good of all. . . .

Given men with an outlook of this sort, inspired by inner conviction, reinforced daily by a search for the will of God for themselves as individuals, one need not fear government or statism. . . . I have complete faith in the democratic process, if and when the conflict of issues is between those who believe it is God's will to use the state as a positive instrument for the betterment of society, and those who fear that such use will undermine the individual's responsibility before God to accept his share and more than his share of the world's work.

The reconciliation of these often incompatible objectives has been a preoccupation of the political theorist since the days of the Greeks. The religious faith of the Western world has potentialities in this reconciliation, for in this faith the individual is end and not means—but an end which includes responsible participating citizenship as not the least of its attributes. Without this faith or its equivalent (and where is this "equivalent" to be found?), I fear many things: the self-centered use of political power, indifference to political action, a footloose, aimless society, reluctance to accept civic responsibility. What are these but cancers eating away at the vitals of our Western world, archenemies of the democracy which we hold as a common and would-be fighting faith.

There is a third motive or principle necessary to sustain democracy. All definitions of democracy have at least this in common: they agree that discussion preceding decision . . . is one of its major attributes. If such a discussion is to be full and free, if ideas are to win their way in the market place of reason, then characteristic institutions such as free press, free communications, open sessions of parliaments and chambers and congresses, judicial processes allowing a man his "day in court" are corollaries. . . . But these are not primary.

What is the primary need is a certain assumption of integrity, the assumption that when a man advances an idea or makes a statement which he expects will influence the decisions of others concerning a governmental problem, he is telling the truth. There may well be "another side" to the question, but as far as it goes his statement is not a lie. And if in the market place of ideas, it turns out not to stand up under criticism, because of either superficiality or error, he must not expect the attention in the future he received in the past. . . .

What shall be the sanctions of integrity; what its motivating forces? . . . The ultimate sanctions are internal; the drive toward honor is of the spirit. Here again the voice of authority speaks, "Let your Yea be Yea, and your Nay, Nay." Jesus by spirit and example unmasked hypocrisy and deceit. He ever sought in simplicity, clarity, and guilelessness to isolate the heart of the matter in each and every issue of life. . . . One must not underrate the force of the example and command of Jesus to His myriad followers today, as among the forces making for that substantial and necessary increment of integrity in discussion which must be added to democratic institutions to make them work.

The fourth prerequisite for a successfully functioning democracy carries one into the economic order.

We all know that the industrial age has brought with it specialization, and that this specialization has divided men into various economic groups—labor, industry, finance, the professions, agriculture, and others—and that these great groups are subdivided, sometimes sharply so, into all sorts of subgroups: coal miners, bankers, physicians, dairy farmers, steel manufacturers, and literally thousands of others. These form the warp and woof of our economic life. We appreciate the extent to which they likewise characterize and at times dominate our political life as well. Each of these groups more or less lives in its own limited world; its members experience the same frustrations, enjoy the same advantages, and thus have come to a considerable extent to share the same political point of view, which in turn diverges to a greater or less extent from that held by other groups. In the United States these divergent points of view of this multitude of economic groups are the greatest single phenomenon in what we call politics and public opinion. . . . In fact, a cynic once defined politics as "the battle of interests masquerading as principles." . . .

There is a striking statement of St. Paul which is relevant at this point: "For the body is not one member, but many. If the foot shall say: Because I am not the hand, I am not of the body; is it therefore not of the body? And if the ear shall say, because I am not the eye, I am not of the body; is it therefore not of the body? If the whole body were an eye, where were the hearing? If the whole were hearing, where were the smelling? . . . But now are they many members, yet but one body. And the eye cannot say unto the hand, I have no need of you. . . . And whether one member suffer all the members suffer with it, or one member be honored, all the members rejoice with it."

The analogy goes to the heart of the problem. Each group performs a specialized function; society as a whole receives the benefit. Essentially this is the Christian insight which gives meaning to daily work. . . . the central problem . . . is the discovery of an altruistic motivation so powerful, that the various economic groups will make the necessary sacrifices to dedicate themselves to the common good—*and do this freely*. . . .

In the fifth place, the office holder, be he elected or appointed, occupies a key place in contemporary society. Leadership seems destined to be more and more concentrated. . . .

Hunger for power, carelessness, self-seeking, intrigue, corruption—these hold dangers for our democracies, if once they come to characterize our men in public life. In the more simple days . . . betrayals of public trust . . . did not have the far-reaching consequences which today follow a lowering of the tone of public life.

I recognize the secular factors making for civic righteousness, and I would not underrate them. I know the white heat of contemporary publicity that spares no nook or cranny even of the private life of any man who stands . . . for public office. I know the growing professionalization. . . . I know the checks and safeguards of audit and accounting. Yet if the spark be lacking, the fire of public service cannot be kindled.

. . . "He that is greatest among you, let him be the servant of all," is a religious insight; it is also a governmental one.

The intellectual abstractions of pure reason may be adequate for the highly educated few, though even this is open to question. They are not adequate for the overwhelming majority who for a greater or less portion of their lives are moved by passion. Basically, the problem of a democracy is one of the acceptance of attitudes and customs which will channel passion into constructive lines. . . . There really remains . . . only a conditioned humanitarianism as an adequate and safe outlet for passion, and only religion has historically been able to evoke this on a sufficiently wide scale to be effective. The record of religion itself is ambivalent on the point. Only when one turns, not to religion's institutional expression, but to its fundamental teachings, does one perceive that in such concepts as "finding one's life by losing it," or "the abundant life," when these are coupled with a recognition of the infinite value of each human being, are there the necessary guide lines which can canalize passion in the direction of love for others. . . .

A final prerequisite for the present atomic age is an attitude toward humanity that transcends nationalism. . . . In such a setting a widespread, deeply felt belief in world brotherhood may well be required, especially in the free world.

Let us summarize the course of argument. . . . I submit the following as the necessary attitudes to sustain democratic institutions:

1. Love for and belief in freedom: best based upon belief in the sacredness of the individual as a child of God.

2. Active and constructive participation in community life: best based upon the obligation of the Christian, the Jew, and other believers to accept responsibilities, cooperating with and working for their brother men.

3. Integrity in discussion: best based upon the inner light of truth being primary in a world God meant to be righteous.

4. The freely assumed obligation of economic groups to serve society: best based upon the Christian insight into the nature of society as set forth, for example, by the parable of the body and its members.

5. Leadership and office holding regarded as public trusts: best based upon or inspired by the example and teachings of religious prophets, such as Jesus, who accepted such a service "to the death."

6. Attitudes assuring that passion will be channeled into constructive ends: best based upon religious faiths that unite an obligation to love and serve with a recognition of the primacy of individual personality.

7. Friendliness and cooperation among nations: best based upon the vision of world brotherhood derived from a faith that we are all children of a common Heavenly Father.

I freely grant that many of these attitudes would be helpful also to non-democratic forms of government, especially the fifth. I seriously doubt, however, that at least the basis of any of them could have anything but the most precarious existence except in a democracy.

JOHN PLAMENATZ

The Case for Religion Re-examined

. . . Hardly anyone will disagree with Griffith when he says that "respect for individual personality" is essential to democracy.

. . . But . . . we must press the question further: what is this "respect for individual personality" essential to modern democracy? Is it the old Greek respect for vitality and self-assertiveness, for the man who can play a fine part in the world, who can attract the admiration of his fellows? Is it the Christian sense that every soul is infinitely valuable in the eyes of God? Both the Greeks and the early Christians accepted slavery and the subjection of women. Were the Christians of the Roman Empire less deeply and less sincerely Christian than they are today? Yet they loyally accepted the absolute power of the Emperor in all temporal matters, and refused him nothing except a worship which they felt was due to God alone. Can we say that Christians, when they are democrats, are, if not more sincerely, then more adequately Christian than when they are not democrats? Surely, we ought to say nothing of the kind. When we are tempted to do so, it is, I think, only because we happen to be both Christians and democrats, who like to see a close connection, logical and psychological, between our two faiths. But in themselves these faiths neither exclude nor suppose one another. The good Christian believes in the "infinite value" of the human soul; and the good democrat

From "Cultural Prerequisites to a Successfully Functioning Democracy: A Symposium" by Ernest S. Griffith, John Plamenatz, and J. Roland Pennock, *American Political Science Review,* L (March 1956), pp. 117–118.

believes in what he calls individualism. But a good Christian need not be a democrat, nor a good democrat a Christian. It may well be, since modern democracy first arose among Christian peoples, that there are important historical connections between democratic ideals and Christian theology and ethics. It does not, however, follow that the individualism of the democrat and that of the Christian have much in common.

☙ CURRIN V. SHIELDS

Democracy as a Secular Belief

Democracy . . . is a political creed of very modest pretensions. Democratic beliefs do not afford solace for all human cares or supply answers for every question the ingenuity of man can propound. Democracy offers no answers whatsoever to any question about "supernatural" or "natural" truth. The realm of religion . . . is outside and beyond the ken of the Democratic theory. Religion is, for the Democrat, a realm of private affairs. A person's private convictions about life in this or another world which none of us knows from public experience are of no concern to the Democrat.

In fact, for the Democrat any appeal to a higher moral law to resolve questions of political value is both unnecessary and futile. He sees no earthly need to postulate an "objective" moral order decreed by God or nature to justify principles of political conduct. Universal principles of political right or reason or truth are not necessary for people to conduct their political lives satisfactorily. The Democrat recognizes no suprahuman laws which prescribe where authority should be located or who should exercise it or how they should exercise it in practice. He denies that the existence of any political laws beyond human control can be demonstrated. Political beliefs derived from such laws cannot be proved valid by any method of reasoning. The notion of validity is in fact meaningless when applied to questions of value. Such questions cannot be answered by means of facts or logic or metaphysics. We may have beliefs about

From *Democracy and Catholicism in America* by Currin V. Shields. New York: McGraw-Hill Book Co., Inc., 1958, pp. 256–258, 271–272.

political right and wrong, but we cannot "know" what is right or wrong political conduct.

This is not to say that Democratic theory contains no value beliefs. It certainly does. Democratic beliefs imply definite normative rules for ordering political conduct. . . . But the value beliefs of a Democrat differ radically in character from the value beliefs entertained by a Catholic. For a Democrat, a political value is not something we ought to accept. It is something we may desire. It is something we can accept, if we choose.

The Democrat's approach to questions of political value is to keep them disentangled from matters of fact or logic or metaphysics. His interest is in political practice. . . . What distinguishes the Democrat is his beliefs about how the members of communities can conduct their political affairs. That is all. He does not claim that these beliefs are right or rational or true. He claims only that they answer some practical questions about the effectiveness of human conduct in political practice, and answer them more satisfactorily than alternative political beliefs do.

This Democratic approach to political morals was not contrived by some creative philosophic genius. It was implicit in the practical purpose that Democratic theory and practice were originated to serve. The felt need was for more meaningful principles to guide political conduct. The established principles were found unsatisfactory. The need was for principles which would enable the members of political communities to achieve greater effectiveness by their common actions. Democratic beliefs were formulated to justify the application of such principles in political practice.

Consequently, we find that the Democrat is not, strictly speaking, concerned with what persons should do. His concern is about the way they can do certain things. They can conduct themselves politically in a Democratic way, which is more effective in practice than any other way. If a person does not want to achieve any political purpose, the Democrat has nothing to say to him. Or if a person does not want to achieve his political purpose effectively, again the Democrat has nothing to say. But if a person does want to achieve a purpose he shares in common with others and wants to be effective in his political activity, then the Democrat has some things to say about how he can get the greatest possible satisfaction from his political life.

. . . A Democrat can be a Protestant or a Jew, an atheist or a true believer. So far as religion is concerned, Democracy is "agnostic," so to speak. It is a set of purely secular beliefs. Democratic beliefs entail no religious or antireligious imperatives. Any conflict between religion and Democratic politics could come only from the intrusion of religious teachings into political affairs. It could not come from Democratic political beliefs in any way penetrating into the area of religion. A Democrat, because of his political beliefs, neither accepts nor rejects any religious teachings.

Catholicism and Democracy are systems of belief and principles which in political practice have no particular relation at all. A Catholic can certainly be a Democrat, but he is a Democrat not because of his religion, only because of his political conviction. The case for Democratic political beliefs can be stated without appealing to Catholicism or any body of religious teachings. In fact, it cannot be very well stated if there is an appeal to religious dogma. For Democratic beliefs are confined to a very narrow area of human conduct. They concern not what people should do, but rather how people can most effectively do certain things. Democracy is merely a method of making collective decisions which members of political communities can use. Catholic religious teachings, it so happens, neither conflict with nor apply to beliefs about this Democratic method of rule. They are simply irrelevant.

This brings us to the close of our inquiry into the relation between Catholicism and Democracy. . . . In closing, let's see now where our inquiry has taken us.

We found that the view that Democracy and Catholicism are incompatible is without warrant. . . . there is no necessary incompatibility between Catholic religious teachings and Democratic beliefs and principles.

We found, too, that the other view, that Democracy is dependent on Catholic moral teachings, is also without warrant. Democracy is a purely secular creed, devoid of religious implications. Democratic beliefs about the principles of political conduct are derived, not from the dogmas of religion, but from the practices of politics. So there is no necessary connection either between Catholicism and Democracy.

I have tried to show how it is that the relation between Catholicism and Democracy is one neither of necessary incompatibility nor of connection, and why this is the case. I hope and trust that the reader . . . now has a clearer understanding than before of the actual relation between Catholicism and Democracy today.

9
Socioeconomic Preconditions

ROBERT A. DAHL and
CHARLES E. LINDBLOM

Polyarchy and Social Pluralism

Polyarchy requires a considerable degree of social pluralism—that is, a diversity of social organizations with a large measure of autonomy with respect to one another. Here again one immediately runs into frustrating problems of measurement. No one can say with much precision how much social pluralism there needs to be, how many social organizations per capita, how autonomous they must be. But the general principle is clear. Social pluralism exists in a society to the extent that there exist a number of different organizations through which control is exerted and over which no unified body of leaders exerts control.

A very high degree of social pluralism does not necessarily mean a very low state of agreement; this is a possible consequence but not an inevitable one. Social pluralism is probably greater in the United States than in France, but agreement is also higher. In the United States a more uniform social indoctrination sufficiently permeates diverse groups so that they can exist with a large measure of agreement on basic method and policy; in France conflicting political norms are indoctrinated in a smaller number of diverse groups and the result is a low state of agreement. . . .

Why is some degree of social pluralism a necessary condition for polyarchy, at least in the modern nation-state? Whatever the case may be in small organizations, in large areas some degree of social pluralism is necessary to polyarchy, for in at least five ways it limits the capacity of officeholders to extend their control over ordinary citizens.

First, social pluralism means the existence of social organizations, organizational loyalties, organizational leaders; in union there is strength. A lone citizen speaking only for himself can often be intimidated by officials; but a spokesman for a body of citizens is less easily cowed. If the official has sanctions, so does the organization leader: publicity, votes, and even the threat of resistance. And besides there is a kind of psychological multiplier effect to organization membership; the knowledge that one is not alone often helps reinforce one's courage and determination. . . . Then, too, organization leaders are likely to have more status than ordinary citizens; they are more likely to move easily in official circles, to command the respect and deference of officials.

Second, social pluralism facilitates competition by insuring the existence of rival leaders with differing loyalties and support. Thus the possibility that officeholders will become uncontrollable is reduced; for officeholders are only one group of leaders, or, more likely, themselves consist of many competing leaders. To wipe out other leaders, revolutionaries must first possess the loyalty and support of more people than they are likely to win over in a pluralistic society; diversified organizational loyalties inhibit this kind of loyalty.

Third, social pluralism facilitates the rise of political

leaders whose main skill is negotiating settlements among conflicting social organizations. Thus the whole cast of the political elites is modified by pluralism; the fanatic, the Messianic type, the leader whose aim is to consolidate the supremacy of some small group tend to trip themselves up on the barrier of groups and group loyalties. . . .

Fourth, social pluralism increases the probability that one is simultaneously a member of more than one social organization; hence action by a leader against what seems to be an enemy organization may in fact strike against his own alliance. . . .

Fifth, social pluralism has some important consequences for information and communication. It increases the probability that alternative sources of information not under direct government control will be technically available to citizens. It is true, of course, that many citizens expose themselves to information that confirms their own norms and those of the group. But as we said earlier, effective criticism of policy or political leaders is a somewhat specialized function; and those who specialize in criticism and communication *can* make use of alternative sources of information. . . .

In these ways social pluralism develops a complex distribution of control. It does not eliminate hierarchical organization but it makes polyarchal government possible. Ordinary citizens control their immediate leaders and are controlled by them. These leaders in turn control other leaders and are controlled by them. Hence a society of reciprocal relationships exists to control government policy. A national political alliance is therefore a vast and slightly shaky enterprise, not a monolith but a pile of billiard balls held together with a poor grade of paste.

SEYMOUR MARTIN LIPSET

Economic Development and Democracy

Perhaps the most widespread generalization linking political systems to other aspects of society has been that democracy is related to the state of economic development. Concretely, this means that the more well-to-do a nation, the greater the chances that it will sustain democracy. From Aristotle down to the present, men have argued that only in a wealthy society in which relatively few citizens lived in real poverty could a situation exist in which the mass of the population could intelligently participate in politics and could develop the self-restraint necessary to avoid succumbing to the appeals of irresponsible demagogues. A society divided between a large impoverished mass and a small favored elite would result either in oligarchy . . . or in tyranny. . . .

As a means of concretely testing this hypothesis, various indices of economic development—wealth, industrialization, urbanization and education—have been defined, and averages (means) have been computed for the countries which have been classified as more or less democratic in the Anglo-Saxon world and Europe and Latin America.

In each case, the average wealth, degree of industrialization and urbanization, and level of education is much higher for the more democratic countries. . . .

The main indices of *wealth* used here are per capita income, number of persons per motor vehicle and per physician, and the number of radios, telephones, and newspapers per thousand persons. The differences are striking on every

From "Some Social Requisites of Democracy: Economic Development and Political Legitimacy" by Seymour Martin Lipset, *American Political Science Review,* LIII (March 1959), pp. 75–79, 83–85.

score. . . . In the more democratic European countries, there are 17 persons per motor vehicle compared to 143 for the less democratic countries. In the less dictatorial Latin American countries there are 99 persons per motor vehicle, as against 274 for the more dictatorial ones. Income differences for the groups are also sharp, dropping from an average per capita income of $695 for the more democratic countries of Europe to $308 for the less democratic ones; the corresponding difference for Latin America is from $171 to $119. The ranges are equally consistent, with the lowest per capita income in each group falling in the "less democratic" category, and the highest in the "more democratic" one.

Industrialization—indices of wealth are clearly related to this, of course—is measured by the percentage of employed males in agriculture, and the per capita commercially produced "energy" being used in the country, measured in terms of tons of coal per person per year. Both of these indices show equally consistent results. The average percentage of employed males working in agriculture and related occupations was 21 in the "more democratic" European countries, and 41 in the "less democratic," 52 in the "less dictatorial" Latin American countries, and 67 in the "more dictatorial." The differences in per capita energy employed in the country are equally large.

The degree of *urbanization* is also related to the existence of democracy. Three different indices of urbanization are available from data compiled by International Urban Research (Berkeley, California), the percentage of the population in places of 20,000 and over, the percentage in communities of 100,000 and over, and also the percentage residing in standard metropolitan areas. On all three of these indices of urbanization, the more democratic countries score higher than the less democratic, for both of the political culture areas under investigation.

Many have suggested that the better educated the population of a country, the better the chances for democracy, and the comparative data available support this proposition. The "more democratic" countries of Europe are almost entirely literate: the lowest has a rate of 96 per cent, while the "less democratic" nations have an average literacy rate of 85 per cent. In Latin America, the difference is between an average rate of 74 per cent for the "less dictatorial" countries and 46 per cent for the "more dictatorial." The educational enrollment per thousand total population at three different levels, primary, post-primary, and higher educational, is equally consistently related to the degree of democracy. The tremendous disparity is shown by the extreme cases of Haiti and the United States. Haiti has fewer children (11 per thousand) attending school in the primary grade than the United States has attending colleges (almost 18 per thousand).

The relationship between education and democracy is worth more extensive treatment since an entire philosophy of democratic government has seen in increased education the spread of the basic requirement of democracy. . . . Education presumably broadens men's outlooks, enables them to understand the need for norms of tolerance, restrains them from adhering to extremist and monistic doctrines, and increases their capacity to make rational electoral choices.

The evidence bearing on the contribution of education to democracy is even more direct and strong in connection with individual behavior *within* countries, than it is in cross-national correlations. Data gathered by public opinion research agencies which have questioned people in different countries with regard to their belief in various democratic norms of tolerance for opposition, to their attitudes toward ethnic or racial minorities, and with regard to their belief in multi-party as against one-party systems have found that *the most important single factor differentiating those giving democratic responses from others has been education.* The higher one's education, the more likely one is to believe in democratic values and support democratic practices. All the relevant studies indicate that education is far more significant than income or occupation.

These findings should lead us to anticipate a far higher correlation between national levels of education and political practice than in fact we do find. Germany and France have been among the best educated nations of Europe, but this by itself clearly did not stabilize their democracies. It may be, however, that education has served to inhibit other anti-democratic forces. Post-Nazi data from Germany indicate clearly that higher education is linked to rejection of strong-man and one-party government. . . .

A number of processes underlie these correlations, observed in many areas of the world, . . . of a high level of education and literacy in creating or sustaining belief in democratic norms. Perhaps most important is the relationship between modernization and the form of the "class struggle." For the lower strata, economic development, which means increased income, greater economic security, and higher education, permit those in this status to develop longer time perspectives and more complex and gradualist views of politics. A belief in secular reformist gradualism can only be the ideology of a relatively well-to-do lower class. Increased wealth and education also serve democracy by increasing the extent to which the lower strata are exposed to cross pressures which will reduce the intensity of their commitment to given ideologies and make them less receptive to supporting extremist ones. . . .

Increased wealth is not only related causally to the development of democracy by changing the social conditions of the workers, but it also affects the poltical role of the middle class through changing the shape of the stratification structure so that it shifts from an elongated pyramid, with a large lower-class base, to a diamond with a growing middle class. A large middle class plays a mitigating role in moderating conflict since it is able to reward moderate and democratic parties and penalize extremist groups.

National income is also related to the political values and style of the upper class. The poorer a country, and the lower the absolute standard of living of the lower classes, the greater the pressure on the upper strata to treat the lower classes as beyond the pale of human society, as vulgar, as innately inferior, as a lower caste. The sharp difference in the style of living between those at the top and those at the bottom makes this psychologically necessary. Consequently, the upper strata also tend to regard political rights for the lower strata, particularly the right to share in power, as essentially absurd and immoral. The upper strata not only resist democracy themselves, but their often arrogant political behavior serves to intensify extremist reactions on the part of the lower classes.

The general income level of a nation will also affect its receptivity to democratic political tolerance norms. The values which imply that it does not matter greatly which side rules, that error can be tolerated even in the governing party, can best develop where (a) the government has little power to affect the crucial life chances of most powerful groups, or (b) there is enough wealth in the country so that it actually does not make too much difference if some redistribution does take place. If loss of office is seen as meaning serious loss for major power groups, then they will be readier to resort to more drastic measures in seeking to retain or secure office. The wealth level will also affect the extent to which given countries can develop "universalistic" norms among their civil servants and politicians (selection based on competence; performance without favoritism). The poorer the country, the greater the emphasis which is placed on nepotism, i.e., support of kin and friends. The weakness of the universalistic norms reduces the opportunity to develop efficient bureaucracy, a condition for a modern democratic state.

Less directly linked but seemingly still associated with greater wealth is the presence of intermediary organizations and institutions which can act as sources of countervailing power, and recruiters of participants in the political process in the manner discussed by Tocqueville and other exponents of what has come to be known as the theory of the "mass society." They have argued that a society without a multitude of organizations relatively independent of the central state power has a high dictatorial as well as a revolutionary potential. Such organizations serve a number of functions necessary to democracy: they are a source of countervailing power, inhibiting the state or any single major source of private power from dominating all political resources; they are a source of new opinions; they can be the means of communicating ideas, particularly opposition ideas, to a large section of the citizenry; they serve to train men in the skills of politics; and they help increase the level of interest and participation in politics. Although there are no reliable data which bear on the relationship between national patterns of voluntary organizations and national political systems, evidence from studies of individual behavior within a number of different countries demonstrates that, independently of other factors, men who belong to associations are more likely to hold democratic opinions on questions concerning tolerance and party systems, and are more likely to participate in the political process—to be active or to vote. Since we also know that, within countries, the more well-to-do and the better educated one is the more likely he is to belong to voluntary organizations, it seems likely that the propensity to form such groups is a function of level of income and opportunities for leisure within given nations.

DANIEL LERNER

Urbanization, Literacy, Participation

. . . The secular evolution of a participant society appears to involve a regular sequence of three phases. Urbanization comes first, for cities alone have developed the complex of skills and resources which characterize the modern industrial economy. Within this urban matrix develop both of the attributes which distinguish the next two phases—literacy and media growth. There is a close reciprocal relationship between these, for the literate develop the media which in turn spread literacy. But, historically, literacy performs the key function in the second phase. The capacity to read, at first acquired by relatively few people, equips them to perform the varied tasks required in the modernizing society. Not until the third phase, when the elaborate technology of industrial development is fairly well advanced, does a society begin to produce newspapers, radio networks, and motion pictures on a mass scale. This, in turn, accelerates the spread of literacy. Out of this interaction develop those institutions of participation (e.g., voting) which we find in all advanced modern societies. . . .

We shall later examine the idea that a common psychological mechanism underlies these phases—that it is the more empathic individuals who respond, in the first place, to the lure of cities, schools, media. Urban residence, schooling, media exposure then train and reinforce the empathic predisposition that was already present. On this view, the modern "style of life" can nowadays be acquired as a whole

From *The Passing of Traditional Society* by Daniel Lerner. New York: The Free Press, pp. 60–62.

by individuals living in modernizing societies. This interpretation is quite plausible, but it does not clarify what happens to empathic individuals who are ready and able to modernize more rapidly and completely than their society permits. . . . Our data on 73 countries, distributed over all the continents of the earth, indicate that many millions of individuals everywhere are in the same position. This further suggests that the model of modernization follows an autonomous historical logic—that each phase tends to generate the next phase by some mechanism which operates independently of cultural or doctrinal variations. To understand the position of those millions who may be caught in some historical lag today, we look more closely at our three phases.

The first phase, then, is *urbanization.* It is the transfer of population from scattered hinterlands to urban centers that stimulates the needs and provides the conditions needed for "take-off" toward widespread participation. Only cities require a largely literate population to function properly—for the organization of urban life assumes enough literacy to read labels, sign checks, ride subways. . . . The primitive social function of literacy, as of all skills, is to reduce waste of human effort. Its higher function is to train the skilled labor force with which cities develop the industrial complex that produces commodities for cash customers, including newspapers and radios and movies for media consumers. Cities produce the machine tools of modernization. Accordingly, increases of urbanization tend in every society to multiply national increases in literacy and media participation. By drawing people from their rural communities, cities create the demand for impersonal communication. By promoting literacy and media, cities supply this demand. . . .

Of this second phase, *literacy* is both the index and agent. To spread consumption of urban products beyond the city limits, literacy is an efficient instrument. The great symbol of this phase is the Sears-Roebuck catalogue. The mail-order house replaces the peddler only when enough people can read catalogues and write letters. In this sense literacy is also the basic skill required for operation of a media system. Only the literate produce the media contents which mainly the literate consume. . . . For, when most people in a society have become literate, they tend to generate all sorts of new desires and to develop the means of satisfying them.

It is this interplay of new desires and satisfactions which characterizes the third phase of modernization, namely *media participation.* Once the people are equipped to handle the new experiences produced by mobility (via their move to the city), and to handle the new experiences conveyed by media (via their literacy), they now seek the satisfactions which integrate these skills. . . . To satisfy this new desire requires the personal skill of empathy which, when spread among large numbers of persons, makes possible the social institution of media participation. [For a discussion of the concept of empathy, see pp. 293–294.] This was the phase in which the West developed the "penny press," early symbol of the accelerating supply and demand for media products, which continues today with the pocket radio and the portable TV. It is characteristic of this phase, as the production-consumption reciprocal of media participation develops, that economists come to find production of radio sets a useful index of growth in total industrial production.

For, rising media participation tends to raise participation in all sectors of the social system. In accelerating the spread of empathy, it also diffuses those other modern demands to which participant institutions have responded: in the consumer's economy via cash (and credit), in the public forum via opinion, in the representative polity via voting.

W. H. MORRIS-JONES

Participation and Apathy

What . . . are the grounds on which it might be argued that there is a duty to exercise the right to vote? This question can be viewed under . . . three heads. . . .

The duty to vote may, in the first place, be a duty to oneself. Duties of this kind are sometimes important and some of them appear to be universal. An obligation not to "neglect oneself" would be widely accepted, and a failure to meet this obligation would be held (by people of quite different fundamental beliefs) to be a moral failure—unless, of course, the neglect was considered necessary in order to fulfill some even more important obligation. But more specific duties to oneself differ from one self to another. What is involved in my not neglecting myself will not be the same as what is involved in your not neglecting yourself. Clearly the duty to vote is a very specific duty which will be real (as a duty to oneself) only in the case of certain people. . . . We may admit that in the *polis* the complete man is the citizen. But where the conditions of the polis do not exist, any attempt to secure active citizenship on the part of all individuals is likely to fail. Nor is this necessarily a matter for regret; the complete man of the large modern State may follow one of several patterns, of which the politically active citizen is but one.

The duty to vote may be a duty to assist in the protection of one's group or section. Here again we may express a skeptical view. Of course it is possible to imagine situations

From "In Defense of Apathy: Some Doubts on the Duty to Vote" by W. H. Morris-Jones, *Political Studies,* II (February 1954), pp. 33–37. Oxford: The Clarendon Press.

in which one's membership of a particular group or section will carry with it an obligation to vote as a means of expressing, presumably for the guidance of the rulers, the views of the group. If a policy of free wheat imports is threatened, then as a wheat farmer I may have a duty to cast a vote (so far as possible) against the proposal, as a way of protecting my fellow farmers from a course which would threaten their livelihood. How far this duty is real depends . . . on circumstances and attitudes. But it is difficult to see that group loyalty can be held to be so important, and so continuously important, as to give rise to a clear and universal duty to vote.

The most serious grounds of a duty to vote are undoubtedly those which arise from a consideration of the needs of the political community as a whole. And here it will be enough if we consider the case of parliamentary democracy. How far do the institutions of such a democracy demand of us that we should exercise our right to vote? The answer to this question may differ to some extent according to which of two general ways of regarding parliamentary democracy we choose to adopt. We may believe that this system of government rests primarily on participation and consent and hold that the more there is of these (measured quantitatively) the better. In that case, considerable emphasis on the duty to vote may be expected, for to withhold one's vote is to make the system as a whole the poorer. . . . But this is not the only way of looking at democracy. We may prefer to regard it as above all a manner of dealing with business, a way of going about things. On this view, parliamentary democracy is distinguished by its love of trial and its willingness to admit error; it demands expression of interests which need to be adjusted, and it requires discussions of viewpoints which are to be exchanged and where possible reconciled. Participation and consent may be useful and desirable, but only as aids to a complete and adequate debate. In this case, the duty to vote appears in a different and less glowing light.

All that is imperative for the health of parliamentary democracy is that the right to vote should be exercised to the extent necessary to ensure that the play of ideas and clash of interests can take place. . . .

There is, however, one special case to consider. It may be felt that a widespread failure to use the right to vote may result in a threat to the continued existence of parliamentary democracy, that the very right to vote can only be secure if a duty to vote is effectively recognized. There is a plausibility about this argument; we have been told often enough that it is the apathy of the electorate that gives dictators their opportunity. But is this really so? Surely the successes of Stalin, Mussolini, and Hitler are sufficiently explained by other factors: inadequate or mistaken notions about the nature of democracy among those who were not apathetic; impatient selfishness of group interests; sheer incompetence of those in power; and so on. When parliamentary democracy fails it is more likely to be because of a failure of vision or of will or of moral courage among those whose business is politics than the consequence of an inadequate interest in politics on the part of the electorate. . . .

A defense of apathy is not, however, exhausted simply by indicating skepticism about the importance or extent of certain political duties. Apathy can be defended on more positive grounds, on the ground that it is a political virtue. . . . The apathetic part of the electorate . . . is a sign of a liberal democracy that is prepared to recognize that "there are and always will be some persons for whom political activity would be largely a waste of time and talent" and is prepared to leave them alone to devote themselves to their gardens, their music, or whatever their passion may be.

But the presence of an apathetic part of the electorate is even more than a sign of understanding and tolerance of human variety; it may also have a beneficial effect on the tone of political life itself. For this group is a more or less vivid reminder of the proper limitations of politics, a more or less effective counter-force to the fanatics who constitute the real danger to liberal democracy. A State which has "cured" apathy is likely to be a State in which too many people have fallen into the error of believing in the efficiency of political solutions for the problems of ordinary lives. It is no part of the job of a student and teacher of politics to preach this doctrine; rather he should recognize that his work makes him prone to commit the error.

MORRIS ROSENBERG

Some Determinants of Apathy

It has been observed that political apathy is a very widespread phenomenon in American culture. Whether one measures apathy by the criterion of political involvement, knowledge or activity, the number of people who satisfy the culturally defined desiderata of participation is small.

There are those who consider this a serious malfunctioning of democracy. If men are to maintain control over their political destinies, they must be aware of what is going on, and must take a hand in determining public policy. On the other hand, there are some political theorists who find such apathy a favorable, rather than an unfavorable, sign. They interpret it to mean that the society is fundamentally contented, is characterized by consensus rather than by broad cleavages, and is basically stable.

If we accept the view that the democratic ideal encourages political interest and participation, then the question naturally arises: what are the factors which bring about this absence of political interest and activity? In order to cast some light on this question, an exploratory study, designed to reveal the range and variation of factors which contribute to political apathy, was undertaken. Seventy qualitative interviews were conducted with a non-random sample of respondents, most of whom resided in Ithaca, New York. The interviews were of an unstructured type, designed to encourage the respondent to reveal his views regarding the political process with a minimum of direction and a maximum of spontaneity. We did not undertake to obtain

From "Some Determinants of Political Apathy" by Morris Rosenberg, *Public Opinion Quarterly*, 18 (Winter 1954), pp. 349–366.

statistically reliable data but, rather, sought to gather ideas and hypotheses for more systematic research. The results presented here, therefore, lay no claim to representing scientific proof, but are designed to serve as suggestive hypotheses.

Limitations of space prohibit a discussion of the total range of factors which were revealed in these interviews and which appeared to contribute to political indifference and inactivity, but three general factors merit discussion: (1) the threatening consequences of political activity, (2) the futility of political activity, and (3) the absence of spurs to interest and participation.

. . . the democratic right of freedom of speech does not insure that people will feel free to express their political convictions publicly at all times. Threats of governmental action will deter some. Others will be blocked from talking or acting in behalf of their political beliefs out of fear of losing friends, alienating neighbors, endangering marriages, jeopardizing their positions in groups, losing business, jeopardizing their jobs, endangering production in their plants, facing community pressures, or exposing their feelings of self-esteem to threat. These are consequences which many people are unwilling to face and, to avoid these consequences, they impose a self-censorship on their political expression, participation, and even emotional involvement. . . . In a democratic society, politics are *controversial*, and controversiality, while it may encourage interest, also has potential interpersonal consequences which may foster political inactivity.

. . . many people may be deterred from political activity by the conviction that their efforts will be futile. An individual may feel that he is but one among so many; that he is a very "little man" compared with very much more powerful agents; that the agents of political decision–representatives, machines, "the government," certain powerful anonymous forces—are unable or unwilling to heed his voice or follow his will; that the political reality is hopelessly remote from the ideal; or that the hopelessness of political victory makes any effort pointless. It may be observed that these consequences of apathy derive from the particular nature of the social and political structure. The *mass nature of the society,* characterized by wide disparities of power, promotes the sense of personal insignificance; the *centralization of government* fosters a sense of remoteness from the key decision-making processes; the *periodic elections* produce a discontinuous exercise of power; the *system of representation* draws power from the citizen and grants it to the representative; and so on. In other words, a political structure established with the aim of implementing democracy may unwittingly establish the conditions for political apathy.

. . . many people are not motivated because of the absence of a shining example by others. Furthermore, whatever guilt they feel may be assuaged by the observation that others (including the most respectable) are equally apathetic. It is reasonable to speculate, incidentally, that an individual who might be ready for action would be discouraged by the spectacle of such widespread apathy; he might feel that he could not carry the burden with so little help. Thus apathy may become self-reinforcing.

People may be members of groups in which apathy is a positive group norm. A young person became associated with a group of cynics who considered concern with political affairs an expression of philistine conformism. She remained inactive partly out of fear of the scorn and ridicule which would greet any manifestation of social responsibility.

Thus, interpersonal factors may operate in several ways to promote political apathy. In the first place, the individual may receive no positive encouragement from others to participate. In the second place, the guilt feelings arising from an individual's inactivity may be assuaged by the observation that others in the community are also inactive.

An individual, ready for action, may be discouraged by the observation that the apathy of other people increases his own burden of political work. Finally, the individual may be a member of a group in which political apathy is a *positive group norm*—a group which would discourage political action.

Apathy may thus be circular and self-reinforcing. The apathetic individual is not encouraged, and actually may be discouraged, from being politically active. Each individual may thus be reassured and reinforced in his political nonparticipation by the observation that others behave in a similar fashion. Thus the individual who, by virtue of his own apathy, encourages apathy in others, may also be influenced in a similar fashion by them.

In this paper we have suggested several factors which in some cases contribute to political apathy. That these factors have some significance is clearly suggested by the data, but their relative importance, their statistical distribution among various population sub-groups, and their interrelationships must remain subjects for more systematic research.

Space limitations prevent us from discussing in detail a number of additional factors which our data suggest might contribute to political apathy. It appears worth noting, however, that some people are apathetic because they feel there is no need to do anything; they are contented with the social and political system, have faith in their representatives, and see no need for change. This basic contentment tends to be linked with a confidence in the basic stability of the society. There are others who would favor change, but who feel that there is no real difference between the two major parties; the outcome of elections, therefore, lacks significance. Some people do not participate actively because of the incertitude of their political convictions; to them politics may be confused, complicated, contradictory; political communications may be rejected as propaganda; or the individuals may be uncertain regarding their own political activity. Others may be too exhausted by the pressure of other activities to pay much attention to it. Certain women express the attitude that political activity would be out of keeping with their social roles. Some people's reluctance to think about political matters ranges from a certain degree of mental laziness to a phobia toward serious thought which borders on the pathological. These and other factors would have to be examined before an adequate understanding of the determinants of political apathy could be achieved.

10
Political Preconditions

☙ SEYMOUR MARTIN LIPSET

Effectiveness and Legitimacy

. . . the stability of a given democratic system depends not only on the system's efficiency in modernization, but also upon the *effectiveness* and *legitimacy* of the political system. By effectiveness is meant the actual performance of a political system, the extent to which it satisfies the basic functions of government as defined by the expectations of most members of a society, and the expectations of powerful groups within it which might threaten the system, such as the armed forces. . . . Legitimacy involves the capacity of a political system to engender and maintain the belief that existing political institutions are the most appropriate or proper ones for the society. The extent to which contemporary democratic political systems are legitimate depends in large measure upon the ways in which the key issues which have historically divided the society have been resolved. . . .

While effectiveness is primarily an instrumental dimen-

From "Some Social Requisites of Democracy: Economic Development and Political Legitimacy" by Seymour Martin Lipset, *American Political Science Review,* LIII (March 1959), pp. 86–91.

sion, legitimacy is more affective and evaluative. Groups will regard a political system as legitimate or illegitimate according to the way in which its values fit in with their primary values. Important segments of the German army, civil service, and aristocratic classes rejected the Weimar Republic not because it was ineffective, but because its symbolism and basic values negated their own. Legitimacy, in and of itself, may be associated with many forms of political organization, including oppressive ones. Feudal societies, before the advent of industrialism, undoubtedly enjoyed the basic loyalty of most of their members. Crises of legitimacy are primarily a recent historical phenomenon, following the rise of sharp cleavages among groups which have been able, because of mass communication resources, to organize around different values than those previously considered to be the only legitimate ones for the total society.

A crisis of legitimacy is a crisis of change, and therefore its roots, as a factor affecting the stability of democratic systems, must be sought in the character of change in modern society. It may be hypothesized that crises of legitimacy occur during a transition to a new social structure, if (a) all major groups do not secure access to the political system early in the transitional period, or at least as soon as they develop political demands; or, if (b) the *status* of major conservative institutions is threatened during the period of structural change. After a new social structure is established, if the new system is unable to sustain the expectations of major groups (on the grounds of "effectiveness") for a long enough period to develop legitimacy upon the new basis, a new crisis may develop. . . .

If, however, the status of major conservative groups and symbols is not threatened during this transitional period even though they lose most of their power, democracy seems to be much more secure. Striking evidence of the link between the preserved legitimacy of conservative institutions and democracy is the relationship between monarchy and democracy. Given the role of the American and French republican revolutions as the initiators of modern democratic political movements, the fact that ten out of twelve of the stable European and English-speaking democracies are monarchies seems a rather ludicrous correlation. Great Britain, Sweden, Norway, Denmark, the Netherlands, Belgium, Luxembourg, Australia, Canada, and New Zealand are kingdoms; while the only republics which meet the . . . conditions of stable democratic procedures . . . are the United States, Switzerland and Uruguay. . . .

The preservation of the monarchy has apparently retained for the system the loyalty of the aristocratic, traditionalist, and clerical sectors of the population which resented increased democratization and equalitarianism. And, by more graciously accepting the lower strata, by not resisting to the point that revolution might be necessary, the conservative orders won or retained the loyalty of the new "citizens." Where monarchy was overthrown by revolution, and orderly succession was broken, those forces aligned with monarchy have sometimes continued to refuse legitimacy to republican successors down to the fifth generation or more.

The one constitutional monarchy which became a Fascist dictatorship, Italy, was, like the French Republic, relatively new and still illegitimate for major groups in the society. The House of Savoy alienated the Catholics by destroying the temporal power of the Popes, and was also not a legitimate successor in the old Kingdom of the Two Sicilies. Catholics, in fact, were forbidden by the church to participate in Italian politics until close to World War I, and the church rescinded its original ban only because of its fear of the Socialists. A similar attitude was taken by French Catholics to the Third Republic during the same period. Both Italian and French democracy have had to operate for much of their histories without loyal support from important groups in their society, both on the left and on the right. Thus, one main source of legitimacy lies in the continuity of primary conservative and integrative institutions during a transitional period in which new social institutions are emerging.

The second general type of loss of legitimacy is, as indicated above, related to the way in which societies handle the "entry into politics" problem. The determination of when new social groups shall obtain access to the political process affects the legitimacy of the political system, either for conservative or for emerging groups. In the 19th century these new groups were primarily industrial workers; the "entry into politics" crisis of the 20th century typically involves colonial elites, and peasant peoples. Whenever new groups become politically active (e.g., when the workers first seek access to economic and political power through economic organization and the suffrage, when the bourgeoisie demanded access to and participation in government, when colonial elites demand control over their own system), comparatively easy access to the *legitimate* political institutions tends to win the loyalty of the new groups to the system, and they in turn can permit the old dominating strata to maintain their own status integrity. In nations such as Germany, where access was denied for prolonged periods, first to the bourgeoisie and later to the workers, and where force was used to restrict access, the lower strata were alienated from the system, and were led to adopt extremist ideologies which, in turn, alienated the more established groups from an acceptance of the workers' political movement as a legitimate alternative.

Political systems which denied new strata access to power except through revolutionary means also inhibited the growth of legitimacy by introducing millennial hopes into the political arena. Groups which feel obliged to push their way into the body politic through forceful means tend to overexaggerate the possibilities which political participation affords. Their hopes are for far more than the inherent limitations of political stability permit. Consequently, democratic regimes born under such stress will not only face the difficulty of being regarded as illegitimate by those groups loyal to the *ancien régime,* but may be also rejected by those whose millennial hopes were not fulfilled by the change. France seems to offer an example of such a phenomenon. Right-wing clericalists have viewed the Republic as illegitimate, while sections of the lower strata still impatiently await millennial fulfillment. Many of the newly independent nations of Asia and Africa face the problem of winning the loyalties of the masses to democratic states which can do little to fulfill the utopian objectives set by nationalist movements during the period of colonialism, and the transitional struggle to independence.

We have discussed several conditions bearing upon the maintenance, or the initial securing of legitimacy, by a political system. Assuming reasonable effectiveness, if the status of major conservative groups is threatened, or if access to the political system is denied at crucial periods, the legitimacy of the system will remain in question. Even in legitimate systems, a breakdown of effectiveness, repeatedly or for a long period, will endanger its stability. . . .

As we have seen, nations may vary in the extent to which their political institutions are viewed as legitimate by different strata. And knowledge concerning the relative degree of legitimacy of a nation's political institutions is of key importance in any effort to analyze the stability of these institutions when faced with a crisis of effectiveness. The relationship between different degrees of legitimacy and effectiveness in specific political systems may be more graphically presented in the form of a four-fold table, with examples of countries characterized by the various possible combinations.

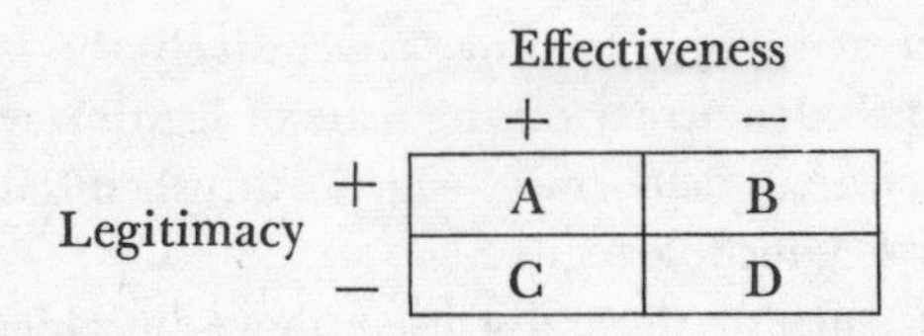

		Effectiveness +	Effectiveness −
Legitimacy	+	A	B
	−	C	D

Societies which fall in box A, those which are high on the scales of both legitimacy and effectiveness, will clearly have stable political systems. Nations like the United States, Sweden, and Britain satisfy the basic political needs of their citizens, have efficient bureaucracies and political decision-making systems, possess traditional legitimacy through long-term continuity of the key symbols of sovereignty, the monarchy or constitution, and do not contain any important minorities whose basic values run counter to those of the system. Ineffective and illegitimate regimes, those which would be found in box D, must, of course, by definition be unstable and break down, unless they are dictatorships maintaining themselves by force such as the governments of Hungary and eastern Germany today. The political experiences of different countries in the early 1930's illustrate the effect of varying combinations of legitimacy and effectiveness. In the late 1920's, neither the German nor the Austrian republics were held legitimate by large and powerful segments of their populations, but nevertheless remained reasonably effective. In the four-fold stable, they fell in box C.

When the effectiveness of the governments of the various countries broke down in the 1930's, those societies which were high on the scale of legitimacy remained democratic, while countries which were low, such as Germany, Austria, and Spain, lost their freedom, and France narrowly escaped a similar fate. Or to put the changes in terms of location in the four-fold table, countries which shifted from A to B remained democratic, while the political systems of those which shifted from C to D broke down. It remained for the military defeat in 1940 to prove conclusively the low position of French democracy on the scale of legitimacy. It was the sole defeated democracy which furnished large-scale support for a Quisling regime.

Situations such as those discussed above in which either legitimacy or effectiveness is high while the other is low demonstrate the utility of this type of analysis. From a short-range point of view, a highly effective but illegitimate system, such as a well-governed colony, is more unstable than regimes which are relatively low in effectiveness and high in legitimacy. . . . The link between the analysis of legitimacy and the earlier discussion of the contribution of economic development to democracy is evident in the processes through which regimes low in legitimacy may gain it, and conversely in those which are related to the collapse of a legitimate system. Prolonged effectiveness which lasts over a number of generations may give legitimacy to a political system; in the modern world, such effectiveness mainly means constant economic development. Thus those nations which adapted most successfully to the requirements of an industrial system had the fewest internal political strains, and either preserved their traditional legitimacy, the monarchy, or developed new strong symbols of legitimacy.

ROBERT A. DAHL

The Opposition

Somewhere in the world, at this moment, a political group is probably engaged in the antique art of imprisoning, maiming, torturing, and killing its opponents. Somewhere, as you read these words, a government and its opponents are no doubt trying to coerce one another by violent means. For without much question the most commonplace way for a government to deal with its opponents is to employ violence.

Of the three great milestones in the development of democratic institutions—the right to participate in governmental decisions by casting a vote, the right to be represented, and the right of an organized opposition to appeal for votes against the government in elections and in parliament—the last is, in a highly developed form, so wholly modern that there are people now living who were born before it had appeared in most of Western Europe.

Throughout recorded history, it seems, stable institutions providing legal, orderly, peaceful modes of political opposition have been rare. If peaceful antagonism between factions is uncommon, peaceful opposition among organized, permanent political parties is an even more exotic historical phenomenon. Legal party opposition, in fact, is a recent unplanned invention that has been confined for the most part to a handful of countries in Western Europe and the English-speaking world. Even more recent are organized political parties that compete peacefully in elections for the votes of the great bulk of the adult population who can

From *Political Oppositions in Western Democracies* by Robert A. Dahl. New Haven: Yale University Press, 1966, pp. xi, xiv, xvi.

exercise the franchise under nearly universal suffrage. Universal suffrage and enduring mass parties are, with few exceptions, products of the past century. It should not be altogether surprising, then, that of the 113 members of the United Nations in 1964, only about 30 had political systems in which full legal opposition among organized political parties had existed throughout the preceding decade. . . .

Political systems with organized political parties protected by law are, as I have already said, a modern development. Historical analogies can generally be found for any innovation; nonetheless, the opposition political party as we know it today represents a radical break with older forms of opposition.

Because some conflict of views seems to be unavoidable in human affairs, political societies have always had to deal somehow with the fact of opposition. Nevertheless, that there might legitimately exist an organized group within the political system to oppose, criticize, and if possible, oust the leading officials of government was until recently an unfamiliar and generally unacceptable notion. When the men at the American Constitutional Convention of 1787 expressed their fear of "factions" as the bane of republics, they spoke the traditional view. . . .

The system of managing the major political conflicts of a society by allowing one or more opposition parties to compete with the governing parties for votes in elections and in parliament is, then, not only modern; surely it is also one of the greatest and most unexpected social discoveries that man has ever stumbled onto. Up until two centuries ago, no one had accurately foreseen it. Today one is inclined to regard the existence of an opposition party as very nearly the most distinctive characteristic of democracy itself; and we take the absence of an opposition party as evidence, if not always conclusive proof, for the absence of democracy.

JAMES W. PROTHRO and CHARLES M. GRIGG

Democratic "Fundamentals"

The idea that consensus on fundamental principles is essential to democracy is a recurrent proposition in political theory. Perhaps, because of its general acceptance, the proposition has never been formulated in very precise terms. When authoritative sources state, for example, that "a successful democracy requires the existence of a large measure of consensus in society," exactly what is meant? We assume that the term "successful democracy," although far from precise, carries a widely shared meaning among political scientists. But we are not told in this typical assertion on what *issues* or *problems* consensus must exist. Presumably they are the basic issues about how political power should be won. Nor are we told what degree of agreement democracy requires. Since the word "consensus" is used to refer to "general agreement or concord," however, a "large measure of consensus" presumably falls somewhere close to 100 per cent. For the purpose of examining the proposition as it is generally formulated, then, we interpret it as asserting: a necessary condition for the existence of a democratic government is widespread agreement (approaching 100 per cent) among the adult members of society on at least the basic questions about how political power is won. Specifically, we propose to submit this proposition to empirical examination in an effort to give it more precise meaning and

From "Fundamental Principles of Democracy: Bases of Agreement and Disagreement" by James W. Prothro and Charles M. Grigg, *Journal of Politics,* 22:2 (May 1960), pp. 276–277, 282–284, 291–293.

to discover bases of agreement and/or disagreement on fundamental principles. . . .

Our research design was based on the major assumption that the United States is a democracy. Taking this point for granted, we prepared an interviewing schedule around the presumably basic principles of democracy and interviewed samples of voters in two American cities to elicit their attitudes toward these principles.

While the general research design was thus quite simple, the preparation of a questionnaire including the basic points on which agreement is thought to be necessary was a difficult and critical step. From the literature on consensus . . . and from general literature on democracy, however, we conclude that the principles regarded as most essential to democracy are majority rule and minority rights (or freedom to dissent). At the abstract level, then, our interviewers asked for expressions of agreement or disagreement on the following statements:

Principle of Democracy Itself

Democracy is the best form of government.

Principle of Majority Rule

Public officials should be chosen by majority vote.

Every citizen should have an equal chance to influence government policy.

Principle of Minority Rights

The minority should be free to criticize majority decisions.

People in the minority should be free to try to win majority support for their opinions.

From these general statements, specific embodiments of the principles of democracy were derived.

Principle of Majority Rule in Specific Terms

1. In a city referendum, only people who are well informed about the problem being voted on should be allowed to vote.

2. In a city referendum deciding on tax-supported undertakings, only tax-payers should be allowed to vote.

3. If a Negro were legally elected mayor of this city, the white people should not allow him to take office.

4. If a Communist were legally elected mayor of this city, the people should not allow him to take office.

5. A professional organization like the AMA (the American Medical Association) has a right to try to increase the influence of doctors by getting them to vote as a bloc in elections.

Principle of Minority Rights in Specific Terms

6. If a person wanted to make a speech in this city against churches and religion, he should be allowed to speak.

7. If a person wanted to make a speech in this city favoring government ownership of all the railroads and big industries, he should be allowed to speak.

8. If an admitted Communist wanted to make a speech in this city favoring Communism, he should be allowed to speak.

9. A Negro should not be allowed to run for mayor of this city.

10. A Communist should not be allowed to run for mayor of this city.

These specific propositions are designed to embody the principles of majority rule and minority rights in such a clear fashion that a "correct" or "democratic" response can be deduced from endorsement of the general principles. The democratic responses to statements 1 and 2 are negative, for example, since a restriction of the franchise to the well-informed or to tax-payers would violate the principle that "Every citizen should have an equal chance to influence government policy." The same general principle requires an affirmative answer to the fifth statement, which applies the right of people to "influence government policy" to the election efforts of a specific professional group. The correct responses to statements 3 and 4 are negative because denial of an office to any person "legally elected" would violate the principle that "Public officials should be chosen by majority vote."

Of the five statements derived from the broad principle of minority rights, 6, 7 and 8 put the right of "the minority . . . to criticize majority decisions" and "to try to win majority support for their opinions" in terms of specific minority spokesmen; agreement is therefore the correct or democratic answer. Disagreement is the correct response to statements 9 and 10, since denial of the right to seek office to members of minority ethnic or ideological groups directly violates their right "to try to win majority support for their opinions."

Since the proposition being tested asserts the existence of consensus, the interviewing sample could logically have been drawn from any group of Americans. . . . The registered voters of two academic communities, Ann Arbor, Michigan, and Tallahassee, Florida, were selected as the sampling population, primarily because they fitted the needs of the hypothesis, and partly because of their accessibility. Although a nation-wide survey was ruled out simply on the ground of costs, these atypical communities offer certain advantages for our problem. First, they do permit at least a limited regional comparison of attitudes on democratic fundamentals. Second, they skew the sample by over-representing the more highly educated, thus permitting detailed comparison of the highly educated with the poorly educated, a comparison that could hardly be made with samples from more typical communities.

The over-representation of the highly educated also served to "stack the cards" in favor of the proposition on consensus. Since our hypothesis holds that consensus is limited, we further stacked the cards against the hypothesis by choosing the sample from registered voters rather than from all residents of the two communities. Although the necessity of consensus is stated in terms of the society as a whole, a line of regression is available in the argument that it need exist only among those who take part in politics. Hence our restriction of the sample to a population of registered voters.

In each city the sample was drawn by the system of random numbers from the official lists of registered voters. The sample represents one per cent of the registered voters from the current registration list in each of the two communities.

The attitudes of voters in selected Midwestern and Southern communities offer no support for the hypothesis that democracy requires a large measure of consensus among the carriers of the creed, i.e., those most consistently in accord with democratic principles. As expected, general consensus was found on the idea of democracy itself and on the broad principles of majority rule and minority rights, but it disappeared when these principles were put in more specific form. Indeed, the voters in both communities were closer to complete discord than to complete consensus; they did not reach consensus on any of the ten specific statements incorporating the principles of majority rule and minority rights; and majorities expressed the "undemocratic" attitude on about half of the statements.

In trying to identify the carriers of the creed, the expected regional and class-related variations were found in attitudes toward democratic principles in specific form, with education having the most marked effect. While attitudes on democratic fundamentals were not found to vary appreciably according to age, sex or party affiliation, they did vary according to education, community, and income. The greatest difference on every statement was between the high-education group and the low-education group, and the high-education group gave the most democratic response to every question, whether compared with other educational, community or income groupings. Education, but not community or income, held up consistently as a basis of disagreement when other factors were controlled. We accordingly conclude that endorsement of democratic principles is not a function of class as such (of which income is also a criterion), but of greater acquaintance with the logical implications of the broad democratic principles. Note, for example, that the highly educated renounce in much greater degree than any other group the restriction of the vote to the well-informed, a restriction that would presumably affect them least of all.

Although high education was the primary basis of agreement on democratic principles, actual consensus was not found even among this segment of the voting population. The approach to consensus is closer among the highly educated in Ann Arbor, where greater agreement exists on extension of democratic rights to Negroes, but in both communities the highly educated are closer to discord than consensus on half of the statements. On the basis of these findings, our hypothesis appears to be invalid.

Assuming that the United States is a democracy, we cannot say without qualification that consensus on fundamental principles is a necessary condition for the existence of democracy. Nor does it appear valid to say that, although consensus need not pervade the entire voting population, it must exist at least among the highly educated, who are the carriers of the creed. Our data are not inconsistent, of course, with the qualified proposition that consensus on fundamental principles in a highly abstract form is a necessary condition for the existence of democracy. But the implication of political theory that consensus includes more specific principles is empirically invalid. Our findings accordingly suggest that the intuitive insights and logical inferences of political theorists need to be subjected more consistently to empirical validation.

∽ HERBERT McCLOSKY

Democratic "Fundamentals" and Democratic Stability

Several observations can be offered by way of summarizing and commenting upon the data just reported:

1. American politics is widely thought to be innocent of ideology, but this opinion more appropriately describes the electorate than the active political minority. If American ideology is defined as that cluster of axioms, values and beliefs which have given form and substance to American democracy and the Constitution, the political influentials manifest by comparison with ordinary voters a more developed sense of ideology and a firmer grasp of its essentials. This is evidenced in their stronger approval of democratic ideas, their greater tolerance and regard for proper procedures and citizen rights, their superior understanding and acceptance of the "rules of the game," and their more affirmative attitudes toward the political system in general. The electorate displays a substantial measure of unity chiefly in its support of freedom in the abstract; on most other features of democratic belief and practice it is sharply divided.

The political views of the influentials are relatively ordered and coherent. As liberals and conservatives, Democrats and Republicans, they take stands on issues, choose reference groups, and express preferences for leaders that are far more consistent than the attitudes and preferences exhibited by the electorate. The latter's opinions do not entirely lack order but are insufficiently integrated to meet

From "Consensus and Ideology in American Politics" by Herbert McClosky, *American Political Science Review*, LVIII (June 1964), pp. 373–379.

the requirements of an ideology. In contrast to the political elite, which tends to be united on basic values but divided on issues by party affiliation (both of which testify to a measure of ideological sophistication), the voters divide on many basic political values and adopt stands on issues with little reference to their party affiliation.

The evidence suggests that it is the articulate classes rather than the public who serve as the major repositories of the public conscience and as the carriers of the Creed. Responsibility for keeping the system going, hence, falls most heavily upon them.

2. Why should consensus and support for democratic ideology be stronger among the political stratum than among the electorate? The answer plainly has to do with the differences in their political activity, involvement and articulateness. . . .

The findings furnish little comfort for those who wish to believe that a passion for freedom, tolerance, justice and other democratic values springs spontaneously from the lower depths of the society, and that the plain, homespun, uninitiated yeoman, worker and farmer are the natural hosts of democratic ideology. . . . Democratic beliefs and habits are obviously not "natural" but must be learned; and they are learned more slowly by men and women whose lives are circumscribed by apathy, ignorance, provincialism and social or physical distance from the centers of intellectual activity. In the absence of knowledge and experience—as we can readily observe from the fidgety course of growth in the newly emerging nations—the presuppositions and complex obligations of democracy, the rights it grants and the self-restraints it imposes, cannot be quickly comprehended. Even in a highly developed democratic nation like the United States, millions of people continue to possess only the most rudimentary understanding of democratic ideology.

3. While the active political minority affirms the underlying values of democracy more enthusiastically than the

people do, consensus among them is far from perfect, and we might well inquire why this is so.

Despite the many forces impelling influentials toward agreement on basic ideological values, counteracting forces are also at work to divide them. Not all influentials are able to comprehend democratic ideas, to apply them to concrete contexts, or to thread their way through the complexities of modern political life. Nor is communication perfect among them either, despite their greater homogeneity. Many things divide them, not least of which are differences in education, conflicting economic and group interests, party competition, factional cleavages and personal political ambitions.

In demonstrating that the influentials are better prepared than the masses to receive and reflect upon political ideas, we run the risk of overstating the case and of exaggerating their capacity for ideological reasoning. Some members of the political class obviously have no more intellectual concern with politics than the masses do; they are in it for "the game," for personal reasons, or for almost any reason except ideology. . . .

4. We turn now to the most crucial question suggested by the research findings, namely, what significance must be assigned to the fact that democratic ideology and consensus are poorly developed among the electorate and only imperfectly realized among the political influentials?

Our first and most obvious conclusion is that, contrary to the familiar claims, a democratic society can survive despite widespread popular misunderstanding and disagreement about basic democratic and constitutional values. The American political system survives and even flourishes under precisely these conditions, and so, we have reason to think, do other viable democracies. What makes this possible is a more conjectural question, though several observations can be offered by way of answering it.

Democratic viability is, to begin with, saved by the fact that those who are most confused about democratic ideas are also likely to be politically apathetic and without significant influence. Their role in the nation's decision process is so small that their "misguided" opinions or non-opinions have little practical consequence for stability. If they contribute little to the vitality of the system, neither are they likely to do much harm. . . . In the United States, at least, their disagreements are *passive* rather than *active,* more the result of political ignorance and indifference than of intellectual conviction or conscious identification with an "alien" political tendency. Most seem not even to be aware of their deviations from the established values. This suggests that there may, after all, be some utility in achieving agreement on large, abstract political sentiments, for it may satisfy men that they share common values when in fact they do not. Not only can this keep conflicts from erupting, but it also permits men who disagree to continue to communicate and thus perhaps to convert their pseudo-consensus on democratic values into a genuine consensus.

I do not mean to suggest, of course, that a nation runs no risks when a large number of its citizens fail to grasp the essential principles on which its constitution is founded. Among Americans, however, the principal danger is not that they will reject democratic ideals in favor of some hostile ideology, but that they will fail to understand the very institutions they believe themselves to be defending and may end up undermining rather than safeguarding them. . . .

Whether consensus among the influentials is either a necessary or sufficient condition for democratic stability is not really known. Since the influentials act, make public decisions, are more organized, and take political ideas more seriously, agreement among them on constitutional values is widely thought to be essential for viability. At present, however, we do not have enough information (or at least we do not have it in appropriately organized form) to state with satisfactory precision what the actual relation is between elite consensus and democratic stability. Some democratic governments, e.g., Weimar Germany, crumbled when faced with ideological conflicts among their political classes; others, e.g., post-war Italy and France, have until now managed to weather pronounced ideological cleavages. The opinion has long prevailed that consensus is needed to achieve stability, but the converse may be the more correct formulation, i.e., that so long as conditions remain stable, consensus is not required; it becomes essential only when social conditions are disorganized. Consensus may strengthen democratic viability, but its absence in an otherwise stable society need not be fatal or even particularly damaging.

It should also be kept in mind that the existence of intellectual disagreements—even among the influentials—does not necessarily mean that they will be expressed or acted upon. In the United States (and doubtless elsewhere as well), numerous influences are at work to prevent ideological cleavages from assuming an important role in the nation's political life. This is certainly the tendency of such political institutions as federalism, checks and balances, separation of powers, bicameralism, the congressional committee system, the judiciary's practice of accommodating one discrepant law to another, and a system of elections more often fought around local issues and personalities than around urgent national questions. Our two-party system also functions to disguise or soften the genuine disagreements that distinguish active Democrats from active Republicans. The American social system contributes to the same end, for it is a model of the pluralistic society, a profuse collection of diverse groups, interests and organizations spread over a vast and variegated territory. Consensus in such a society becomes difficult to achieve, but by the same token its absence can also more easily be survived. The complexities of a highly pluralistic social and political order tend to diminish the impact of intellectual differences, to compel compromise, and to discourage the holders of divergent views from crystalizing into intrasigent doctrinal camps. Thus it seems, paradoxically enough, that the need for consensus on democratic rules of the game increases as the conflict among competing political tendencies becomes sharper, and declines as their differences become more diffused. Italy, by this reasoning, has greater need of consensus than the United States, but has less chance of achieving it. A democratic nation may wisely prefer the American model to the Italian, though what is ideally desired . . . is a balance between cleavage and consensus—the one to give reality and force to the principle of opposition, the other to furnish the secure framework within which that principle might be made continuously effective. Countervailing power within a structure of shared political values would, by this logic, be the optimal condition for the maintenance of a democratic society.

5. But even giving this much weight to consensus may exaggerate the role which intellectual factors play in the attainment of democratic stability. The temptation to assign a controlling influence to the place of ideas in the operation of democracy is very great. Partly this results from our tendency to confuse the textbook model of democracy with the reality and to assume the high order of rationality in the system that the model presupposes. . . .

Research from many different lines of inquiry confirms unequivocally that the role heretofore assigned to ideas and to intellectual processes in general has been greatly exaggerated. . . . Witness, for example, the research on the nonrational factors which govern the voting decision. . . . We now have evidence that . . . the strength of one's attachment to a political community need not depend upon one's approval of its intellectual, cultural, or political values. . . .

6. To conclude, as we have in effect, that ideological awareness and consensus are over-valued as determinants of democratic viability is not to imply that they are of no importance. While disagreements among Americans on fund-

amental values have tended to be passive and, owing to apathy and the relative placidity of our politics, easily tolerated; while they do not follow party lines and are rarely insinuated into the party struggle; and while no extremist movement has yet grown large enough to challenge effectively the governing principles of the American Constitution, this happy state of affairs is not permanently guaranteed. Fundamental differences could *become* activated by political and economic crises; party differences could *develop* around fundamental constitutional questions, as they have in France and other democracies; and powerful extremist movements are too familiar a phenomenon of modern political life to take for granted their eternal absence from the American scene. . . .

There is, however, reason to believe that ideological sophistication and the general acceptance of liberal democratic values are increasing rather than declining in the United States. . . . democratic ideology in the United States, linked as it is with the articulate classes, gives promise of growing as the articulate class grows. Many developments in recent American life point to an increase in "articulateness": the extraordinary spread of education, rapid social mobility, urbanization, the proliferation of mass media that disseminate public information, the expansion of the middle class, the decline in the size and number of isolated rural groups, the reduction in the proportion of people with submarginal living standards, the incorporation of foreign and minority groups into the culture and their increasing entrance into the professions, and so on. While these developments may on the one side have the effect of reducing the tensions and conflicts on which extreme ideologies feed, they are likely on the other side to beget a more articulate population and a more numerous class of political influentials, committed to liberal democracy and aware of the rights and obligations which attend that commitment.

11
Psychocultural Preconditions

KARL MANNHEIM

Integrative Behavior and Democratic Personality

As a matter of fact, the easiest way to express the democratic pattern of life, action, and personality is to contrast it with the authoritarian or domineering pattern.

On a simple plane, what it is has always been obvious. As everybody will agree, it is part of our democratic creed to call "democratic" behavior that implies the person's readiness for cooperation, especially with his equals. Everyone also realizes that this equality means readiness to respect our neighbor's personality, never using him as a tool or as a means to our own ends. . . . Similarly, an essential feature of democratic as contrasted with dominative behavior is minimal use of violence, pressure, or power; and if we have recourse to the latter, it will be under the control of peers with equal controlling influence.

Although people have long been more or less aware of these main features of democratic behavior, a recent development to my way of thinking has greatly strengthened the

From *Freedom, Power, and Democratic Planning* by Karl Mannheim. New York: Oxford University Press, and London: Routledge & Kegan Paul, 1950, pp. 200–203, 230–232.

concept of that basic pattern which ought to serve as a measuring rod for understanding human behavior. The psychologists . . . H. H. Anderson and D. W. Harding called "integrative behavior" what I would term the archetype of democratic behavior. I think there are good reasons for adopting this term because it refers to something more fundamental than simple co-operation and contains the key to various facets characteristic of democratic behavior.

The important element in this conception of integrative behavior is that the person who acts in its spirit is not only unwilling to superimpose his own view and will upon the other fellow—the essence of the domineering attitude—but he is tolerant of disagreement. He is tolerant not for the sake of compromise, but in the expectation of enlarging his own personality by absorbing some features of a human being essentially different from himself. Practically, this means that the democratic personality welcomes disagreement because it has the courage to expose itself to change. Going to the root of the matter, we find that openness to change is only within reach of the person who really feels secure, and therefore is unafraid of losing either status or individuality by having his probity exposed to the testing powers of co-operation and exchange of ideas.

The most important point in this observation is realization of the link between authoritarian superimposition of one's view and fear of losing status. In an authoritarian relationship it stands to reason that one of the parties has a higher status than the other and in his activities is concerned with maintaining that status, whereas in the ideal case of democratic partnership the question of status is ruled out by acknowledgment of essential equality: in other words, the desire for prestige stands less in the way of willingness to learn from another person than under an authoritarian system. Indeed, there is no greater obstacle to real learning . . . than the fear of losing one's status. A status-ridden person cannot really learn. . . .

Once this close interconnection between the pattern of

behavior and the pattern of personality structure is recognized, all differences in modes of conduct and personality types become more intelligible. The pattern of action is, then, part and parcel of the personality structure. A society that creates the status-ridden type, incessantly afraid of losing face, is bound to express this concern for social esteem in an endless number of rituals in which the "superior" person can continually reassure himself of the submissiveness of his subordinates. Moreover, in such societies social approval, the most fundamental weapon of conditioning behavior, is always given to self-assertive behavior, especially on the part of those who are expected to rule. In contrast, in a really democratic society, public approbation tends to discourage the would-be domineering person who refuses to treat his fellow men as equals or even tries to humiliate them.

From the very beginning of this discussion we left no doubt about considering integrative behavior not as an already established reality, but as an *ideal* of democracy. Setting up an ideal does not mean we shall ever attain it completely, but rather lends direction to education and to mutual controls. . . .

We saw that co-operation, properly understood, means continuous integration of different purposes. One who has never been trained in integrating purposes has never experienced true democratic cooperation, since the essence of democracy is the integration of purposes and not mere compromise. Even dominative people may achieve a compromise. They try to suppress each other, to impose their will upon each other, and only when this fails will they try to reach a compromise. . . .

Integrative behavior is more than compromise. It means that people, though fully aware of the fact that differences of constitution and social position, of drives and interests, shape their experience and attitude to life in different ways, yet transmute their different approaches for the purpose of co-operating in a common way of life. Such transmutation is a creative form of integration: out of the process of common living and co-operative pursuits, a new purpose emerges which the partners come to cherish even more than their original aims. From the very outset this kind of integration offers scope for the dissenter or the man of initiative whose contribution, which may differ from ours, is to be absorbed, not excluded. Only the Anglo-Saxon countries, where the dissenters have contributed importantly to the new idea of creative compromise, could develop this conception.

Behavior, as noted above, is rooted in a specific personality type. Democratic behavior is characterized by openmindedness and readiness for co-operation, which not only enables the individual to face disagreement but prepares him to expect substantial enrichment of his own personality by absorbing differences in the process. Thus integrative or basic democratic behavior means exposure to change and criticism. But, as we have seen, only the type of person who is himself secure, and does not fear loss of either status or individuality, is capable of such behavior.

Here the deep bond between simple behavior and personality type becomes apparent. In our earlier discussion integrated behavior appeared to have been achieved by external influences, by habit formation or by holding up appropriate models. However, the more deeply we probe the question, the more obvious it becomes that integrative behavior is not simply peripheral, or merely the sum of acquired habits, but is deeply rooted in a definite type of personality structure.

The latter statement seems to take us back to a psychology of individual variations, suggesting that democratic integration is not a problem of sociology, or social psychology, but rather of individual psychology. . . . Any such conclusion, however, would be misleading. Though integrated behavior is rooted in personality structure, the patterns of personality integration can be socially induced and to a large extent are the products of cultural environment. It is from society that we derive even the patterns of personality integration. Although allowances must be made for individual deviations, the predominant personality types of any society are also its products. If this is true, we may say that a society is democratic only so long as its members, consciously or unconsciously, are motivated by the ideal of democratic personality and try to abide by this ideal.

The underlying principle, that there is a correlation between social organization and personality pattern, applies, of course, *mutatis mutandis* to the interrelation between authoritarian society and the authoritarian personality type as well. As we have briefly outlined above, authoritarian society is bound to produce the dominative type of character. The very existence of an authoritarian order is based upon the socially guaranteed and absolute control of a commanding individual and his retinue, all other authority being derived from them. Thus by its very structure this society produces the status-ridden personality who draws all his strength and confidence from this pre-established status and not from the continuous approval of his authority by his equals. . . .

Hampered by this necessity for maintaining an artificially enhanced status, the status-ridden person cannot perform the function of integrating groups from within, nor can he, in his foreign policy, do anything but strive to subject greater territories to his rule. He may master material techniques, but cannot learn the art of evolving creative—not dominating—patterns of social integration, simply because his imagination is limited to concepts of suppression and exploitation.

It would, however, be wrong to assume that no such authoritarian and status-ridden character-types exist in our democratic societies. It cannot be pretended that the latter are thoroughly permeated by the democratic spirit. As they exist at present, they are only partly democratic and still contain remnants of the feudal order, an older elaboration of the dominative attitude. This does not, however, negate the fact that it was through the democratic way of life that we first moved away from the hierarchy of ranks and estates. Today, on many different levels, experiments are being carried out for meeting people on a more equalitarian footing. In a democratic atmosphere the person who formerly found security in his inherited status must emancipate himself from this crutch.

HAROLD D. LASSWELL

Democratic Character

THE SELF-SYSTEM IN DEMOCRATIC CHARACTER: THE OPEN EGO

. . . our conception of democratic character . . . falls in two grand divisions, the first of which has to do with the self-system, the second with the energy system. The initial step in characterizing the self-system is to select the system of identifications which appears to be consonant with democratic character. . . .

Let us take as the outstanding characteristic of democratic character, in reference to identifications, *the maintenance of an open as against a closed ego.* By this expression our intention is to convey the idea that the democratic attitude toward other human beings is warm rather than frigid, inclusive and expanding rather than exclusive and constricting. We are speaking of an underlying personality structure which is capable of "friendship," as Aristotle put it, and which is unalienated from humanity. Such a person transcends most of the cultural categories that divide human beings from one another, and senses the common humanity across class and even caste lines within the culture, and in the world beyond the local culture. . . .

The conception of the open ego is something other than the capacity to enter into an intense and all-embracing sentimental bond with another person. Often such passionate attachments represent a socialization of fears and hostilities directed against other human beings. It operates as a preventive of the degree of detachment which enables the individual to sense the feelings and viewpoints of others in the life of an entire group, such as appears to be characteristic of those persons who are well-equipped to function in a democratic manner. . . .

THE SELF-SYSTEM IN DEMOCRATIC CHARACTER: VALUES MULTIPLE AND SHARED

. . . Let us speak of the democratic character as *multi-valued, rather than single-valued, and as disposed to share rather than to hoard or to monopolize.* In particular, little significance is attached to the exercise of power as a . . . value.

The characteristics of democratic character have often been cast into relief by the study of individuals who are infatuated with the pursuit of one value to such a point that the integrity of the common life is imperiled thereby. This is perhaps most obvious in studies that have been made of the *homo politicus,* the man who, when compared with others similarly situated in culture and class, relies with relish upon the "pursuit of power by the use of power." Since we understand that power relationships have, or are assumed by the participants to possess, the element of severe deprivation, it is apparent that the human being who is fascinated by power is out of harmony with our basic concept of human dignity. . . . To the power-centered person all human beings and all contacts with others are opportunities for imposing his will, or for enlisting the other person in some manner that contributes to the imposition of his own will in some future situation. Hence he imposes a wall of insulation and isolation between himself and others, with the result that a growing sense of alienation from mankind becomes one of the recurring complaints of those who attain power, or only aspire with all the intensity of their being to acquire it.

When the demand for respect is the consuming passion,

other values are sacrificed for the sake of receiving symbolic acknowledgments of eminence. The vain man has a special position of dependence upon the human beings by whom he is surrounded, seeking to elicit a continuing flow of those reassuring postures, gestures and symbolic expressions which sustain the inflated image of the ego. We are speaking of the individual who is so sensitized to the admiration of others that he may react with wounded pride to fancied slights, and burn with fierce jealousies and resentments against those who receive the plaudits to which he fancies himself entitled, or against those from whom he believes that the plaudits ought to come. The respect-centered character is often disposed to poison human relations "by taking everything personally" and by needing a perpetual stream of reassurance about "how am I doing." The clinician is accustomed to see in the over-sensitive neurotic, or in the grandiose delusions of the paranoid, the extreme manifestation of what is known to common sense as abnormal pride. The secret image is not necessarily connected with power, since coercive intentions are not always the cherished means of obtaining boundless admiration. . . .

THE SELF-SYSTEM OF THE DEMOCRATIC CHARACTER: CONFIDENCE IN HUMAN POTENTIALITIES

When we turn from the demand-structure of the democratic character to the consideration of the pattern of expectation we note at once that it is essential to have *deep confidence in the benevolent potentialities of man.* This affirmative trust is very different from the apathetic endurance of life in the manner of the apathetic orphan.

Unless there is some early basis for trust in the benevolence of the surrounding world, we can hardly expect that the individual will develop predispositions capable of carrying him through adverse experiences. This is the deep significance of the "good mother" image in contributing to the formation of a perspective that fosters inclusive identifications with other people. It has become amply apparent in the course of research on the infant that the expectation of benevolence is a factor enabling the infant to put forth the energy to live. . . .

THE ENERGY SYSTEM OF THE DEMOCRATIC CHARACTER: FREEDOM FROM ANXIETY

The ideal conception of democratic character *includes the specification that the self-system shall have at its disposal the energies of the unconscious part of the personality.* The deviations from this standard are in several directions. The energies may be so divided and opposed to one another that little is available to the ego, which may be relatively immobilized into the performing of an impoverished social role. The super-ego system of restriction and compulsion may remain at war with the recurring initiatives of the id-system, resulting in immobilization through physical incapacitation.

. . . When we speak of democratic character, of course, we have in mind the development of self and energy systems which withstand adversity on behalf of democratic patterns of value and practice.

The task is nothing less than the drastic and continuing reconstruction of our own civilization, and most of the cultures of which we have any knowledge. Since the basic postulate of behavior is the maximization of indulgences over deprivations, our task is to consolidate democratic conduct by directing the indulgences toward those who act democratically, and the deprivations toward those who do not. . . . The aim is to bring into being a democratic equilibrium in societal relations in which deviations are promptly rectified. If we were designing a machine, it would be possible to "build in" a set of servo-mechanisms which perform this re-stabilizing operation. Since human relations are not mechanized, our task of creating and sustaining a democratic equilibrium is more complex. And the complexity is augmented by the prevailing anarchy in the world community, which keeps alive the expectation and the application of violence in the arena of world affairs, and also in the civic arena of police states. Hence the tremendous task of reconstruction must proceed in the face of adverse contemporary conditions and of anti-democratic inheritances from the past.

☙ DANIEL LERNER

The Mobile Personality

The mobile personality can be described in objective and technical fashion. . . . The mobile person is distinguished by a high capacity for identification with new aspects of his environment; he comes equipped with the mechanisms needed to incorporate new demands upon himself that arise outside of his habitual experience. These mechanisms for enlarging a man's identity operate in two ways. *Projection* facilitates identification by assigning to the object certain preferred attributes of the self—others are "incorporated" because they are like me. (Distantiation or negative identification, in the Freudian sense, results when one projects onto others certain disliked attributes of the self.) *Introjection* enlarges identity by attributing to the self certain desirable attributes of the object—others are "incorporated" because I am like them or want to be like them. We shall use the word *empathy* as shorthand for both these mechanisms. This condensation of psychoanalytic terminology has a pragmatic, not theoretic, intent—since our materials are simply not amenable to the more highly differentiated categories of Freudian vocabulary. Our interview data does not permit systematic discrimination between the introjective and projective mechanisms. Nor does empathy denote sympathy or antipathy. In particular cases it may lead to either—"understanding" may breed dislike as well as affection.

We are interested in empathy as the inner mechanism which enables newly mobile persons to *operate efficiently* in a changing world. Empathy, to simplify the matter, is the

From *The Passing of Traditional Society* by Daniel Lerner. Copyright 1958 by The Free Press, a Corporation. New York: The Free Press, pp. 49–51.

capacity to see oneself in the other fellow's situation. . . .

It is a major hypothesis of this study that high empathic capacity is the predominant personal style only in modern society, which is distinctively industrial, urban, literate and *participant*. . . . Modern society is participant in that it functions by "consensus"—individuals making personal decisions on public issues must concur often enough with other individuals they do not know to make possible a stable common governance. Among the marks of this historic achievement in social organization, which we call Participant Society, are that most people go through school, read newspapers, . . . vote in elections which actually decide among competing candidates, and express opinions on many matters which are not their personal business.

Especially important, for the Participant Style, is the enormous proportion of people who are expected to "have opinions" on public matters—and the corollary expectation of these people that their opinions will matter. It is this subtly complicated structure of reciprocal expectation which sustains widespread empathy. . . .

For, in any society, only when the accepted model of behavior is emulated by the population at large does it become the predominant personal style. The model of behavior developed by modern society is characterized by empathy, a high capacity for rearranging the self-system on short notice. Whereas the isolated communities of traditional society functioned well on the basis of a highly constructive personality, the interdependent sectors of modern society require widespread participation. This in turn requires an expansive and adaptive self-system, ready to incorporate new roles and to identify personal values with public issues. This is why modernization of any society has involved the great characterological transformation we call psychic mobility. The latent statistical assertion involved here is this: In modern society *more* individuals exhibit *higher* empathic capacity than in any previous society.

GABRIEL A. ALMOND and SIDNEY VERBA

The Political Culture of Democracy

THE STUDY OF POLITICAL CULTURE

Our study grows out of this body of theory about the characteristics and preconditions of the culture of democracy. What we have done amounts to a series of experiments intended to test some of these hypotheses. Rather than inferring the properties of democratic culture from political institutions or social conditions, we have attempted to specify its content by examining attitudes in a number of operating democratic systems. And rather than deriving the social-psychological preconditions of democracy from psychological theory, we have sought to determine whether and to what extent these relations actually exist in functioning democratic systems. We do not argue that our study will shut off speculation and provide the precise and tested propositions of a complete theory of democracy, but, rather, that some of these propositions will survive the test of empirical-quantitative analysis and some will not. This stage of experiment should focus and direct inquiry by providing some answers to old questions and suggesting some new questions.

In still another respect we hope to contribute to the development of a scientific theory of democracy. By far the greatest amount of empirical research on democratic attitudes has been done in the United States. In our study we

From *The Civic Culture* by Gabriel A. Almond and Sidney Verba. Princeton, N.J.: Princeton University Press, 1963, pp. 11–20, 22–23, 24–26, 31–32, 492–493.

have included, in addition to our own country, Britain, Germany, Italy, and Mexico. . . . Our five-country study offers us the opportunity to escape from this American parochialism and to discover whether relations found in the American data are also encountered in democratic countries whose historical experiences and political and social structures differ from one another.

POLITICAL CULTURE: DEFINITION AND TYPES

In our comparison of the political cultures of five contemporary democracies, we employ a number of concepts and classifications which it will be useful to specify and define. We speak of the "political culture" of a nation rather than the "national character" or "modal personality," and of "political socialization" rather than of child development or child rearing in general terms. This is not because we reject the psychological and anthropological theories that relate political attitudes to other components of personality, or because we reject those theories that stress the relationship between child development in general terms and the induction of the child into his adult political roles and attitudes. . . .

We employ the term "political culture" for two reasons. First, if we are to ascertain the relations between political and nonpolitical attitudes and developmental patterns, we have to separate the former from the latter even though the boundary between them is not as sharp as our terminology would suggest. The term political culture thus refers to the specifically political orientations—attitudes toward the political system and its various parts, and attitudes toward the role of the self in the system. . . . It is a set of orientations toward a special set of social objects and processes.

But we also choose political *culture,* rather than some other special concept, because it enables us to utilize the conceptual frameworks and approaches of anthropology, sociology, and psychology. Our thinking is enriched when we employ, for example, such categories of anthropology and psychology as socialization, culture conflict, and acculturation. . . .

We appreciate the fact that anthropologists use the term culture in a variety of ways, and that by bringing it into the conceptual vocabulary of political science we are in danger of importing its ambiguities as well as its advantages. Here we can only stress that we employ the concept of culture in only one of its many meanings: that of *psychological orientation toward social objects.* When we speak of the political culture of a society, we refer to the political system as internalized in the cognitions, feelings, and evaluations of its population. People are inducted into it just as they are socialized into nonpolitical roles and social systems. . . .

The political culture of a nation is the particular distribution of patterns of orientation toward political objects among the members of the nation. Before we can arrive at such distributions, we need to have some way of systematically tapping individual orientations toward political objects. In other words, we need to define and specify modes of political orientation and classes of political objects. Our definition and classification of types of political orientation follow Parsons and Shils. . . . Orientation refers to the internalized aspects of objects and relationships. It includes (1) "cognitive orientation," that is, knowledge of and belief about the political system, its roles and the incumbents of these roles, its inputs, and its outputs; (2) "affective orientation," or feelings about the political system, its roles, personnel, and performance; and (3) "evaluational orientation," the judgments and opinions about political objects that typically involve the combination of value standards and criteria with information and feelings.

In classifying objects of political orientation, we start with the "general" political system. We deal here with the system as a whole and include such feelings as patriotism or alienation, such cognitions and evaluations of the nation as "large" or "small," "strong" or "weak," and of the polity as "democratic," "constitutional," or "socialistic." At the other extreme we distinguish orientations toward the "self" as political actor; the content and quality of norms of personal political obligation, and the content and quality of the sense of personal competence vis-à-vis the political system. In treating the component parts of the political system we distinguish, first, three broad classes of objects: (1) specific *roles* or *structures,* such as legislative bodies, executives, or bureaucracies; (2) *incumbents* of roles, such as particular monarchs, legislators, and administrators; and (3) particular public *policies, decisions,* or *enforcements* of decisions. These structures, incumbents, and decisions may in turn be classified broadly by whether they are involved either in the political or "input" process or in the administrative or "output" process. By political or input process we refer to the flow of demands from the society into the polity and the conversion of these demands into authoritative policies. Some structures that are predominantly involved in the input process are political parties, interest groups, and the media of communication. By the administrative or output process we refer to that process by which authoritative policies are applied or enforced. Structures predominantly involved in this process would include bureaucracies and courts.

We realize that any such distinction does violence to the actual continuity of the political process and to the multi-functionality of political structures. Much broad policy is made in bureaucracies and by courts; and structures that we label as input, such as interest groups and political parties, are often concerned with the details of administration and enforcement. What we are referring to is a difference in emphasis, and one that is of great importance in the classification of political cultures.

. . . the political orientation of an individual can be tapped systematically if we explore the following:

1. What knowledge does he have of his nation and of his political system in general terms, its history, size, location, power, "constitutional" characteristics, and the like? What are his feelings toward these systemic characteristics? What are his more or less considered opinions and judgments of them?

2. What knowledge does he have of the structures and roles, the various political elites, and the policy proposals that are involved in the upward flow of policy making? What are his feelings and opinions about these structures, leaders, and policy proposals?

3. What knowledge does he have of the downward flow of policy enforcement, the structures, individuals, and decisions involved in these processes? What are his feelings and opinions of them?

4. How does he perceive of himself as a member of his political system? What knowledge does he have of his rights, powers, obligations, and of strategies of access to influence? How does he feel about his capabilities? What norms of participation or of performance does he acknowledge and employ in formulating political judgments, or in arriving at opinions?

Characterizing the political culture of a nation means, in effect, filling in such a matrix for a valid sample of its population. The political culture becomes the frequency of different kinds of cognitive, affective, and evaluative orientations toward the political system in general, its input and output aspects, and the self as political actor.

Parochial Political Culture. When this frequency of orientations to specialized political objects of the four kinds specified . . . approaches zero, we can speak of the political culture as a parochial one. The political cultures of [certain] African tribal societies and autonomous local communities

. . . would fall into this category. In these societies there are no specialized political roles: headmanship, chieftainship, "shamanship" are diffuse political-economic-religious roles, and for members of these societies the political orientations to these roles are not separated from their religious and social orientations. A parochial orientation also implies the comparative absence of expectations of change initiated by the political system. The parochial expects nothing from the political system. . . .

What we have been describing is extreme or pure parochialism that occurs in simpler traditional systems where political specialization is minimal. Parochialism in more differentiated political systems is likely to be affective and normative rather than cognitive. That is to say, the remote tribesman in Nigeria or Ghana may be aware in a dim sort of way of the existence of a central political regime. But his feelings toward it are uncertain or negative, and he has not internalized any norms to regulate his relations to it.

The Subject Political Culture. The second major type of political culture . . . is the subject culture. Here there is a high frequency of orientations toward a differentiated political system and toward the output aspects of the system, but orientations toward specifically input objects, and toward the self as an active participant, approach zero. The subject is aware of specialized governmental authority; he is affectively oriented to it, perhaps taking pride in it, perhaps disliking it; and he evaluates it either as legitimate or as not. But the relationship is toward the system on the general level, and toward the output, administrative, or "downward flow" side of the political system; it is essentially a passive relationship, although there is . . . a limited form of competence that is appropriate in a subject culture.

Again we are speaking of the pure subject orientation that is likely to exist in a society where there is no differentiated input structure. The subject orientation in political systems that have developed democratic institutions is likely to be affective and normative rather than cognitive. Thus a French royalist is aware of the democratic institutions; he simply does not accord legitimacy to them.

The Participant Political Culture. The third major type of political culture, the participant culture, is one in which the members of the society tend to be explicitly oriented to the system as a whole and to both the political and administrative structures and processes: in other words, to both the input and output aspects of the political system. Individual members of the participant polity may be favorably or unfavorably oriented to the various classes of political objects. They tend to be oriented toward an "activist" role of the self in the polity, though their feelings and evaluations of such a role may vary from acceptance to rejection. . . .

This threefold classification of political cultures does not assume that one orientation replaces the others. The subject culture does not eliminate diffuse orientations to the primary and intimate structures of community. To the diffuse orientations to lineage groups, religious community, and village it adds a specialized subject orientation to the governmental institutions. Similarly, the participant culture does not supplant the subject and parochial patterns of orientation. The participant culture is an additional stratum that may be added to and combined with the subject and parochial cultures. Thus the citizen of a participant polity is not only oriented toward active participation in politics, but is subject to law and authority and is a member of more diffuse primary groups.

To be sure, adding participant orientations to subject and parochial orientations does not leave these "earlier" orientations unchanged. The parochial orientations must adapt when new and more specialized orientations enter into the picture, just as both parochial and subject orientations change when participant orientations are acquired. Actually, some of the most significant differences in the political cultures of the five democracies included in our study turn on the extent and the way that parochial, subject, and participant orientations have combined, fused, or meshed together within the individuals of the polity.

Another caution is necessary. Our classification does not imply homogeneity or uniformity of political cultures. Thus political systems with predominantly participant cultures will, even in the limiting case, include both subjects and parochials. The imperfections of the processes of political socialization, personal preferences, and limitations in intelligence or in opportunities to learn will continue to produce subjects and parochials, even in well-established and stable democracies. Similarly, parochials will continue to exist even in "high" subject cultures.

. . . We have already suggested that all political cultures (with the exception of the simple parochial ones) are mixed. Thus a participant culture contains individuals who are oriented as subjects and parochials; and a subject culture will contain some parochials. We use the term "systemically mixed" political cultures to refer to those in which there are significant proportions of both the simpler and more complex patterns of orientations.

. . . we may distinguish three types of systemically mixed political cultures: (1) the parochial-subject culture, (2) the subject-participant culture, and (3) the parochial-participant culture.

The Parochial-Subject Culture. This is a type of political culture in which a substantial portion of the population has rejected the exclusive claims of diffuse tribal, village, or feudal authority and has developed allegiance toward a more complex political system with specialized central governmental structures. This is the classic case of kingdom building out of relatively undifferentiated units. The chronicles and histories of most nations include this early stage of shift from local parochialism to centralized authority. But the shift may stabilize at a point that falls short of a fully developed subject culture. The loosely articulated African kingdoms, and even the Ottoman Empire, are examples of stable, mixed subject-parochial cultures where the latter predominates and central authority takes the form of a primarily extractive, dimly cognized set of political objects. The problem of cultural change from parochial to subject patterns is a difficult one, and unstable moves back and forth are common in the early history of nations. . . .

The Subject-Participant Culture. The way in which the shift from a parochial to a subject culture is solved greatly affects the way in which the shift from a subject to a participant culture takes place. . . . the inculcation of a sense of national loyalty and identification, and of a propensity to obey the regulations of central authority, is the first priority problem in the emerging nations. In the shift from a subject to a participant culture, the parochial and local autonomies, if they survive, may contribute to the development of a democratic infrastructure. Certainly this is what happened in the British case. Local authorities, municipal corporations, religious communities, and merchant groups in which the tradition of guild freedoms still persisted became the first interest groups in the developing British democracy. The lesson is a significant one. Precisely because the development of a subject culture in England stopped short of destroying local and parochial structures and cultures, these could become available at a later time and in modified form as an influence network that could relate Britons as competent citizens to their government. . . .

In the mixed subject-participant culture a substantial part of the population has acquired specialized input orientations and an activist set of self-orientations, while most of the remainder of the population continue to be oriented toward an authoritarian governmental structure and have a relatively passive set of self-orientations. In the Western European examples of this type of political culture—France, Germany, and Italy in the nineteenth and present centuries

—there was a characteristic pattern of structural instability with an alternation of authoritarian and democratic governments. But more than structural instability results from this kind of cultural mix. . . . Because participant orientations have spread among only a part of the population, and because their legitimacy is challenged by the persisting subject subculture and suspended during authoritarian interludes, the participant-oriented stratum of the population cannot become a competent, self-confident, experienced body of citizens. They tend to remain democratic aspirants. That is, they accept the norms of a participant culture, but their sense of competence is not based on experience or on a confident sense of legitimacy. Furthermore, the structural instabilities that frequently accompany the mixed subject-participant culture, the frequent ineffectiveness of the democratic infrastructure and of the governmental system, tend to produce alienative tendencies among the democratically oriented elements of the population. . . .

The Parochial-Participant Culture. In the parochial-participant culture we have the contemporary problem of cultural development in many of the emerging nations. In most of these countries the political culture is predominantly parochial. The structural norms that have been introduced are usually participant; for congruence, therefore, they require a participant culture. Thus the problem is to develop specialized output and input orientations simultaneously. It is not surprising that most of these political systems, always threatened by parochial fragmentation, teeter like acrobats on tightropes, leaning precariously at one time toward authoritarianism, at another toward democracy.

THE CIVIC CULTURE

The civic culture is not the political culture that one finds described in civics textbooks, which prescribe the way in which citizens ought to act in a democracy. The norms of citizen behavior found in these texts stress the participant aspects of political culture. The democratic citizen is expected to be active in politics and to be involved. Furthermore, he is supposed to be rational in his approach to politics, guided by reason, not by emotion. He is supposed to be well informed and to make decisions . . . on the basis of careful calculation as to the interests and principles he would like to see furthered. This culture, with its stress on rational participation within the input structure of politics, we can label the "rationality-activist" model of political culture. The civic culture shares much with this rationality-activist model; it is, in fact, such a culture *plus something else*. . . .

In the first place, the civic culture is an allegiant participant culture. Individuals are not only oriented to political input, they are oriented positively to the input structures and the input process. In other words, . . . the civic culture is a participant political culture in which the political culture and political structure are congruent.

More important, in the civic culture participant political orientations combine with and do not replace subject and parochial political orientations. Individuals become participants in the political process, but they do not give up their orientations as subjects or as parochials. Furthermore, not only are these earlier orientations maintained, alongside the participant political orientations, but the subject and parochial orientations are congruent with the participant political orientations. The nonparticipant, more traditional political orientations tend to limit the individual's commitment to politics and to make that commitment milder. In a sense, the subject and parochial orientations "manage" or keep in place the participant political orientations. Thus attitudes favorable to participation within the political system play a major role in the civic culture, but so do such nonpolitical attitudes as trust in other people and social participation in general. The maintenance of these more traditional attitudes *and their fusion* with the participant orientations lead to a balanced political culture in which political activity, involvement, and rationality exist but are balanced by passivity, traditionality, and commitment to parochial values.

In sum, the most striking characteristic of the civic culture . . . is its mixed quality. It is a mixture in the first place of parochial, subject, and citizen orientations. The orientation of the parochial to primary relationships, the passive political orientation of the subject, the activity of the citizen, all merge within the civic culture. The result is a set of political orientations that are managed or balanced. There is political activity, but not so much as to destroy governmental authority; there is involvement and commitment, but they are moderated; there is political cleavage, but it is held in check. Above all, the political orientations that make up the civic culture are closely related to general social and interpersonal orientations. Within the civic culture the norms of interpersonal relationships, of general trust and confidence in one's social environment, penetrate political attitudes and temper them. The mixture of attitudes found in the civic culture . . . "fits" the democratic political system. It is, in a number of ways, particularly appropriate for the mixed political system that is democracy.

Conclusion

This volume has been devoted to a consideration of some major theories of democracy. In the opening chapter we examined briefly the historical evolution of democratic ideas from ancient Greece to the twentieth century. We saw that pre-twentieth-century theories were characteristically normative in orientation. They idealized certain values without systematic reference to actual reality; they looked to a utopian state of affairs in which natural law, natural rights, popular sovereignty, self-government, common good, common will, prevailed. The net result was the creation of a serious gap between democratic theory and political actuality.

Part One was devoted to a consideration of a large number of democratic theories under a fourfold typology. We found that although the normative conceptions continue to be represented in the neoclassicists, the main focus of contemporary theories represents a shift away from metaphysical speculation and a tendency toward empirical analysis of actual democratic systems. A third variety of democratic theory was distinguished by an attempt to reconcile the normative and empirical conceptions. The value components of most of these formulations, however, were stated in relative and conditional terms. We identified as the distinctive feature of a final group of democratic theories the emphasis on a certain ideological outlook, on a series of shared beliefs and habits. We concluded that on the whole democratic theory has undergone something of a metamorphosis, that in departing from the main precepts of the older conceptions, most contemporary writers on democracy have sought to close the gap between theory and reality.

Contemporary democratic theory remains nonelitist in character, although substantial concessions to the elitist critique of the classical theory are made. Seldom, for instance, is the assumption of human rationality to be found in the literature of democratic theory. Seldom is it assumed that the rational political man is a necessary requisite of democracy.[1] Similarly, seldom is it assumed that democratic government is "government by the people," although it is recognized that it continues to remain "government of the people and for the people."

Contemporary democratic theory stipulates a competitive political environment in which a number of leaders and organizations define the issues of the day and contend for public support. Democratic politics, in other words, unfolds in a pluralistic context. A democratic society is one in which power is diffused among contending parties and groups; no single entity is permitted to monopolize power for any length of time.

An important implication of the foregoing proposition is that in democratic societies power and leadership are subject to regular and fairly rapid alternations. The electorate is provided with frequent opportunities for changing (and thereby controlling) the leadership groups. The elitist attack upon the classical theories of democracy has not led to the denial of leadership; it has led to an increasing recog-

1 Obvious exceptions are John H. Hallowell (pp. 79–81) and Anthony Downs (157–161). It should perhaps be stressed that to question the classic assumption of human rationality (see Chapter 1) is not the same as saying that the political man is completely irrational. For an important study of rationality in presidential voting, for example, see V. O. Key, Jr., *The Responsible Electorate* (Cambridge, Mass.: Harvard University Press, 1966).

nition of the necessity of its control. In this sense, the core of democratic political rule may be summed up in two words: responsiveness and responsibility.

It is worth reiterating at this point that our use of these two terms has been nonethical and nonevaluative. By responsiveness we refer to the willingness and ability of democratic government to express, reflect, and meet the reasonable demands of the citizenry. Our formulation is necessarily somewhat imprecise, but the point generally holds that democratic government must be sensitive and receptive to the intense, persistent, and reasonable demands of the influential segments of the population; otherwise, it will run the risk of instability and eventual collapse.

The word "responsibility" has been traditionally used in two broad senses: ethical and descriptive—or alternatively, moral and relational, personal and impersonal, subjective and objective.[2] Our use of the term has been descriptive, relational, impersonal, and objective; it is analogous to the definition developed by Harold D. Lasswell and Abraham Kaplan: "the formal commitment to practices in behalf of specified interests."[3]

In Part Two we examined some of the many preconditions regularly associated with the emergence and survival of democratic political systems. These preconditions were grouped under five principal headings: physical, religious, socioeconomic, political, and psychocultural. Some of them (for example, those relating to size) were not supported by empirical evidence and thus we had no alternative but to reject them. Others, while highly plausible, lacked convincing evidence and our attitude toward them was one of "agnosticism," as it were. The psychocultural preconditions

2 See, for example, Carl J. Friedrich, ed., *Responsibility, Nomos III* (New York: Liberal Arts Press, 1960).

3 *Power and Society* (New Haven: Yale University Press, 1950), p. 161.

may fall in this category. A third group of prerequisites appeared to be strongly supported by empirical data and we were inclined to accept them on a provisional basis. The socioeconomic and political prerequisites may be listed in this area.

Even by itself, however, the last group of preconditions involves a large number of complex variables, among which industrialization, urbanization, literacy, participation, political parties, political groups, and so on, are included. The basic proposition underscoring the entire enterprise, of course, is that in the absence of a suitable social, political, and economic environment, the emergence of democracy remains highly dubious. What is sought, in effect, is an evidential base for democracy, a series of propositions that can be ascertained empirically. As such, no longer is it assumed that democracy can grow in most any place, at most any time, and under most any set of conditions. The assumption of transplantability of democracy to nondemocratic political circumstances is explicitly rejected.

Although it is difficult to pinpoint the genesis of the notion that democratic government is a universally applicable phenomenon, the proposition can be found in the works of Jefferson and Lincoln, for example. In his optimistic enthusiasm regarding the future of man and the destiny of democratic government, Jefferson regarded American democracy as an experiment of global significance, one involving mankind in its entirety. He wrote: "It is impossible not to be sensible that we are acting for all mankind. . . ."[4] A similar line of thought persisted in Lincoln. In the American Revolution, he wrote, "was the germ which has vegetated, and still is to grow and expand into the universal liberty of mankind."[5] Half a century later, however, it

4 "To Doctor Joseph Priestley," June 19, 1802. *The Writings of Thomas Jefferson,* VIII, collected and edited by Paul L. Ford (New York: G. P. Putnam's Sons, 1899).

5 "Temperance Address," delivered before the Springfield Washington Temperance Society, February 22, 1842. *The Collected Works of Abraham Lincoln,* I, edited by Roy P. Basler (New Brunswick, N.J.: Rutgers University Press, 1953).

remained for Woodrow Wilson to set out self-consciously to universalize the American system, to make the world safe for democracy.

As is common knowledge, these dreams were shattered in the postwar mushrooming of the new states. As country after country shunned democracy of the Western type, disillusionment inescapably set in. It was finally recognized, in explicit terms, that the Western experience with democracy is not directly relevant to non-Western political contexts, that Western democracy cannot be thrust upon a country that does not meet at least some of its preconditions. The precise constellation of prerequisites that makes democracy possible is not easy to specify; we do know, however, that in the absence of any exposure to democratic ideas and practices, the emergence of democratic government in the new states is highly unlikely. Within the next century, however, it may be possible for some of the preconditions to develop and mature in a limited number of emerging countries.

To conclude, a series of constraints and limitations has come to be placed on democratic theory in its applicability to both Western and non-Western environments. These modifications may be looked upon, at least in part, as concessions to the elitist critique of the classical theory. As a consequence, democratic theory has been transformed. In this transformation, it must be admitted, democratic theory has lost much of its idealistic charm and visionary appeal. At the same time, this loss has been more than offset by concrete improvements in the theory of democracy. Democratic theory has been "improved" in that it is now more faithfully descriptive of actual political conditions. We say this in the belief that the acid test of a viable theory lies in its consonance with political reality. In this sense, the elitists may be viewed as having done democracy an important service. From a long-term perspective, the elitist attack upon the classical theories of democracy was one of the most constructive functions they performed.

Further Readings

NOTE: This bibliography contains for the most part items not covered in the volume at all, or briefly mentioned in the introductory chapters.

For further exploration of the historical evolution of democratic ideas, the following references (some of which include extensive bibliographies) are especially helpful: A. N. Hattersley, *A Short History of Democracy* (Cambridge: Cambridge University Press, 1950); L. Lipson, *The Democratic Civilization* (New York: Oxford University Press, 1964); R. McKeon, ed., *Democracy in a World of Tensions* (Chicago: University of Chicago Press, 1951); S. K. Padover, *The Meaning of Democracy* (New York: Frederick A. Praeger, 1963); W. H. Riker, *Democracy in the United States,* second edition (New York: The Macmillan Co., 1965); A. Ross, *Why Democracy?* (Cambridge, Mass.: Harvard University Press, 1952); H. Tingsten, *The Problem of Democracy* (Totowa, N.J.: Bedminster Press, 1965).

Further statements of the classical theory of democracy are found in Ross, *op. cit.*; M. Salvadori, *Liberal Democracy* (New York: Doubleday & Co., 1957); T. V. Smith and Eduard C. Lindeman, *The Democratic Way of Life* (New York: The New American Library, 1951); T. L. Thorson, *The Logic of Democracy* (New York: Holt, Rinehart and Winston, 1962).

For some criticisms of normative theory on empirical grounds, the following are useful: S. H. Beer, "New Structures of Democracy: Britain and America," in W. N. Chambers and R. H. Salisbury, eds., *Democracy in the Mid-Twentieth Century* (St. Louis, Mo.: Washington University Press, 1960); B. R. Berelson,

"Democratic Theory and Public Opinion," *Public Opinion Quarterly,* XVI (Fall 1952), pp. 313–330; B. R. Berelson *et al., Voting* (Chicago: University of Chicago Press, 1954), especially Chapter 14; R. A. Dahl, "Further Reflections on 'The Elitist Theory of Democracy,'" *American Political Science Review,* LX (June 1966), pp. 296–305; R. A. Dahl, *Who Governs?* (New Haven: Yale University Press, 1961); J. W. Fulbright *et al., The Elite and the Electorate: Is Government by the People Possible?* (Santa Barbara: Center for the Study of Democratic Institutions, 1963); L. Hartz, "Democracy: Image and Reality," in Chambers and Salisbury, *op. cit.*; V. O. Key, Jr., *Public Opinion and American Democracy* (New York: Alfred A. Knopf, 1961), especially Part VI; McKeon, *op. cit.*; L. W. Milbrath, *Political Participation* (Chicago: Rand McNally, 1965), especially Chapter VI; T. D. Weldon, *The Vocabulary of Politics* (Baltimore: Pelican Books, 1953); H. Wheeler, *The Rise and Fall of Liberal Democracy* (Santa Barbara: Center for the Study of Democratic Institutions, 1966).

For some criticisms of empirical theory on normative grounds, the following should be consulted: L. Davis, "The Cost of Realism: Contemporary Restatements of Democracy," *Western Political Quarterly,* 17 (March 1964), pp. 37–46; G. Duncan and S. Lukes, "The New Democracy," *Political Studies,* 11 (June 1963), pp. 156–177; Fulbright *et al., op. cit.*; C. B. MacPherson, "Post-Liberal Democracy," *Canadian Journal of Economics and Political Science,* 30 (November 1964), pp. 485–498; McKeon, *op. cit.*; J. L. Walker, "A Critique of the Elitist Theory of Democracy," *American Political Science Review,* LX (June 1966), pp. 285–295.

Further normative-empirical conceptions of democracy are found in E. Barker, *Principles of Social and Political Theory* (New York: Oxford University Press, 1951); C. L. Becker, *Modern Democracy* (New Haven: Yale University Press, 1941); C. W. Cassinelli, *The Politics of Freedom* (Seattle: University of Washington Press, 1961); J. Dewey, "Democracy and Educational Administration," in J. Ratner, ed., *Intelligence in the Modern World* (New York: Random House, 1939); H. K. Girvetz, *Democracy and Elitism* (New York: Charles Scribner's Sons, 1967); P. Herring, *The Politics of Democracy* (New York: W. W. Norton & Co., 1940); J. D. Lewis, "The Elements of Democracy," *American Political Science Review,* XXXIV (June 1940), pp. 467–478; Lipson, *op. cit.;* Padover, *op. cit.;* N. Riemer, *The Revival of Democratic Theory* (New York: Appleton-Century-Crofts, 1962); Riker, *op. cit.*; Y. R. Simon, *Philosophy of Democratic Government* (Chicago: University of Chicago Press, 1951); Tingsten, *op. cit.*

Two further ideological conceptions of democracy are R. G. McClosky, "The American Ideology," in Marian D. Irish, ed., *Continuing Crisis in American Politics* (Englewood Cliffs, N.J.: Prentice-Hall, 1964); McKeon, *op. cit.*, especially pp. 2–3.

Some general preconditions of democracy are explored in H. Eckstein, *A Theory of Stable Democracy,* Research Monograph No. 10 (Princeton University, Center for International Studies, 1961); W. Kornhauser, *The Politics of Mass Society* (New York: The Free Press, 1959); S. M. Lipset, *The First New Nation* (New York: Basic Books, 1963); S. M. Lipset, *Political Man: The Social Bases of Politics* (New York: Doubleday & Co., 1960); McKeon, *op. cit.*

Further discussion of religious preconditions of democracy are found in J. H. Hallowell, *The Moral Foundation of Democracy* (Chicago: University of Chicago Press, 1954); Reinhold Niebuhr, *Christian Realism and Political Problems* (New York: Charles Scribner's Sons, 1943); L. Sturzo, "The Philosophic Background of Christian Democracy," *Review of Politics,* 9 (January 1947), pp. 3–15.

Discussion of socioeconomic preconditions of democracy is pursued in R. A. Dahl and C. E. Lindblom, *Politics, Economics, and Welfare* (New York: Harper and Brothers, 1953); Milbrath, *op. cit.*; E. Shils, *Political Development in the New States* (The Hague: Mouton & Co., 1962); Walker, *op. cit.*

Discussions of political preconditions of democracy are contained in D. E. Apter, "Some Reflections on the Role of a Political Opposition in New Nations," *Comparative Studies in Society and History,* IV (November 1961), pp. 154–168; P. Bachrach, "Elite Consensus and Democracy," *Journal of Politics,* 24 (August 1962), pp. 439–452; C. J. Friedrich, *The New Belief in the Common Man* (Boston: Little, Brown and Co., 1942); McClosky, *op. cit.*; G. Myrdal, *An American Dilemma* (New York: Harper and Brothers, 1944), Chapter 1; J. N. Perryman, "On the Meaning of 'Democracy,'" *Public Opinion Quarterly,* 17 (Spring 1953), pp. 47–60; Shils, *op. cit.*

Further studies of the psychocultural preconditions of democracy include Z. Barbu, *Democracy and Dictatorship* (New York: Grove Press, 1956); A. Inkeles, "National Character and Modern Political Systems," in Francis L. K. Hsu, ed., *Psychological Anthropology: Approaches to Culture and Personality* (Homewood, Ill.: Dorsey Press, 1961); D. Spitz, *Democracy and the Challenge of Power* (New York: Columbia University Press, 1958), Chapter X.

Finally, some miscellaneous references: J. R. Beery, *Current Conceptions of Democracy* (New York: Teachers College, Columbia University, 1943); C. Brinton, "Utopia and Democracy," *Daedalus,* 94 (Spring 1965), pp. 348–366; E. Cahn, *The Predicament of Democratic Man* (New York: The Macmillan Co., 1961); H. W. Ehrmann, ed., *Democracy in a Changing Society* (New York: Frederick A. Praeger, 1964); D. C. Hodges, "Political Democracy: Its Informal Content," *American Journal of Economics and Sociology,* 24 (January 1965), pp. 12–20; B. Lippincott, *Democracy's Dilemma* (New York: Ronald Press, 1965).

Index